THE PARATROOPERS

THE ELITE
The World's Crack Fighting Men

THE PARATROOPERS

Ashley Brown, Editor

Jonathan Reed, Editor

Editorial Board

Lisa Mullins, Managing Editor, NHS edition

A Publication of
THE NATIONAL HISTORICAL SOCIETY

Published in Great Britain in 1986 by Orbis Publishing

Special contents of this edition copyright © 1989 by the
National Historical Society

Library of Congress Cataloging-in-Publication Data
The Paratroopers / Ashley Brown, editor, Jonathan Reed, editor.
    p.   cm.—(The Elite : the world's crack fighting men ; v. 8)
  ISBN 0-918678-46-3
    1. Parachute troops—History—20th century.   2. Military history,
Modern—20th century.   I. Brown, Ashley.   II. Reed, Jonathan.
III. National Historical Society.   IV. Series: Elite (Harrisburg,
Pa.) ; v. 8.
UD480.P37   1989
356'.166'0904—dc20   89-12496
                                                           CIP

CONTENTS

INTRODUCTION

Imagine hearing a door thrown open, the roar of air rushing past at hundreds of miles an hour, then standing in the doorway looking down at an eternity of clouded airspace, with the earth a dimly seen object below. Imagine standing there, then leaping out of the door! There were those—there *are* those—who don't have to imagine it. They did—and do—it. They are THE PARATROOPERS, a special kind of ELITE who have been braving the skies for half a century and more. In Spain's civil war, in World War II, Korea, Vietnam, at Suez and South Africa, the Falklands, and more, they have floated down silently from the heavens to take command on the ground.

Picture participating in the February 1942 raid on Bruneval as part of the 2d Para Raiders, officially the 2d Battalion, 1st Parachute Brigade. Incredible aerial reconnaissance, combined with intelligence provided by French resistance fighters, had pinpointed a German radar installation near the Channel coast. Even the strength of the enemy garrison had been determined, and that was important, for the mission was not just to attack and destroy. The raiders had to take the position, and hold it long enough to dismantle the radar equipment, then get themselves *and* the radar apparatus to safety via Royal Navy landing craft. Just how the operation went is only one of the incredible stories of heroism found in THE PARATROOPERS.

But it is hardly more remarkable than the taking of the Merville Battery on June 6, 1944, as part of the D-Day operations. Or Marcel Bigeard's paratrooper regiment's exploits in the Sahara, facing the FLN in 1957. Or the German paratroopers who swept through the skies in gliders before falling out of the darkness on Norway in 1940. At a little-known place called Chinese Farm, the Israeli 35th Paratroop Brigade took on the hardest-fought engagement of the 1973 Yom Kippur War. As far back as 1929, the Russian military began parachute training, with airships not even designed for such a purpose. The intrepid paras had to climb out of the top of the ship, then jump off for a free fall. But they did it.

THE PARATROOPERS have always done it. It is what makes them a part of . . . THE ELITE.

THE ISRAELI PARACHUTE CORPS

The Israeli Parachute Corps, whose badge is shown above, was created by Major Yoel Palgi in the months leading up to the 1948 War of Independence. His assignment was fraught with difficulties: nowhere in Palestine was there a usable parachute and the IAF had only one aircraft suitable for dropping paratroopers. Palgi, however, overcame these initial problems and was able to establish a training base at Ramat David.

His call for volunteers was answered by over 100 men, most of whom had never even seen a parachute. Inevitably, there was a series of accidents and several senior officers began to doubt the wisdom of setting up a parachute unit.

It was decided, however, to give the unit another chance. Following Palgi's resignation in 1949, command of the Corps was given to Yehuda Harari, who then tightened discipline and introduced a rigorous 36-day training course. Under his watchful eye, the Corps blossomed into a well-schooled force but, much to his chagrin, it remained untested in combat.

This state of affairs persisted until 1956, when the unit participated in an attack with a commando force, Unit 101, on an Arab base. The raid was a major success and the Israeli high command ordered the Corps to be amalgamated with Unit 101. Overall command was given to Ariel Sharon.

The Parachute Corps fought its first large-scale action at Mitla Pass in 1956 where it displayed all the hallmarks of an elite fighting force. Subsequently, the paras fought with distinction in all of Israel's wars with its Arab neighbours, most notably, in the capture of Mount Hermon in the Six-Day War of 1967.

DEATH IN THE PASS

Isolated and far behind enemy lines, the Israeli paratroopers of Ariel Sharon's 202nd Brigade battled against the Egyptian forces holding the Mitla Pass in Sinai, in 1956

1659 HOURS, 29 October 1956. Sixteen DC-3 Dakotas of the Israeli Air Force (IAF) skimmed low over the sun-baked hills of western Sinai, evading Egyptian radar surveillance. Above them, 10 Gloster Meteor jet fighters rode shotgun, their pilots keeping a wary eye peeled for enemy interceptors while, to the west, 12 Dassault Mystère IVA fighters patrolled the length of the Suez Canal. Inside the Dakotas, with only the monotonous drone of the aircraft engines to keep their thoughts from straying to the probable dangers they would face in a deep-penetration raid behind enemy lines, 395 men of the 1st Battalion of the newly-formed Israeli 202nd Parachute Brigade made their final preparations. Parachute harnesses and weapons, including the relatively untried Uzi sub-machine gun, were checked.

The battalion's commander, Lieutenant-Colonel Rafael 'Raful' Eitan, a battle-scarred veteran of many border clashes with the Arabs, was keenly aware of the importance of this drop on the strategically vital Mitla Pass, and he prayed that the scheduled link-up with the rest of the brigade, travelling overland under the command of Colonel Ariel 'Arik' Sharon, would take place before the Egyptians could respond to their landing. Moments later, however, the time for reflection was over; the aircraft climbed to 1500ft and, once at that altitude, Eitan led his men into the unknown. The pilots had done their job and now it was the turn of the paratroopers. Phase 1 of Operation Kadesh was underway.

Kadesh was the codename for the Israeli invasion of Sinai, to precede and provide the pretext for Anglo-French air and seaborne landings in the recently nationalised Suez Canal Zone. All the parties concerned were trying to unseat Egyptian leader Gamal Abdel Nasser, whose aggressive brand of Arab nationalism ran contrary to British and French interests in the Middle East, and posed a threat to the very existence of the state of Israel.

The political background to the seizure of the Mitla Pass, the defile through which the main road to central Sinai ran, did not concern Eitan as he parachuted down to the drop zone. He, like any experienced commander, was considering the chances of success. Although his young charges had received the finest training the Israeli Defence Forces (IDF) could provide and exuded an air of casual confidence in both themselves and their officers, Eitan was acutely aware that this mission was their first large-scale operation and that its outcome depended on the reception they received on landing.

If the pre-drop preparations had gone according to plan, his paratroopers should land unopposed at the Parker Memorial, a local landmark lying on a rocky outcrop at the eastern end of the pass. Surprise was the key to success. To ensure the maximum disruption of Egyptian communications and delay any response they might try to mount, four P-51 Mustangs of the IAF, flying at a hair-raising 12ft above the ground, had cut overhead telegraph lines with their propellers, before the drop took place.

Left: Young paratroopers of Israel's 202nd Brigade digging trenches at the eastern end of Mitla. The lack of natural cover made unprotected troops very vulnerable to strafing attacks by enemy jets. The seizure of the pass, the main point of entry into central Sinai, was the opening phase of Operation Kadesh, Israel's plan to defeat Egyptian forces east of the Suez Canal Zone. Below left: Final preparations before the mission; men check their parachutes before boarding one of the 16 Dakotas earmarked for the drop. Although of World War II vintage, the Dakota was an ideal choice as it could carry up to 28 fully-equipped men. Below: After a 200km journey over enemy territory, the landings took place exactly on schedule.

ARIEL SHARON

Ariel Sharon, the driving force behind the occupation of the Mitla Pass in 1956, was a controversial figure, who was destined to become a legend in the IDF. A heavily-built, no-nonsense type, he was renowned for his great drive, but also an unwillingness to accept any criticism of his style of leadership.

Sharon's rise to prominence began in the early 1950s when he was given the task of raising a specialist commando force, known as Unit 101, to carry out cross-border raids against Jordanian targets. Unit 101 rapidly established itself as a first-rate combat force and set the standards by which other IDF troops were judged. A joint raid against the village of Kalkilya in 1956 proved so successful that Unit 101 was amalgamated with the fledgling Israeli Parachute Corps and Sharon was given a free hand to mould the two forces into a single body,

which proved its worth in 1956.

In the Six-Day War of 1967, Sharon led an armoured division in the Sinai desert and played a key role in the defeat of the Egyptian 2nd Division at Abu Aweigila. It was in the Yom Kippur War of 1973, however, that Sharon's heavy-handed independence brought him into direct confrontation with his fellow officers. He was accused of disobeying orders and there were calls for his resignation. However, he weathered the storm and played an important part in the Israeli counter-attack of 15-24 October that pushed the Egyptians back across the Suez Canal.

In the years since 1973, Sharon has devoted his time to politics.

Eitan hit the ground and rolled over, expecting the worst. To his surprise, the area was clear of the enemy. The landing, however, was not entirely unobserved; a motley group of Egyptian workers appeared and believing the Israelis to be Egyptians, applauded their skilful descent and then offered the paratroopers mugs of coffee. The discovery that they had landed five kilometres from the target was a less welcome surprise. Time being of the essence, Eitan gathered his command and marched them to the eastern end of the pass which, after a brief firefight with a few Egyptian sentries, was captured. The paratroopers dug in and then settled down to await the arrival of their heavy equipment under Sharon.

Sharon's force, consisting of the other two battalions of the 202nd Brigade, two battalions of half-tracks, 13 AMX-13 tanks, a battery of 25-pounders and a heavy mortar company, had left its base on the Jordanian border a few hours before Eitan's departure and, although they had travelled across the Negev desert at breakneck speed, they crossed into Sinai 18 minutes behind schedule. Sharon knew that the outcome of the operation depended on meticulous timing, and he drove his men forward with redoubled vigour towards their first objective, the frontier post at El Kuntilla.

The leading elements of the column arrived outside the post at 1600 on 29 October. There was no time for fancy planning or protracted combat – El Kuntilla had to be taken in minutes rather than hours. Sharon quickly appraised the situation and then unleashed two companies, travelling in machine-gun armed half-tracks, to the west of the Egyptian positions. With the benefit of the sun setting behind their backs, these men charged the enemy with guns blazing, while a handful of tanks and a single howitzer pounded the defenders who, blinded by the sun, were unable to pinpoint the Israeli attack. The ferocity of the assault was too much for the Egyptians, who fled into the desert. The battle was a morale-boosting success, but Sharon did not allow his men the luxury of self-congratulation. Instead, he goaded them to their next target, El Thamad, 60km west.

Sharon knew that this outpost would be a tougher nut to crack; intelligence reports had indicated that two Sudanese companies equipped with machine guns and recoilless rifles had strengthened the position's natural defences, a rock-strewn escarpment, with minefields and barbed wire. The Israelis arrived at dawn on the 30th with the sun at their

Below: An M3 half-track of Sharon's force drives into Sinai. Ahead lay a tough journey that was to include three lightning attacks against enemy-held posts. Despite these delays, and interdiction from Egyptian ground-attack aircraft, the link-up with Eitan's men at the pass was achieved at 1630 hours on 30 October. Bottom: A group of Israeli officers including a buoyant Sharon (left) pose by a French 120mm Brandt mortar.

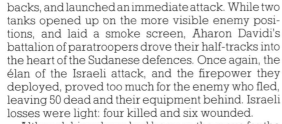

backs, and launched an immediate attack. While two tanks opened up on the more visible enemy positions, and laid a smoke screen, Aharon Davidi's battalion of paratroopers drove their half-tracks into the heart of the Sudanese defences. Once again, the élan of the Israeli attack, and the firepower they deployed, proved too much for the enemy who fled, leaving 50 dead and their equipment behind. Israeli losses were light: four killed and six wounded.

Although his column had been on the move for the greater part of a day and had fought two large skirmishes, Sharon could ill-afford any further delay. The Mitla Pass was still over 135km distant and the Egyptians, having recovered from their surprise at the attack, were closing in. But his men were exhausted and many of their vehicles were showing signs of wear and tear. Sharon had to order a halt.

A few hours after dawn, the advance recommenced and, after brushing aside a strafing attack by enemy jets, the Israelis reached Nakhl, the headquarters of an Egyptian frontier force battalion, at 1630 hours on the 30th. Barely pausing to assess the situation, Sharon launched a head-on charge backed by an artillery barrage, but the garrison fled before battle could be joined. At 1700 the Israelis entered the village, swapped some of their battered trucks for the Soviet-built BTR 152 armoured personnel carriers left in the compound and then drove off towards Mitla, 65km to the west.

The fall of Nakhl assured the success of the Israeli plan and, despite the strain that the final lap of the journey placed on both men and machines, Sharon linked up with Eitan at 2230 hours. In a truly remarkable drive that owed much to the indomitable personality and dogged determination of Sharon, the column had travelled through 200km of inhospitable, enemy-held territory in less than 32 hours.

The situation at the pass, however, was considerably less secure than either Eitan or Sharon believed. Although the paratroopers had spotted Egyptian aircraft in their vicinity, they remained unaware that the response to their incursion was gathering momentum. On the morning of 30 October, the Egyptians had despatched the 2nd Brigade from Suez to confront the Israelis and, despite heavy attacks launched by the IAF, the brigade's 5th Battalion and a company of the 6th reached the area and deployed near the eastern end of the pass.

At Mitla, the road from Suez meanders through a sheer-sided 32km-long defile that is little more than 50m wide. Unbeknown to the Israelis, the Egyptians had taken up position around and in some caves on the Jebel Heitan that lay along the southern edge of the road, and in dug-outs along a ridge to the north. Their defences bristled with heavy machine guns, 12 six-pounder anti-tank guns and dozens of Alpha light machine guns. Every section of the pass was turned into a lethal killing ground.

Although unaware of the Egyptian occupation of the pass, Sharon recognised that his paratroopers were dangerously over-exposed and, in view of their vulnerability to air attack, he sought to move deeper into the pass. After discussing the matter with Lieutenant-General Moshe Dayan, the Israeli chief of staff, he received permission to send out a small patrol to reconnoitre the ground on condition that they avoid large-scale combat. The fire and dash which had carried him through the desert now proved to be Sharon's undoing. Despite Dayan's explicit orders, he dispatched two reinforced companies under Mordechai 'Motta' Gur into the defile.

Gur's force motored into Mitla, blithely unaware of the Egyptian presence in the caves on either side of the track. Coolly, the enemy waited until the leading Israeli vehicles were well inside their prepared killing grounds. As the column rounded a sharp bend, the leading half-track was met by a devastating fusillade. The driver and his commander fell,

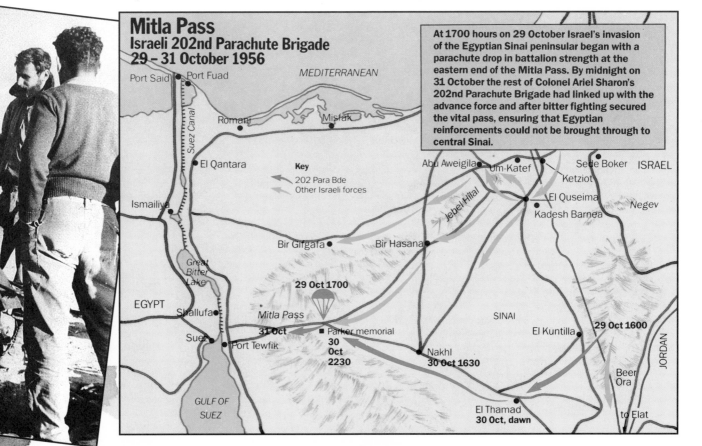

Mitla Pass
Israeli 202nd Parachute Brigade 29 – 31 October 1956

At 1700 hours on 29 October Israel's invasion of the Egyptian Sinai peninsular began with a parachute drop in battalion strength at the eastern end of the Mitla Pass. By midnight on 31 October the rest of Colonel Ariel Sharon's 202nd Parachute Brigade had linked up with the advance force and after bitter fighting secured the vital pass, ensuring that Egyptian reinforcements could not be brought through to central Sinai.

riddled with bullets, and their vehicle skidded across the path of the following trucks. Undaunted, Gur pressed on, believing the opposition to be light. He was quickly disillusioned; his own half-track was hit by a well-aimed anti-tank round and its dazed crew was forced to shelter in a ditch.

The blazing wreckage of the leading vehicles, however, did not halt the Israelis' progress. The rest of Gur's men drove on, their guns blazing away indiscriminately, until they reached a saucer-shaped depression in the middle of the pass, where they were forced to halt. By 1300 hours, the whole column was pinned down by sustained fire from the surrounding cliffs. Desperate measures were needed if the trapped men were to survive.

Sharon ordered Davidi, one of his most trusted officers and the victor of El Thamad, to attempt the rescue of Gur's men. Recognising the futility of any further attempt to advance down the pass, he despatched the brigade's reconnaissance company to a hill north of the visible Egyptian positions. As the company began its advance downhill, it was met by fierce fire from hitherto unseen enemy bunkers. The Israelis, unable to pinpoint the source of the withering fire, were forced to concede ground since any further advance would have been suicidal.

Davidi was forced to make a fateful decision; he asked for a volunteer to drive into the pass to draw the enemy's fire, thereby enabling his paratroopers to pinpoint the Egyptian positions. His call was answered by many brave men, including Eitan, but Davidi chose a young recruit for the task. Gathering an unarmoured jeep, the volunteer sped down the road into a deadly cross-fire. The driver, riddled with bullets, crashed his vehicle, but his sacrifice was not in vain. The enemy-held caves were noted.

Below: After the ferocious battle on the night of 30/31 October, the Israelis fell back from Mitla. Although the mission was an overall success and the Egyptians had been denied access to central Sinai in the first crucial hours of Operation Kadesh, the paratroopers had paid a fearful price – over 150 casualties. Their heavy losses might have been avoided if Sharon had not attempted to push deeper into the pass. Despite the dangers of a deep raid behind enemy lines, Sharon's men had displayed great courage in attacking a series of heavily fortified positions. These Israelis, waiting for the order to withdraw, have been provided with a motley collection of weapons, clothing and transport including American jeeps and half-tracks, German machine guns, and British battledress.

As darkness fell, small groups of Israelis edged along the scree-slopes beneath the Egyptian emplacements. Carrying only sub-machine guns and plentiful supplies of hand grenades, the paratroopers crept into positions around the mouths of the caves. Then, they began their grim, bloody task. Grenades were lobbed and Uzis were fired; the noise of countless explosions rent the night air. For two-and-a-half hours the battle raged; neither side asked for quarter. One by one, the paratroopers took the enemy positions and, by midnight, the pass was firmly in Israeli hands. More than 260 Egyptians died that night. Later, the brigade regrouped and had a roll-call; they were shocked to find that they had lost 38 men killed and a further 120 wounded in an unnecessary action, brought about by Sharon's disobedience. The brigade withdrew from the pass next morning and needed 48 hours' rest before it was fit for action again. Nevertheless, the battle allowed other Israeli columns to meet and defeat the Egyptians in northern Sinai.

Mitla Pass was a bloody debut for the 202nd Parachute Brigade. Faced with an ambush of such intensity, a lesser unit would have crumbled, but the training and courage of Sharon's men saved the day. The battle was the first of many tests that Israel's paratroopers would meet with skill and resolution.

THE AUTHOR Ian Westwell, a graduate of St Catherine's College, Oxford, has contributed articles on post-war conflicts to a number of magazines; he is a specialist on the 19th-century British Army.

A short, hard-hitting campaign on the Solomon Island of Choiseul by a battalion of US Marine Corps paras drew Japanese forces away from the main target island of Bougainville

THE GROWL OF a field telephone jarred me into consciousness at 0200 hours, 19 October 1943. I was ordered to report to the 1st Marine Amphibious Corps Headquarters on Guadalcanal, 250 miles south of my base on the Solomon Island of Vella Lavella. The next day, climbing out of the medical evacuation aircraft I had used for the flight, I was met by Major Jim Murray, the staff secretary. He told me that, after months of chasing the few Japanese left on Vella Lavella, my unit, the 2nd Battalion of the 1st Parachute Regiment, US Marine Corps, had been chosen for an operation vital to the campaign to retake the Solomon Islands.

Following a good deal of planning for a large-scale assault on the island of Choiseul, the strategic approach had been changed. Choiseul was to be bypassed, and neighbouring Bougainville was to be seized by a direct assault beginning on 1 November. The original plans were to be used to good advantage by landing a force on Choiseul, five days in advance of the Bougainville attack, to deceive the Japanese on Bouganville into thinking that Choiseul was the main objective. I was instructed by the corps commander, Major General Alexander Vandegrift, to do everything possible to create the illusion of being a much larger force, in the hope that the enemy would redeploy forces from Bougainville to reinforce the Choiseul garrison. The Japanese currently had about 5000 troops on Choiseul, mainly landing party personnel (marines), based at Choiseul Bay, Sangigai and Kakasa.

We needed boats for movement along the coast, and native bearers to help us move inland

Midway between the Japanese strongpoints of Sangigai and Choiseul Bay was a break in the island's coral reef which intelligence reports had described as undefended. Our force was to be landed there, at the village of Voza, by four converted destroyers. We had to be ready to begin the operation in exactly one week, when the destroyer-transports would arrive at Vella Lavella for an immediate pick-up. It was my plan to land at night at Voza, then initiate operations on a broad front – 20 or 30 miles – engaging the enemy wherever possible. There were to be attacks on the main enemy concentrations at Sangigai and Choiseul Bay, co-ordinated with numerous smaller offensive actions.

Bearing in mind the mountainous terrain and dense banyan forest of Choiseul, where heavy rains daily turn the ground underfoot into deep mud, I realised that we needed boats for movement along the coast, and native bearers to help us move inland. I requested four landing craft, to be transported aboard the destroyers and left with the battalion, and 40 Choiseul islanders to be recruited as bearers.

When I returned to Vella Lavella I was met by an expectant staff who enthusiastically began preparations for the operation. Three days later we were joined by an Australian Coastwatcher, a 250lb, red-bearded giant of a man named Carden Seaton. Seaton brought a great deal of information from Choiseul, most of which tallied with what we already knew, and he informed me that 50 bearers had been found to help us on the island. Then, two days before embarkation, we were advised by Corps Headquarters that we were to be augmented by a force of 24 marines armed with 60 large experimental rockets. Though glad of the extra firepower, I wondered how easy it would be to move the heavy rockets around, each one weighing 45lb with the container that also served as its launcher.

By 27 October, embarkation day, all our material was organised into loads for the four ships. With Japanese aircraft flying freely and frequently over Vella Lavella, it was necessary to load the ships at night, and this was to be accomplished within 45 minutes of the ships' arrival – without our ever having

The Allied campaign to regain control of the Pacific islands from their Japanese occupiers was marked by vicious jungle warfare on an unprecedented scale. The Japanese had had ample time to consolidate their defences on many of the islands, and their determination to fight to the death rather than be taken prisoner imposed a terrible strain on the mental and physical resources of the US ground units deployed against them. Below: A US Marine, armed with an M1 carbine, shows a war-weary face to the camera during the struggle to drive the Japanese out of the vast area of the Pacific that they had seized for Japan's 'new order'.

MISSION: TO RAISE HELL

Having already volunteered for service in the US Marines, numbers of marines were to volunteer again to join the Corps' parachute units. They were initially trained at Lakehurst, New Jersey, and then at Camp Gillespie, near San Diego in California, and at Camp Lejeune, North Carolina.

The first parachute unit of the US Marines, a company, was raised in 1941, and it participated in combined US Army/Marine Corps manoeuvres at Camp Lejeune in August that year. Two additional companies were formed and, as the 1st Parachute Battalion, Fleet Marine Force, the unit participated in the attacks by the 1st Marine Division on the Solomon Islands of Guadalcanal, Tulagi and Gavutu in August 1942. Following these actions, three additional battalions were formed. The 2nd and 3rd Battalions were united with the original battalion as the 1st Parachute Regiment at New Caledonia in early 1943. The 4th Battalion was never deployed as a unit from the United States.

None of the US Marine parachute units jumped in combat. The regiment, less the 2nd Battalion, was committed to a conventional amphibious infantry role in the recapture of Bougainville in November 1943. The 2nd Battalion took part in operations on Vella Lavella, while under the command of the 8th New Zealand Brigade. Although the battalion was not involved in any serious fighting on Vella Lavella, it suffered substantial casualties when, during the initial landing, the ship carrying the battalion headquarters was sunk. In October 1943, the 2nd Battalion conducted the diversionary raiding operation on Choiseul. In 1944 the 1st Parachute Regiment was disbanded and its elements became part of the 5th Marine Division that fought in 1945 at Iwo Jima.

seen them!

One hour after dark, the ships had been loaded up and we were under way on the five-hour trip to Choiseul. It was a crystal-bright night, and half-way there our flourescent wakes were spotted by Japanese aircraft. Although they made four bombing runs, which blasted up cascades of water around our ships, we sustained no damage. The landing was scheduled for 0100 hours on the 28th, and at about midnight I was advised that we had reached the designated launch position, 5000yds off Voza. A reconnaissance party was sent ashore to check for Japanese, with orders to return immediately if enemy troops were found: if the area was clear they were to beckon in the battalion with a shaded light. Enemy aircraft were circling in the darkness, obviously searching for the convoy, but our ships were lying dead in the water with all lights extinguished and were near invisible. Nevertheless, the ships' commanders were understandably anxious, and it came as a great relief when, 45 minutes after midnight, the long-awaited 'All clear' lantern signal appeared on the shore.

Empty boxes and cartons were to be strewn on a dummy beach to mislead the Japanese reconnaissance aircraft

Once ashore, we found Voza village, little more than five grass huts, and set up a defensive perimeter around it. The jungle lay 150yds beyond, a black and almost impenetrable wall. Leaving us with our four landing craft, the destroyers lost no time in disappearing into the darkness. We used the hours before daylight to conceal our vessels under overhanging mangrove trees on the small offshore island of Zinoa, and we tried to remove all traces of our landing on Voza beach.

Meanwhile, Carden Seaton moved up the coast to find his team of bearers. He was accompanied by a detail carrying empty boxes and cartons, which were to be strewn on a dummy beach to mislead Japanese reconnaissance aircraft as to our point of entry onto the island. The bearers, wiry little men with their hair dyed red with lime, were located, and at first light on 28 October they helped move us into an inland stronghold, situated in a river bend with steep cliffs on three sides. Our dummy beach failed to deceive the Japanese, however, and three bombers made two runs over the Voza beach area, luckily causing only little damage.

That morning, reconnaissance patrols set out to the north and south along the beach trail. Returning before dark, they reported that the areas were clear of the enemy for at least five miles in both directions. It was imperative to lock horns with the enemy if our mission was to succeed, however, and, hearing from the bearers that the Japanese were closer in the south, we planned to launch a strong combat patrol early on 29 October, going as far south as necessary to gain contact. The patrol was also to reconnoitre the route to Sangigai, where we planned to stage a large-scale attack against the settlement's 300-man Japanese garrison on the 30th.

Shortly before dawn on the 29th, a small patrol moved north to find a more secure hideout for our boats, since we suspected that the enemy had located the present one. Also, a strong patrol, consisting of 19 marines with a pair of machine guns, set off towards Sangigai. I went with the latter patrol to inspect the terrain we would face on the following day. Going was difficult through thick jungle, and the

Above: General Alexander Vandegrift, overall commander of the US Marine paras on Choiseul. Bottom right: seeking out Japanese patrols.

trail often petered out. Here and there we saw an abandoned Japanese camp, and sometimes some discarded equipment.

Seven miles to the south of Voza we reached Vagara village, where a three-man detachment broke off to move up the Vagara river and reconnoitre an inland route for our attack on Sangigai. Then, just as the main body of the patrol passed through the deserted village, the leading element signalled, 'Enemy in sight'. We crawled forward and saw, through the undergrowth, a detachment of 10 Japanese unloading a landing barge in the river mouth about 50yds away.

When all was in readiness, I gave the signal. Everyone opened up at once, and seven of the men dropped. The remaining three bolted for the jungle without returning our fire. We moved in quickly, set the landing barge alight, frisked the dead and set off back to base. We had announced our presence.

Manchester's column would move down the trail carrying mortars, with bearers carrying 20 of the rockets

On the return route we set up a six-man ambush about a mile south of Voza. It turned out to be a good idea, for two hours after our return a Japanese platoon waded straight into it. Achieving total surprise, the ambush killed seven of them and the rest withdrew. There were no American casualties.

Back at base, the final plans for the Sangigai attack were formulated. One company would remain behind to hold the base, while the rest of the battalion would strike the village from two directions at 1400 hours. Company A, under Captain Bobby Manchester, was to move off down the coast trail to Vagara at first light, driving any enemy patrols southward. The remainder of the force was to follow to Vagara by boat, and then move up the Vagara river in order to curve round in the jungle and approach Sangigai from the north. Meanwhile, Manchester's column would move down the trail carrying mortars, with bearers carrying 20 of the rockets. It was estimated

Choiseul Island
Oct – Nov 1943

1 October 1943 Vice-Admiral William Halsey, commander of the South Pacific Area, ordered an invasion of the island of Bougainville in the Solomon Islands. The date set for the landing by units of the 1st Marine Corps (IMAC) was 1 November. To fool the Japanese IMAC decided to mount a diversionary operation on another island in the chain, and Choiseul was chosen. The 2nd Battalion, 1st Marine Parachute Regiment was assigned the task of creating the impression that a major amphibious landing was underway on the island. The 'paramarines' of the 2nd Battalion had only five days to prepare for the operation, but on 27 October they were ready. They embarked aboard four fast troop carriers at Vella Lavella and sailed to Choiseul.

The paramarines land at Voza

28 Oct Shortly after midnight Companies F and G make the initial landings near the village of Voza. During the day a base camp is established to the northwest.

29 Oct A patrol reconnoitres towards the Sangigai river and meets Japanese troops.

The Pacific war Campaign in the Solomons 1942–1943

Maximum extent of Japanese advance, July 1942

Raid on Sangigai

30 Oct At dawn the paramarines set off for the Sangigai river.

1430 Japanese troops are encountered at the village of Sangigai. They attempt to withdraw to a prepared defensive position, but the paramarines had planned a flanking attack which catches the retiring Japanese in the rear.

1 Nov IMAC's 3rd Marine Division lands on the island of Bougainville. The paramarines' landing on Choiseul convinced the Japanese commanders on Bougainville that no landing would be likely to take place until the end of November.

3 Nov After further patrolling activity to the north of the Voza position, the paramarines are withdrawn from the island of Choiseul.

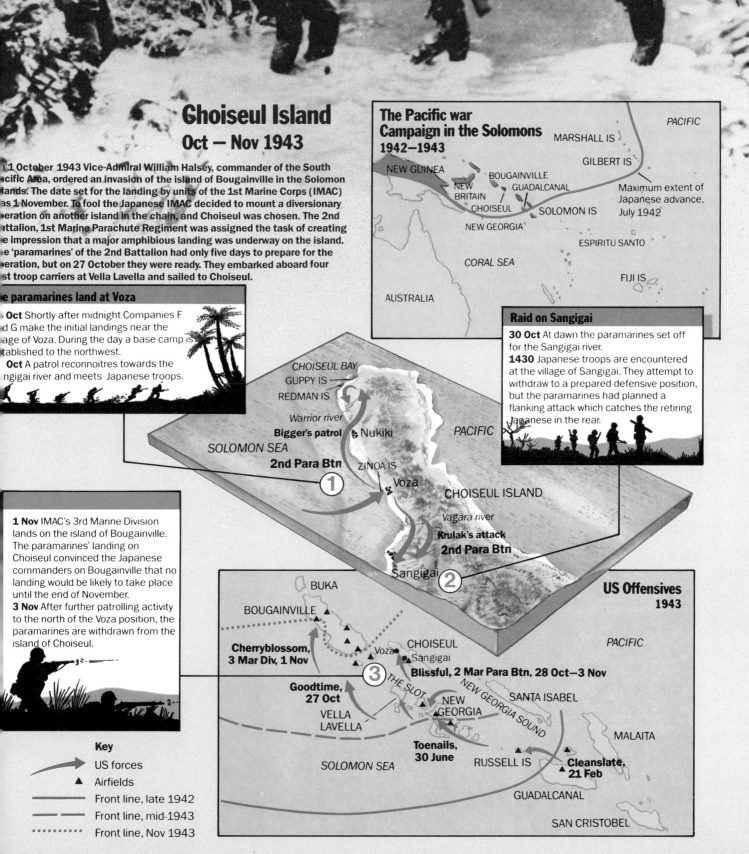

US Offensives 1943

Cherryblossom, 3 Mar Div, 1 Nov

Blissful, 2 Mar Para Btn, 28 Oct–3 Nov

Goodtime, 27 Oct

Toenails, 30 June

Cleanslate, 21 Feb

Key
→ US forces
▲ Airfields
— Front line, late 1942
– – Front line, mid-1943
···· Front line, Nov 1943

15

PARATROOPERS ON CHOISEUL

The 2nd Battalion, 1st Parachute Regiment, US Marine Corps, selected for the diversionary operations on Choiseul, consisted of a headquarters company, which included a headquarters section, supply section and a communications platoon, and three rifle companies. These each consisted of three rifle platoons, plus a weapons platoon that comprised a light machine gun section (three squads with six guns) and a light mortar section (three squads with six mortar tubes).

The basic smallarms of the rifle companies included the version of the Garand that was standardised in 1936 for service in the US forces, the 0.3in M1 rifle, which was fed by an eight-round magazine, and the 15- or 30-round M1 carbine. These weapons also had launch attachments (the M7 and M8 respectively) for the M9A1 anti-tank grenade. The Johnson 0.3in M1941 semi-automatic rifle, with a 10-round rotary, non-detachable magazine, also saw service, together with the Reising 0.45in 12- or 20-round sub-machine gun, which was one of the weapons developed during World War II to replace the complex and expensive Thompson. The rifle companies were also equipped with H.E. hand grenades and HC-M8 smoke grenades.

The machine-gun sections were armed with the Browning 0.3in 1919A4 light machine gun, selected for deployment in the difficult jungle conditions of Choiseul. The mortar sections had the 60mm Mortar M2, the standard infantry mortar of the US forces.

Additional weapons included the 2.36in 'Bazooka' anti-tank rocket launcher and a new form of experimental rocket with a 29lb shell.

that these men should also be able to reach Sangigai by 1400.

With unreliable radio communications in the jungle, we planned to co-ordinate the attack by the opening of a rocket and mortar barrage, to begin no earlier than 1400. My command group would be with the enveloping force moving through the jungle.

At dusk on the 29th, our effort to announce a heavy force on Choiseul received an unexpected windfall. Lieutenant Douglas Morton, in charge of the security detachment on Zinoa Island, reported over the radio that a Japanese submarine had surfaced just 200yds from them. I told him to attempt a rocket attack, and the second round exploded square on the conning-tower. The submarine immediately submerged and, although no great damage was done, there was no doubt that a report would be filed of an American

Background: A US Marine holds out with an M1 carbine against suicidal Japanese banzai assaults. Top: A patrol sets out carrying experimental rockets and their launchers. Above right: A mortar is used to bombard a Japanese bivouac.

attack from Choiseul.

At dawn on 30 October we suffered an unforeseen setback. Four US planes dived onto our landing craft on Zinoa Island and damaged three of them before the pilots realised their error. The whole of the force now had to go overland. We took off down the trail in single file under a steady rain.

The seven miles to Vagara were covered without contact with the enemy. The force then split to follow our scheme of manoeuvre. The force moving northward inland struggled past the 100ft banyan trees, chopping their way through the thick undergrowth. Deep, black streams crossed our path in the steep hills and there was an all-pervasive stink of rotting vegetation. The pressure of having to gain our positions before 1400 hours made the task still more fatiguing, and when the hour arrived we could see nothing of the Sangigai base. In growing apprehension, I worked my way forward to the leading platoon – where the battalion commander has no business being. There I met Captain Spencer Pratt, the commander of the leading company, who was sharing my impatience.

Suddenly, at about 1430, we heard the crash of mortar and rocket explosions over the hill no more than 200yds to our front. At the same time we heard screaming and shouting, and in a moment we struck the enemy head on at close range. Our troops deployed with great difficulty and the fire on both sides grew in intensity. We heard the familiar slow rattle of the Japanese Nambu machine guns and the explosions of their 50mm 'Knee Mortars'. What we did not know was that Manchester's force, moving down the beach, had surprised the enemy, who had withdrawn back through the village and directly into the face of our enveloping column.

The fighting was sharp, at ranges as little as 15yds. Grenades were flying in both directions. Some of the enemy occupied foxholes, which had been dug previously as part of their perimeter, while others scurried up trees to gain better visibility. One of these elevated snipers hit Captain Pratt in the shoulder, and my runner, Corporal Albert Hoffman, located him and knocked him out of the tree with a burst of automatic fire, but not before the sniper had hit me in the arm. We pressed on, however, making slow progress as we flushed the Japanese, one by one, from their emplacements. After half an hour the Japanese launched a 'banzai' attack which was broken up by our machine guns. During this attack I was hit a second time, this time in the jaw.

As the remnants of the garrison tried to withdraw to the southeast, Manchester's column drove into Sangigai, capturing everything of value, destroying all the installations and barges, and burning food and other supplies. A bag of documents was collected, and 70 Japanese dead were left behind. Of our forces, four were dead and nine wounded.

Knowing that Japanese aircraft and reinforcements would soon arrive, we pulled out by two routes and headed for Vagara. We were to rendezvous there at between 1800 and 1900 hours with any boats that had been repaired during the day. Manchester's column arrived at 1830 and was evacuated to Voza, but our column was delayed by the terrain, and darkness found us about a mile short of Vagara. Arriving at 1930, we found no boats and spent an apprehensive but uneventful night dug in by the river mouth. The boats appeared 30 minutes after daylight on the 31st, having ceased to operate in the darkness for fear of reefs.

Back at Voza, we examined the pile of documents captured at Sangigai. Among them was a large naval chart of the region, with symbols indicating the locations of minefields around southern Bougainville. We immediately sent a message to Corps Headquarters, informing them of the approximate positions. An answer was not long in coming: 'What are exact locations of minefields including all channels? Expedite answer.' As a result, we laboriously encoded the latitudes and longitudes of the corners of each minefield and radioed them out. It was not until 10 days later that we learned that, using our information, Admiral William Halsey had sent in mine-layers to close the entrances to the channels through the minefields, and two Japanese ships had been sunk as a result.

Having struck hard at the Japanese outpost at Sangigai, it was now imperative to keep up the pressure in order to keep the Japanese guessing as to our strength. Accordingly, on 31 October we sent a platoon combat patrol southward to prevent the Japanese from gaining intelligence of us and to keep them on the defensive. The men met a Japanese patrol near Vagara, and nine of the enemy soldiers were killed during the ensuing fierce firefight. Concurrently, another patrol reconnoitred northward by boat as far as the Warrior River, spying out the terrain for an attack on Choiseul Bay on 1 November. Led by Major Tom Bigger, my executive officer, the attacking force was to land at the mouth of the Warrior River and move inland to positions from which the Japanese Choiseul Bay supply base on Guppy Island could be bombarded by mortars. The force would then pull back to be evacuated by our boats which, thanks to the ingenuity of their crews, were now all serviceable again.

At dawn on 1 November, D-day for the landings on Bougainville, the Choiseul Bay force set out. A platoon also moved south to set up an ambush near Vagara. There, three of the large experimental rockets were armed and strung up in trees directly over the beach trail, secured by a slip knot to vines lying across the path. Four hours later the trap was sprung. A 20-man enemy patrol tripped two of the rockets and they performed exactly as planned. When the smoke cleared, eight of the enemy lay dead and four more were wounded.

The Choiseul Bay force, meanwhile, landed at the Warrior River and, leaving a four-man radio detachment at the mouth, pressed inland through the jungle until nightfall. The landing was observed, however, and during the night of 1/2 November a Japanese reconnaissance patrol stumbled into the radio detachment, but was beaten off. The men found that they could not reach the main force on the radio to warn them, but they managed to contact me and I requested fighter and PT boat cover for the withdrawal of the force, which was scheduled for the afternoon of 2 November.

A savage firefight broke out, but suddenly our four landing craft, covered by four PT boats, arrived

Two hours after dawn on the 2nd, the main force at Choiseul Bay ran into the Japanese outpost positions. After driving the enemy back during the morning they got close enough to put 142 mortar rounds into the Guppy Island base. Two big fires were blazing behind them as they turned back down the trail, but just as they approached the Warrior River they encountered about 200 Japanese to their front and left. A savage firefight broke out, but suddenly our four landing craft, covered by four PT boats, arrived on the scene. The men aboard opened up with all their weapons, and their fire turned the tide of the battle. The enemy slowly retreated, leaving 42 dead behind them.

As the landing craft withdrew, one of them piled up on a coral head. Its bottom was torn out and it went down in an instant. Luckily, everyone aboard was resuced by a PT boat captained by Lieutenant John F. Kennedy, who was later to become President of the United States.

The Choiseul Bay force was back at Voza by 2100 hours, and we were advised that we were to be withdrawn from the island at midnight. Natives then reported that a battalion of Japanese was landing about five miles to our north. Obviously the Bougainville attack had shown them the true size of our force, and now they were after us. We sent out men on both flanks, setting up minefields and rocket ambushes and, around each outpost, we worked razor blades into the trees to discourage snipers from climbing into them.

With darkness, we withdrew to a defensive perimeter around Voza beach. The outposts were all reporting Japanese probing the positions in

strength, and at about 2200 we heard the crash of a rocket and firing from one of the outposts. Firing broke out from one outpost after another then and it was clear that a major attack was imminent.

The landing ships did not appear until 0100 on the 3rd. We began loading immediately, and at 0200 we began pulling in the outposts. Seaton insisted that his job was to remain on the island and he refused to come, arguing that he and the bearers could elude the enemy. I had my doubts, but I shook the hand of that brave and dedicated man and walked aboard the last landing ship. Next day, he reported by radio that the Japanese had launched a co-ordinated attack on both flanks of the Voza position at daybreak. It took them half a day to make their way through the booby traps and mines, only to discover that the Americans had gone.

THE AUTHOR Lieutenant-General Victor H. Krulak commanded the 2nd Battalion, 1st Parachute Regiment, US Marine Corps, during the diversionary operations on Choiseul. He was awarded the Navy Cross for his heroic leadership of the force.

Above: The rescue of a boat load of US Marine paras on Choiseul was just one episode in the eventful wartime career of Lieutenant John F. Kennedy. Below: Admiral William F. Halsey presents Lieutenant-Colonel Victor Krulak with the Navy Cross. The award was for 'extraordinary heroism displayed against an armed enemy as commanding officer of a unit of a marine parachute regiment during operations on Choiseul Island'.

In February 1942, 2 Para launched a raid on the German radar installation at Bruneval. Major-General John Frost, who led the paras, tells the story of their audacious first mission

EMPLANED IN THE belly of a black Whitley, slow, draughty, uncomfortable, cold and seemingly most vulnerable, we sat on Thruxton Aerodrome waiting for take-off on a raid on the coast of enemy-occupied France. So many men have since described what it feels like to go by air to battle that I hesitate to mention our feelings on the way to France. This was no armada. We were so very much by ourselves.

The whole object of the operation was to dismantle the essential parts of the latest German radar station at Bruneval and bring them back to England. Our force, which consisted of 120 all ranks, was to drop about half a mile inland in three main parties, starting at 0015 hours on 28 February 1942. This was to be a combined operation par excellence with the navy, army and RAF all intimately concerned, and we had named each party after a famous sailor; we hoped the Senior Service would appreciate our gesture.

Below: Whitley bombers, known affectionately as 'Flying Barn Doors', were tasked to drop the paras over Bruneval, aerial photo-reconnaissance (bottom right) having first pinpointed the villa and radar station. Bottom left: Mission accomplished. In the aftermath of a successful raid, Major Frost (right), commander of 2 Para, discusses the raid with an airborne officer.

BRUNEVAL RAIDERS

A COMBINED OPERATION

In January 1942, Admiral Lord Louis Mountbatten (below), the Chief of

Combined Operations, approached HQ 1st Airborne Division with a plan for a combined operation par excellence, pivoting on the men of the 1st Airborne.

In late 1941, RAF photographic reconnaissance aircraft had pinpointed a radio-location site at Bruneval, near Le Havre, one of a series of such installations on the western seaboard of Europe to give the enemy warning of incoming Allied aircraft.

A sophisticated combination of vertical and oblique photographs indicated that this station was one of the most advanced in design and construction, and the decision was made for an immediate raid, not merely to put it out of action, but to dismantle and bring back to England the essential parts of the Würzburg radio-location apparatus for study. Much of the success of the operation must be attributed to the remarkable reconnaissance work of the RAF, supplemented with information gathered by the French Resistance – the exact location of every enemy defensive position was plotted.

This is not, however, to underestimate the contribution of the pilots of Bomber Command who took the paras to their destination nor the Royal Navy crews who brought them home – without them the raid could never have been mounted.

Raid on Bruneval
Feb 1942

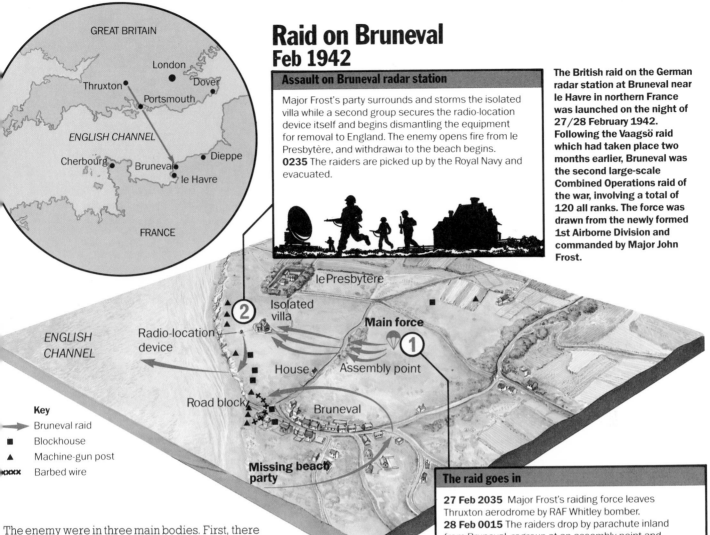

Assault on Bruneval radar station

Major Frost's party surrounds and storms the isolated villa while a second group secures the radio-location device itself and begins dismantling the equipment for removal to England. The enemy opens fire from le Presbytère, and withdrawal to the beach begins.
0235 The raiders are picked up by the Royal Navy and evacuated.

The British raid on the German radar station at Bruneval near le Havre in northern France was launched on the night of 27/28 February 1942. Following the Vaagsö raid which had taken place two months earlier, Bruneval was the second large-scale Combined Operations raid of the war, involving a total of 120 all ranks. The force was drawn from the newly formed 1st Airborne Division and commanded by Major John Frost.

Key
- → Bruneval raid
- ■ Blockhouse
- ▲ Machine-gun post
- ✕✕✕ Barbed wire

The raid goes in

27 Feb 2035 Major Frost's raiding force leaves Thruxton aerodrome by RAF Whitley bomber.
28 Feb 0015 The raiders drop by parachute inland from Bruneval, regroup at an assembly point and move off to their targets, a villa outside Bruneval and the radio-location device nearby.

The enemy were in three main bodies. First, there were the signallers and guards on duty at the main radar station itself, which was built near a lonely clifftop villa – thought to be about 30 men all told. Then, at 'Le Presbytère', a wooded enclosure containing some buildings 300yds north of the villa, the reserve signallers and coast defence troops were billeted, totalling possibly over 100 men. Lastly, there was the garrison of the village of Bruneval itself, through which a narrow road led from the beach to the hinterland, the beach being defended by pillboxes and earthworks both on top of the cliffs flanking the beach, and also down below. Some 40 men lived in the village and were responsible for manning these positions.

Our first party was to be 'Nelson', consisting of 40 men under Lieutenant John Ross and Lieutenant Euen Charteris. Their task was to capture the beach defences from the rear, so that we could subsequently be evacuated from the shore. Then came my lot, which was further subdivided into three parties, 'Jellicoe', 'Hardy' and 'Drake'. Included here were Flight-Sergeant Cox, an RAF expert in radar, and a section of 1st Parachute Field Squadron, RE, under Captain Dennis Vernon. Our task was to capture the villa and the radar equipment, while the sappers and Cox dismantled all the parts that were needed, and photographed what couldn't be removed.

Finally, a reserve party called 'Rodney', under John Timothy, was to be interposed between the radar station and the most likely enemy approach, so as to prevent interference with the dismantling. The pilots who were to fly us to our objective belonged to a crack bomber squadron commanded by Wing

Left: Remarkable photo-reconnaissance work by the RAF was supplemented by information gathered by the French Resistance. Using this intelligence, the operational planners were able to construct a scale model of the target (top), and could ascertain the exact strength and disposition of the enemy. Once the radar equipment had been captured, the paras were to be evacuated from the beach by Royal Navy landing craft. On the bridge of one of these craft (centre) can be seen Major John Frost (second from left), who led the raid. The deployment of airborne troops had been necessitated by Bruneval's steep cliffs, and a string of machine-gun posts which would have pinned down a direct beach assault. Commanding the force of Whitley bombers was Squadron Leader Charles Pickard (bottom left), seen here talking to the men he had dropped a few hours earlier.

Commander Charles Pickard. We were in no doubt as to their efficiency and we felt that if anybody was going to put us down in the right place, they were the people to do it.

Success depended on complete surprise. Elaborate precautions had been taken in the interests of security and it did not require much imagination to predict what the enemy's reception would be if he had obtained an inkling of our intentions. We had been presented with an alarming close-up photograph of our objective, which had obviously been taken by a Spitfire or some such aircraft at nought feet, and my attention had been drawn to the fact by one of the men: 'If they're going to go flashing cameras in their faces in that sort of way, how can we possibly surprise them?' he said. 'Oh, telephoto lens, you know, telephoto lens, taken from miles away,' I replied. 'Nothing to worry about at all.'

However, we did worry as we sat in silence enforced by the alternating roar and hush of the Whitley's engines, passing round a water bottle filled with tea well laced with rum. My stomach contracted as the aircraft began to move and bump

The raid on Bruneval was centred around the men of C Company, 2nd Battalion, 1st Parachute Brigade, which formed part of the 1st Airborne Division under General 'Boy' Browning. The 2nd Battalion had begun to form in the autumn of 1941, to be ready for war by midsummer 1942.

However, the men had barely completed parachute training when, in January 1942, they were earmarked for the special operation at Bruneval. 1st Battalion had already been in existence for over a year, but General Richard Gale, then Brigadier, deliberately chose one of the newly formed battalions, to show that his whole brigade was ready for action at any time.

And so they proved. Commanded by a Cameronian, Major John Frost, C Company, which bore the brunt of the fighting, was almost entirely Scottish. Black Watch and Cameron Highlanders dominated in numbers, with Scottish Riflemen, Fusiliers and Bordermen a close second; but all regiments were represented, including a small contingent of London Scottish, who were nicknamed 'The Piccadilly All-Sorts'. An outstanding body of men, fully 95 per cent of the company had decided to become parachutists as, they thought, the quickest way of seeing action. In the absence of an enemy, the healthy rivalries that existed between their parent regiments proved a useful way of letting off steam during training. A feather in the cap for HQ Combined Operations, their successful sortie into enemy-occupied France really put airborne forces on the map.

along the perimeter track. Then came the surge forward with full throttle and all doubting went as, soon after 2030 on 27 February, my aircraft took off.

It was difficult to talk. The noise and vibration were considerable. We sat side by side on the floor, which was of ribbed aluminium and not at all comfortable. We were jammed close together and our legs were covered with blankets. Sometimes we sang, and then above all that din the voice of Flight-Sergeant Cox filled that gloomy fuselage with ringing cheery tones. So we have sung many times since on long flights over other countries, when the engines seem to play the music of an unseen band.

The tempo of the aircraft quickened perceptibly when we took the cover off the hole. Those sitting beside it looked down into the Channel and watched the water moving gently in the moonlight. This opening made the inside of the fuselage very cold and we drew our blankets closely about us and began to count the minutes. Suddenly we were over land. Our enemies were now only 600ft below us. Soon we saw lights moving slowly up towards us which increased their speed viciously as they flashed beyond the limits of our view.

There was no wind and all was silent apart from the noise of our aircraft stealing away into the night

'Action stations!' came soon after. Away went our blankets and other comforts. The noise of the engines abated to a gentle humming. I dangled my legs in the hole. Then someone shouted, 'Go!'

As I jumped, I was able to recognise the ground as being identical with that depicted by the model, maps and photographs we had seen of the landscape. All the features one expected to see were standing out in the bright moonlight. I landed very softly in the snow. There was no wind and all was silent apart from the noise of our aircraft stealing away into the night.

We collected at the rendezvous and in about 10 minutes we were ready to move off. We met no opposition nor any obstacles other than wire fences on our way. We heard a few stray bursts of machine-gun fire in the distance, but from the area of the radar station, which we could see plainly, there was no sign of alarm. According to plan, silently and stealthily we surrounded the villa, and when everybody was in position I walked towards the door. It was open. I blew my whistle, the signal for battle to commence. Immediately, explosions, yells and the sound of automatic fire came from the proximity of the radar set and my party rushed into the house. It was devoid of furniture and we found only one German in a top room who was firing at our people down below.

Having left a couple of men inside, we went to reinforce the men near the set. By this time they had dealt with the enemy on the site and had two prisoners. We questioned them about their comrades. It seemed that our original information was correct. However, they were vague about reserves based further inland and were almost incoherent with surprise and shock.

So far so good, but fairly soon the enemy opened fire on the villa from 'Le Presbytère' and one of our men was killed coming out of the door. Dennis Vernon with his sappers arrived soon after this and he, with Flight-Sergeant Cox, began to inspect and dismantle the parts of the radar set that they wanted. Gradually the fire from the edge of 'Le Presbytère' increased and it became extremely uncomfortable

A smooth evacuation from the beach was vital to the operation's success, and rigorous combined training exercises were held beforehand. Landing craft were put through their paces (left) and paratroopers were drilled in covering their approach to the beach (below left). Troops in the craft (below) would cover the paras' retreat using Bren light machine guns and anti-tank rifles.

in our area. Fortunately this fire was most inaccurate and caused no further casualties. However, some time later we noticed vehicles moving up behind the wood. If the enemy began to mortar us in the open it would be difficult to get the equipment away.

I told Dennis that it was time to go. His men had been loading the pieces of equipment they had dismantled onto canvas trolleys and we all moved off towards the beach. When we reached a pillbox on the shoulder of the cliff, a machine gun opened up on us from the other shoulder and we suffered casualties. Company Sergeant-Major Strachan was badly wounded in the stomach. We pulled him into cover and gave him some morphia. This machine gun opened up each time we moved, but it was possible to make contact with the Rodney party, who were further inland.

At this stage, some confusion was caused by an unidentified voice shouting from below: 'Come on down! Everything is alright and the boats are here.' But this was immediately contradicted by John Ross who was near the beach: 'Do not come down. The beach defences have not been taken yet.'

Obviously something was seriously wrong. I started to go across to John Timothy of Rodney to order him to put in an immediate attack from his position. Then a man came from behind to say that the Germans had reoccupied the villa and were advancing against us from that direction. Here again we were at a disadvantage. My men were armed only

Para, Bruneval 1942

This para wears a steel helmet, gaberdine jump smock and '37 pattern web anklets. He carries a Lee-Enfield .303in rifle (right) and a captured German Mauser 98K carbine.

with grenades and with Sten guns which had just been produced and had many teething problems. The unorthodox formations we had adopted meant that I had to lead the party back to deal with this new threat, when I had many other things to take care of.

Fortunately this threat did not amount to very much, for the Germans were still very confused and were up against they knew not what. As we returned to the pillbox, we found that the sappers were on the move again, skidding and sliding with their heavily laden trolleys down the steep frozen path to the beach. The Sergeant-Major was being dragged along at the same time. The troublesome machine gun was silent now, so one could presume that the beach defences had been taken. All the main features showed up well in the moonlight, but one could see men and movement only when they were close at hand.

I found Euen Charteris, the commander of Nelson party, near the main beach pillbox. He told me that he and two of his sections had been dropped about two miles short of the correct place. They had had a very difficult time finding their way across country through woods and hedges to Bruneval and had fought a tricky little battle with a German patrol en route. It was Euen and his party who had dealt with the machine gun on the cliffs and then swept down on to the beach with great aplomb. He quickly collected the remainder of Nelson and every defender who showed himself was speedily despatched.

There was now time to take stock. So far, the object had been achieved. We had very few casualties. We had given the enemy a good hammering and so far they had produced no effective counter-measures. It was about 0215 in the morning. All we wanted now

...e raiders return. With their ...ecious cargo on board, the ...tilla of landing craft ...ossed the Channel ...hampered by the Luftwaffe. ...s they neared Portsmouth ...rbour, the triumphant ...ders received a chorus of ...eers and victory waves ...elow) from two passing ...stroyers. The operation ...d been a resounding ...ccess; in addition to the ...ürtzburg's secrets, the ...sault force captured a ...mber of German prisoners ...elow left), seen here ...aving one of the landing ...aft. Far left: Captain H.B. ...ate of the *Prinz Albert* ...scusses the operation with ...e of the radio experts who ...ok part in the raid.

was the navy.

I found the signallers and told them to send for the boats, but to my disgust they said they could not make contact. Then we tried to summon them with a lamp, and still got no reply. There was a slight mist out to sea and visibility was no more than half a mile. We had arranged one last emergency means of communication, which was a red Verey light fired first to the north and then to the south along the beach. Even after this had been fired several times, there was no sign of recognition from the sea.

'Sir, the boats are coming in! The boats are here! God bless the ruddy navy, sir!'

The great cliffs each side of the little beach seemed to lean over and dominate us with ever-growing menace. It looked as though we were going to be left high and dry; the thought was hard to bear. With a sinking heart, I moved off the beach with my officers to rearrange our defences in the entrance to the village and on the shoulders of the cliff. But then there came a joyful shout from one of the signallers. 'Sir, the boats are coming in! The boats are here! God bless the ruddy navy, sir!'

A sense of relief unbounded now spread amongst us all as we saw several dark shapes gliding in across the water towards us and we began to assemble in our various parties to embark. But then the men who manned the landing craft opened fire on the cliffs when they were about 50yds from the beach. The

noise was terrific as the echoes rang from cliff to cliff. We shouted and screamed at them to stop as some of our men were still in position to defend the beach from landward attack.

We had planned that only two boats would come in at a time, so that we could make an orderly withdrawal in three phases, but now all six landing craft came in together and some looked as though they might be beached, as the sea was beginning to run fairly high. Amidst the noise and confusion, it was impossible to control the embarkation. Meanwhile, when they saw we were going, the Germans began to emerge from some of their hiding places and lobbed grenades and mortar bombs onto the beach.

Fortunately, we were able to get the wounded and enemy radar equipment onto one landing craft very quickly, but the rest of our evacuation plan went by the board, and it was a case of getting as many as possible onto each boat in turn. As far as we could tell, all our men were away, most of us soaked to the skin, for we had had to wade and scramble through the waves to reach the boats. But we had not been able to check everybody in and, as we reached the gunboats which were to bring us home, we heard a pathetic message from two signallers who had lost their way and reached the beach too late.

Aboard the gunboats, we went below to warm ourselves, where we learnt that the navy had been having troubles of its own. While they had been waiting motionless for us offshore, a German destroyer and two E-boats had passed by less than a mile away and by God's good grace had failed to spot them. It was no wonder that they had been unable to answer our signals and that they had been in a hurry to take us off.

There were destroyers now on either side of the flotilla and they came by at speed and saluted us

The sailors make us as comfortable as they could and made a great fuss of us, which I began to feel we did not deserve. In worrying about the fate of the unfortunate few, I almost forgot that the object had been achieved. We were considerably cheered therefore to get a message from the ship which carried the radar equipment to say that we had managed to get practically everything that was wanted.

As daylight came, a squadron of Spitfires flew from England to meet us, ready to beat off any attempt by the enemy to destroy us and our cargo on the way home, but the crossing passed without incident. I went up to the bridge as we approached Portsmouth. There were destroyers now on either side of the flotilla and they came by at speed and saluted us. The strains of 'Rule Britannia' rang out from their loudhailers while Spitfires dived down in turn.

At about six that evening we boarded the *Prinz Albert*, the parent ship of our flotilla, where we found Charles Pickard with his pilots and a great welcome. The ship was crowded with staff officers, photographers, reporters and all who had taken part in the raid. The limelight was strange after weeks of secrecy and stealth. All we really wanted was dry clothes, bed and oblivion; but before that there was some serious drinking to be done.

THE AUTHOR Major-General John Frost commanded the 2nd Battalion of The Parachute Regiment from 1940 to 1945. He retired from the army in 1968 and his books include *A Drop Too Many* and *2 Para Falklands: The Battalion at War*.

6 June 1944: the men of the 9th Battalion, The Parachute Regiment, drifted down into France, their target the well-defended Merville Battery

AIRBORNE OPERATIONS have always been considered risky undertakings: for success, the troops involved have to be professional, the preparations exhaustive, and the timing precise. If an assault starts to go wrong, the men are likely to pay with their lives. Consequently, the ability to make sudden adjustments to unexpected circumstances has long been seen as crucial to the outcome of a mission. Although the men of the 9th (Home Counties) Battalion, The

D-DAY LANDING

After months of intensive and realistic training (below right), smiling paras of the 6th Airborne Division emplane for Normandy (below, left and centre).

Parachute Regiment (9 Para) may not have considered their operation on D-day in quite the same terms, they had to start making changes to their plans from about 0230 hours on the morning of 6 June 1944.

At about 0100 hours on that fateful morning, the Allied invasion of Europe began. The story of Operation Overlord and of D-day itself is well known, but many people fail to appreciate just how marginal some of the operations were that took place that day. The assault by 9 Para on the German gun battery at Merville and that of the US Rangers on the battery at Point du Hoc rank as the two classic small-unit actions of the entire operation.

9 Para was part of the 6th Airborne Division's 3rd Parachute Brigade. Commanded by Brigadier James Hill, a former commanding officer of 1 Para who had served in North Africa, the brigade's job was, very simply, to seal the left flank of the invasion beaches by destroying bridges over the river Dives and its tributaries over which German reinforcements would have to pass, and to destroy the

German gun battery at Merville. This battery posed one of the greatest threats to the British landings on Sword, Juno and Gold beaches, just five miles to the west. Its four heavy guns, buried under 12ft of concrete, could engage the ships out at sea, the landing craft coming in to the shore, or the men, tanks and vehicles already ashore but under heavy fire on the beaches. The job of taking the battery and destroying the guns was given to 9 Para, under the command of Lieutenant-Colonel T.B.H. Otway.

A hard-driving perfectionist, Terence Otway was not a man to court popular affection, but made up for this by the respect in which he was held by his subordinates and fellow officers. Like Hill, Otway was an archetypal airborne commander: tough, energetic, capable of generating violence himself and inspiring others to do the same, and quite unwilling to accept defeat until it was rammed down his throat. He received his orders on 2 April 1944, leaving just two months to plan and rehearse the attack.

The battery at Merville consisted, it was believed, of four 150mm guns (later found to be of 75mm calibre), protected by a clutch of near-

Below: Capable of carrying 25 men, the Horsa was the main glider used by the paras on D-day. Below inset: A senior para officer. Note the Glider Pilot's badge on his Denison smock.

impregnable concrete casemates. The RAF had made no impression on the guns with their high-level precision bombing, so Otway was given carte blanche to plan the attack and prepare for the operation. Aerial photographs and information supplied by the French Resistance showed him just how tough a nut the Merville battery was going to be.

Otway began by setting a record for any soldier in any war. Some fine agricultural land near Newbury in the Thames valley closely resembled the area around the battery; he wanted to plough it up and turn it into a full-scale replica of the target. To do so meant getting written permission from no less than seven government ministries. This apparently impossible feat was accomplished in just under 48 hours.

To both Otway and Brigadier Hill, the detailed planning for this operation was vitally important. Besides the four guns, the garrison of

PARAS IN NORMANDY

The 6th Airborne Division, under the leadership of Major-General Richard Gale, had some of the most complex and dangerous missions to perform of any unit during the opening stages of D-day. The division's parachute battalions and support arms were to land several hours in advance of the main invasion force, seize or destroy several bridges over two rivers and the Caen canal, and silence enemy positions in an area along the eastern edge of Sword, Gold and Juno beaches, where the British Second Army was to come ashore a few hours later.

The division's two parachute brigades, the 3rd and 5th, had to land in the very heart of the enemy's defences and, after securing their primary objectives, prevent German forces from striking at the beach-heads.

Each brigade had specific tasks to perform: the 3rd Parachute Brigade had to destroy the Troarn, Varaville, Robehomme and Bures bridges across the Dives river, and another of its battalions, 9 Para, had to silence the Merville battery. The 5th Brigade was given a similar brief: to hold the bridges north of the village of Ranville over the river Orne and the Caen canal, and to prepare landing zones for glider troops.

At 0020 hours on the 6th, the first units of the 5th Brigade glided down to their targets: the canal and river bridges near Ranville. The canal crossing was seized in quick time and, a few hundred yards to the east, the second bridge was captured. Despite these successes, the battle for control lasted throughout the morning. As the fighting continued, the main force of the brigade landed. The 7th Battalion reinforced the hard-pressed men holding the bridges, the 12th seized the village of Le Bas de Ranville and the 13th began its advance on Ranville.

Further to the east, the battalions of the 3rd Brigade were moving on their objectives. The 8th Battalion destroyed two of its three targets but the third, at Troarn, took longer due to a temporary lack of explosives. The 1st Canadian Parachute Battalion sent out parties to blow the crossings at Varaville and Robehomme; they soon succeeded. Meanwhile, the most important attack, by 9 Para at Merville, had also been accomplished.

Left above: Major-General Richard Gale, the creator and commander of the 6th Airborne Division, on D-day, holds a last-minute conference with some of his officers before they join their men. Precise attention to detail at the frequent and exhaustive briefings prior to 6 June ensured that every man knew what was expected of him. Left below: Pathfinders learn their objectives. Landing in advance of the main airborne force, these men had to guide transports and gliders to their destinations.

some 130 men had nearly 20 machine guns, one 20mm dual-purpose gun and huge amounts of barbed wire, all sited in depth to give interlocking fire zones and mutual support to aid their defence. With typical German thoroughness, many of the guns pointed inland in case of attack from the rear. To compound 9 Para's problems, a cattle fence surrounded the battery. Inside the fence was a minefield 100yds deep, and inside this obstacle there was a barrier of barbed concertina wire some 15ft thick and five feet high, covered by the machine guns. Finally, much of the surrounding terrain was quite flat and, apart from a nearby orchard, treeless. Any direct assault in daylight would be detected long before the attacker could even get close to the mines and wire.

Such carefully planned defences meant that a surprise attack from the air and the resulting free-for-all was out of the question. Otway had therefore to make a highly complicated plan involving no less than 11 separate parties of paratroopers and engineers from 591 Parachute Squadron RE. Most of the groups would land by parachute some distance from the battery to preserve the element of surprise; some would land by glider, carrying heavy equipment, and others would land on the battery itself.

Otway's plan was to have Rendezvous (RV) Control and Battery Recce Parties land by parachute; the former to mark the drop zones (DZs) for the remainder, then reconnoitre routes to the battalion's main RV point and the battery itself; the latter to scout around the battery's defences and select the best assault points. Whilst they were doing this, 400 Lancaster bombers of the RAF would plaster the battery with high explosive, both to keep the enemy's heads down and to try and destroy some of the defences. At the same time, 11 gliders would land near the main RV carrying all the heavy equipment and engineering stores for the assault. Simultaneously, a Royal Engineer Taping Party would land by parachute and mark cleared routes through the defensive minefields, having probed them with special mine detectors.

The commander of the RV Organisation Party would then meet the rest of the battalion at the main RV and lead it to a firm base, 300 yds southeast of the battery, from where the attack would be mounted.

Three platoons of the Breaching Company would lead the assault, using bangalore torpedoes to blow gaps in the wire, then the Assault and Reserve Companies would sprint through and go for the guns, covered by two separate sniping parties. At the same time, a diversionary assault would go in against the main gate, which faced north, and three Horsa Mark II gliders carrying 58 volunteer sappers and paratroopers would crash-land on the battery itself.

Securing the British flank
6th Airborne Division, 6 June 1944

On D-Day, 6 June 1944, the massed troops of two Allied armies poured onto the beaches of Normandy: the drive to push the occupying German forces out of France had begun. The British 6th Airborne Division was tasked with securing the Allied left flank – and as part of this operation, the 9th Para Battalion was deployed to take the battery at Merville.

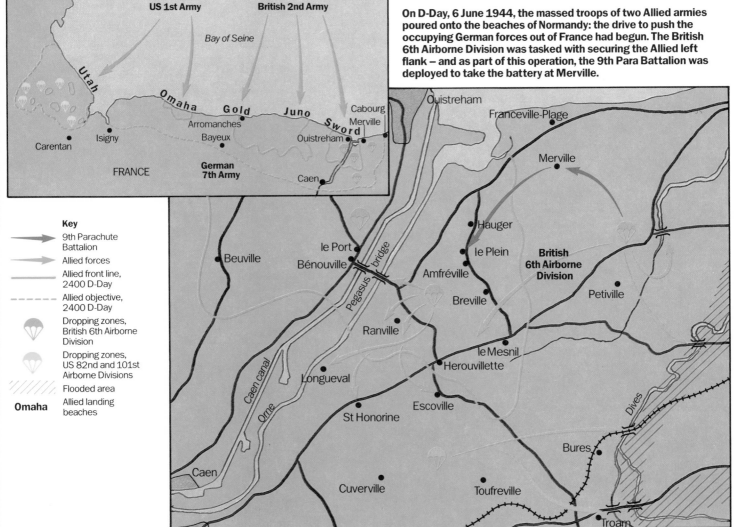

Operation Overlord

US 1st Army

British 2nd Army

Bay of Seine

Utah

Omaha Gold Juno Sword

Cabourg
Merville
Arromanches
Bayeux
Ouistreham

Carentan Isigny

FRANCE

German 7th Army

Caen

Ouistreham

Franceville-Plage

Merville

Hauger

le Port

Bénouville

Pegasus bridge

le Plein

British 6th Airborne Division

Amfréville

Petiville

Beuville

Breville

Ranville

le Mesnil

Herouvillette

Caen canal

Orne

Longueval

Escoville

St Honorine

Dives

Bures

Caen

Cuverville

Toufreville

Troarn

Key

→	9th Parachute Battalion
→	Allied forces
—	Allied front line, 2400 D-Day
---	Allied objective, 2400 D-Day
⛟	Dropping zones, British 6th Airborne Division
⛟	Dropping zones, US 82nd and 101st Airborne Divisions
////	Flooded area
Omaha	Allied landing beaches

at exactly 0430 hours. Their attack was to be the signal for the main assault to commence.

If the attack failed, Otway was told that HMS *Arethusa* would begin shelling the target at exactly 0530 hours. Success was to be signalled by the firing of yellow flares, whereupon the battalion would pull out and get on with its secondary tasks.

Nine separate rehearsals for the assault, four of them at night and all of them using live ammunition, were concluded by a minutely detailed five-day briefing in which every man learned the layout of the battery. As it was impossible to conduct a briefing of such detail in complete secrecy, Brigadier Hill put 9 Para to the test by infiltrating a number of good looking and specially trained girls into the battalion area. They tried to wheedle and seduce information out of the men by any means that came to mind but despite the fact that only the date and exact location of the target were unknown to the men, the girls learned nothing.

Brigadier Hill summed it all up in the conclusion of his final briefing to 3 Para Brigade: 'Gentlemen,' he said, 'in spite of your excellent training and orders, do not be daunted if chaos reigns. It undoubtedly will.' The GOC 6th Airborne Division, Major-General Richard Gale, told 9 Para: 'The Hun thinks only a bloody fool will go there. That's why we're going'. Truer words were never spoken, even in jest.

The battalion took off at 2310 hours on 5 June 1944, the 11 cargo gliders having set off some time before. The fly-in, despite bad weather which had already delayed the invasion by 24 hours, went well. Just four minutes from the DZ, however, things started to go wrong. For a start, the Germans had flooded the low-lying ground alongside the Dives and Orne rivers, so identifying landmarks became difficult and, for some Dakota crews, impossible. Then the flak started, and the Dakota transports of 46 Group RAF started weaving and turning to avoid being shot down with their passengers aboard.

The passengers did not like it. Laden with up to 90lb of weapons and equipment and another 35lb of parachute, those who were flung to the floor of the aircraft had a real problem trying to get up again. Others fell out of the open doors by accident as they stood there, hooked up and waiting for the green light, the signal to jump.

Otway was tipped out of his aircraft, as it bobbed and weaved through the flak, and realised immediately that he was nowhere near the DZ. In fact, he was heading straight for a German headquarters, which he recognised from air photographs! He and another man landed near the building and became the targets for a fusillade of pistol shots. Otway's companion heaved a brick through the window and, as the German officers inside ducked in the face of what they thought was a grenade, the two men doubled away. As they did so, a crash of breaking glass from the back of the building marked the arrival of Otway's batman in the greenhouse. Mira-

Main picture: Three Dakotas from the RAF's No. 46 Group unleash their cargoes of paras over Normandy. The descent was often the most dangerous part of an air assault. Unable to reply to enemy fire, many paras died before reaching the ground. Right: Paras take a break after three days' bitter action around Ranville. German resistance was stubborn. Far right: Hidden machine guns took a fearful toll.

culously, he was to meet up with Otway at the RV.

Things seemed to be going badly wrong. Otway's worst fears were confirmed when he finally reached the RV. The Battery Recce and RV Parties had arrived safely, but not many others, and the RAF bombers had missed the target. Otway's report on the situation remains to this day a minor classic of terse understatement:

'By 0250 hours the battalion had grown to 150 strong with 20 lengths of bangalore torpedo. Each company was approximately 30 strong. Enough signals to carry on – no 3in mortars – one machine gun – one half of one sniping party – no six pounder guns – no jeeps or trailers or any glider stores – no sappers – no field ambulance, but six unit medical orderlies – no mine detectors – one company commander missing.'

Otway, in a foul temper and in no mood to mess around, decided to advance at once.

The gliders had, in fact, all arrived in the wrong place. Low cloud, and the smoke and haze created

by the bombing had hidden key landmarks and made navigation impossible. Unable to find the Landing Zone (LZ), they came down widely separated and out of sight of the battalion. The men and stores the gliders were carrying were thus denied to Otway and the rest of the division until daybreak.

As time was running short and there was nothing to be done about the gliders, Otway sent A Company off towards the main RV. He and his tiny HQ following,

with the rest of the battalion trailing behind their furious colonel. A herd of stampeding bullocks did nothing to stop him, and the battalion met up with the Battery Recce Party at the main RV. This party had cut the outer fence and crawled through the minefield to spend half an hour listening to the German sentries and machine-gun crews whispering and coughing in their weapon pits. The Taping Party had arrived without their white tape but had scratched heel marks in the dust with their boots to mark corridors in the minefield. Things were not quite so bad after all. Otway took stock of the situation and ordered a complete reorganisation of the tiny force now left to him.

B Company, divided into two teams, would force the breach so that A and C Companies, divided into four parties of 12 men each, could deal with the guns. A six-man team under the command of a sergeant would carry out the diversionary attack. As this last team moved out, the Germans opened fire with 10 machine guns. The battalion's lone Vickers .303in medium machine gun returned fire and took out three of the enemy guns. The diversionary party took out three more with Bren-gun and rifle fire.

While this contest was going on, two of the three assault gliders appeared over the battery, bang on time. Here, again, luck deserted the battalion. The radio beacon which was supposed to guide the gliders in (code-named Eureka) was normally fitted with a demolition charge in case it fell into enemy hands. This particular one had decided to self-destruct as it hit the ground, nearly killing the paratrooper carrying it. A back-up had been arranged: illuminating rounds fired from a 2in mortar. But none had landed with the battalion. 9 Para watched, agonised, as the gliders circled the bat-

Given the likely scale of enemy opposition to its landings in the early part of D-day, the 6th Airborne Division had to be a large, all-arms force capable of sustained independent action.

With a strength of over 10.000 men, the division was divided into three self-contained brigades: the 3rd and 5th Parachute Brigades, and the 6th Air-Landing Brigade. Each contained three battalions which, with the exception of the glider-borne 6th Brigade, could be parachuted into battle. The brigades also received heavy support from field and anti-tank batteries, and could call on Royal Engineer and medical detachments.

At the divisional level, the commanding officer had larger engineer and artillery units as well as full logistical back-up under his direct control.

Although less well provided with heavy equipment than more conventional forces, the division was capable of generating a great deal of firepower. The provision of sub-machine guns was lavish, and up to 1000 Bren-guns and around 500 mortars of varying calibres were also available. Artillery support included six-pounder anti-tank guns and the much-liked 75mm pack howitzer.

Apart from the specially designed Welbike, the division's transportation requirements were met by bicycles, light trucks and the ubiquitous jeep. During the battles around the beach-head perimeter, however, the division was deployed in a conventional ground role to hold defensive positions, and made little use of its potential mobility.

tery, searching through the smoke and dust for a clear view of the target, taking a horrific amount of smallarms fire. They came down eventually, only four miles away, with no casualties, one, piloted by Staff-Sergeant Kerr, with some drama. Kerr was carrying four wounded men and the glider was beginning to smoulder from the effects of German tracer ammunition when he thought he could see the battery. He aimed straight for it, and his wheels had already touched the ground before he discovered that the smoke and haze had been playing tricks on his eyes. Ahead of him, there loomed a sign post, black on white, which carried a skull and crossbones and the word 'MINEN'. The terrified pilot hauled back the control column, the glider lurched into the air again, and landed 200yds further on, in an orchard. The trees tore the wings off the flimsy aircraft.

When the stunned survivors baled out of the now-burning wreckage, they were engaged by a platoon of Germans who were rushing to reinforce the battery. However, a four-hour gun battle beside the burning glider kept the Germans at bay and ensured that Otway's men were left undisturbed as they attacked the battery.

As the last chance of any support from the glider assault team went careering into the orchard under the horrified gaze of 9 Para, Otway gave the order for the attack to commence: 'Everybody in.

We're going to take this bloody battery!' One of the battalion's officers sounded the charge on his hunting horn and the breaching parties went in to clear the wire with bangalore torpedoes. The rest moved up, some men stepping outside the corridors through the minefield to suffer terrible injuries as they stormed the wire.

The four assault teams sprinted for the guns, trading rifle and sub-machine gun fire with the defenders as they went. Otway had ordered each paratrooper to paint a luminous skull and crossbones on the left breast of the sleeveless jacket that each man wore over his Denison smock. These emblems, together with the blackened faces and scrimmed helmets of the British parachutist did as much to frighten the enemy as anything else.

Although the fighting lasted for only a few minutes, it was hard and brutal, with no quarter given by either side. Hand-to-hand battles were fought in the gun

Bottom left: Manned by paras, a Vickers heavy machine-gun is used to hold captured ground. Once they had taken their initial objectives, the British airborne troops had to beat off a succession of increasingly desperate German attacks until relieved. Bottom: Despite heavy interdiction by the Allied aircraft and naval gunfire, small assault groups were able to hit back against the invasion troops.

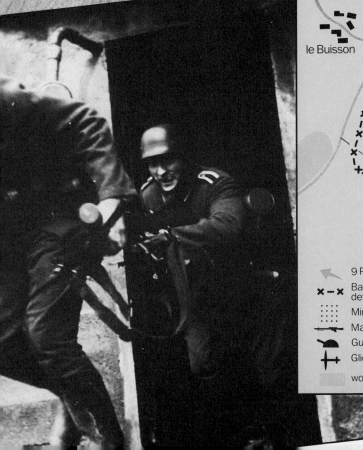

emplacements and the underground corridors. Subterranean galleries were cleared using grenade, Sten-gun and bayonet. In one gallery, ammunition was detonated by a grenade, killing one of the assault troops, but, despite the explosion, the fighting went on.

Suddenly, it was all over. With the back of the German resistance broken, one of the defenders spotted the skull and crossbones on the jacket of a paratrooper and shouted out 'Fallschirmjägern!' before surrendering. Others took up the cry and within minutes the Germans had surrendered. Otway was marching around the battery reorganising his men when news came that the guns had been spiked. Without their engineering stores the paratroopers had used Gammon bombs, a kind of anti-tank grenade, to destroy three of them and had blown the fourth by firing two shells through the barrel at once.

At almost exactly 0500 hours Otway ordered a yellow flare to be fired, just half an hour before *Arethusa* was to start lobbing shells into what was still an almost impregnable position. It was now four hours since 9 Para had started to jump from their Dakotas; in that time a battalion of 635 officers and men had been reduced to a mere 80. Some 65 men and five officers had been killed or wounded during the assault.

Otway gave orders for the wounded to be left with the battalion medical officer, and then he and the survivors set out for their secondary objective, the high ground close by the village of Le Plein to the south. On the way they met a Frenchman who warned them that nearly 200 German troops (conscripted Russians, in fact) were defending a château in the village of Hauger, which lay just ahead. Otway knew that his depleted command could not mount an attack on such a heavily fortified position, and he deployed his men in defensive positions around it; 10 yards between each man so that nobody could break out from the château or from further east towards the beaches. With the arrival of stragglers and lost

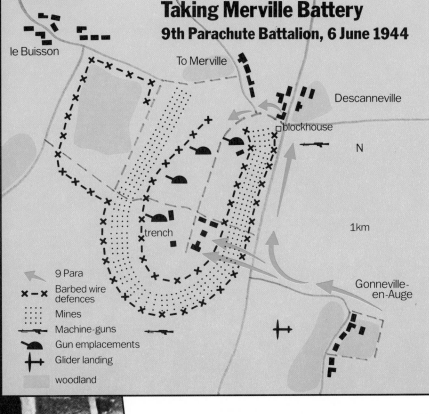

Taking Merville Battery
9th Parachute Battalion, 6 June 1944

le Buisson

To Merville

Descanneville

blockhouse

N

trench

1km

Gonneville-
en-Auge

→ 9 Para
×–× Barbed wire defences
∶∶∶ Mines
⊢ Machine-guns
◖ Gun emplacements
✛ Glider landing
woodland

Below left: The bitter harvest of D-day; a lone German lies where he fell in defence of Hitler's Festung Europa. Bottom: Shadowed by the mightiest invasion fleet ever seen and unhindered by enemy fire, British troops move off the Normandy beaches.

paratroopers from all points of the compass, 9 Para built up its strength during D-day itself, before being thrust into one of the hardest slogging matches of the entire Normandy campaign – the battle of Breville.

9 Para had secured one of the most dangerous threats to the Allied invasion fleet

9 Para's achievement in taking the battery at Merville must not be underestimated. Conventional wisdom states that when the defender is well equipped and dug-in on ground of his own choosing, it takes a numerical superiority of at least three-to-one to dislodge him. The assault must be planned carefully, the men must be rehearsed and properly equipped, and surprise must be maintained up to the last possible minute. Without exception, all of these elements were missing from 9 Para's final assault: the numbers were even; the plan had fallen apart and needed to be re-made at the very last minute; the men had no specialist equipment or support weapons, and they were only too aware of the risks they were running.

It was a magnificent tribute to both Otway and the men of 9 Para that the objective was taken in spite of all the problems, and that the battalion was still in some semblance of order to carry out its secondary task. By the morning of 6 June 1944, Terence Otway and 9 Para had secured one of the most dangerous threats to the assault craft of the Allied invasion force. They had paid a high price, but, in doing so had saved many more lives. As the first landing craft came ashore, the guns at Merville remained silent.

THE AUTHOR Gregor Ferguson is the editor of *Defence Africa and the Middle East* and has contributed to several publications. His most recent work is a short history of The Parachute Regiment.

On 29 November 1942 the men of 2 Para were dropped into Tunisia to attack the Axis airfield at Oudna. Major-General John Frost, who commanded the battalion, tells the story of the ensuing engagement

IT WAS CLEAR and cloudless as we flew between the peaks of the mountains, but it was a rough passage, with sudden gusts of wind buffeting the aircraft. Up above us were American Lightnings and far away on the flanks came British Hurricanes, but no enemy approached. I jumped as soon as we had swept over Depienne in Tunisia, and, having landed, I made for a small mound at the edge of the dropping zone and signalled my position to the men. Dominating the whole scene was a great rocky peak rising abruptly some 5000ft above the surrounding plain; this, the Djebel Zagouan, was so prominent a landmark that it helped us keep direction during the whole operation. Gradually, the battalion sorted itself out, and I sent orders to the companies that they were to take up positions on the edge of the dropping zone. I took stock of the situation and then summoned the company commanders. Six men were injured and one killed as a result of heavy landings, and it seemed best to leave the injured in Depienne, from where they could be evacuated later.

It was now just after 1600 hours. Suddenly three armoured cars appeared on the road leading east from Depienne. To our great relief they were friendly and belonged to the 56th Recce Regiment. I had not expected to meet any of our own forces in the area so soon, and my optimism regarding our mission

Right: Douglas Dakotas, carrying men of the 2nd Battalion, The Parachute Regiment, head for the Axis airfield at Oudna in Tunisia.

soared. The armoured cars trundled off down the road in the direction that we would take later on, while we set about requisitioning every vehicle – mostly mule carts – from the locals. The troop of armoured cars came back through our positions about an hour later, and informed us that there was an enemy road block near a place called Cheylus. The troop commander said that they hoped to catch up with us at Oudna the next day and that they would do what they could for our dropping casualties. I reckoned it was about 12 miles to Oudna and that if we started at midnight, we should be able to attack at first light. By exploiting the darkness and avoiding the main road, the possibility of encountering enemy patrols on the way would be minimised. Leaving one stick of C Company behind to salvage the parachutes, we formed up and moved off.

Lieutenant Ken Morrison was leading the column as it wound through the hill tracts towards our objective. The bad going caused the column to stretch out snake-wise, and all shoulders within reach had to be employed to ensure that the mule carts and trollies we had commandeered kept going. Gradually, our maps began to make sense as we spotted the outskirts of Tunis in the distance. During most of the night, streams of tracers, feeling their way up towards Allied bombers, had shown where the capital lay – in the backs of our minds was the proud hope that somehow we should get there. By 1100 hours on 30 November we were deployed on low hills overlooking the airfield that we had come such a long way to deal with. Our briefing had been very hurried, but there had been mention of a thrust by the 6th Armoured Division. Now our meeting with the armoured cars the previous day made me feel there was little need for caution, and I decided to press on to the airfield with the whole battalion. Frank Cleaver's B Company was detailed to keep watch from the high ground on the left flank, while Dick Ashford's A Company moved down the valley in open formation. John Ross's C Company, followed by

On 12 November 1942 the 2nd Battalion, The Parachute Regiment, commanded by Lieutenant-Colonel John Frost, landed at Algiers as part of the eastward thrust of the British First Army, under Lieutenant-General Sir Kenneth Anderson, towards Tunis and Bizerta. The British Eighth Army, commanded by General Sir Bernard Law Montgomery, had defeated Axis forces at the second battle of El Alamein, and on 8 November Allied forces landed in northwest Africa as part of Operation Torch. The capture of Tunis and Bizerta would effectively cut off German and Italian supply lines, and consolidate the Allied position in Tunisia before the winter rains began. When the 2nd Battalion arrived in Algiers, therefore, the leading elements of the First Army were confronting Axis forces some 600 miles further east.

The Allied advance was being hampered by enemy aircraft operating from airstrips to the west of Tunis, and, on 28 November, Frost was briefed to take the battalion to a German airstrip at Pont du Fahs in Tunisia and destroy any enemy aircraft that he could find. The battalion would then move on to airstrips at Depienne and Oudna and

perform the same task. The final objective was to link up with the First Army at St Cyprien.

As the battalion prepared to leave, there was a last-minute change of plan. New information, indicating that neither Pont du Fahs nor Depienne was being used by the Luftwaffe, meant that the drop would now be at Depienne. From here the battalion would advance on Oudna.

WINGS OVER OUDNA

The advance on Tunisia
Nov 1942 – Jan 1943

On 8 November 1942 the Allies launched Operation Torch. Three task forces landed in Morocco and Algeria and began an eastward drive along the North African coast towards the vital ports and airfields of Tunisia. Axis forces moved into Tunisia in strength, establishing a defensive line including Tunis and Bizerta by 10 November. In late November, an Allied offensive reached as far as Tebourba, and 2 Para dropped near Oudna with orders to seize the airfield and link up with the advancing Allies at St Cyprien.

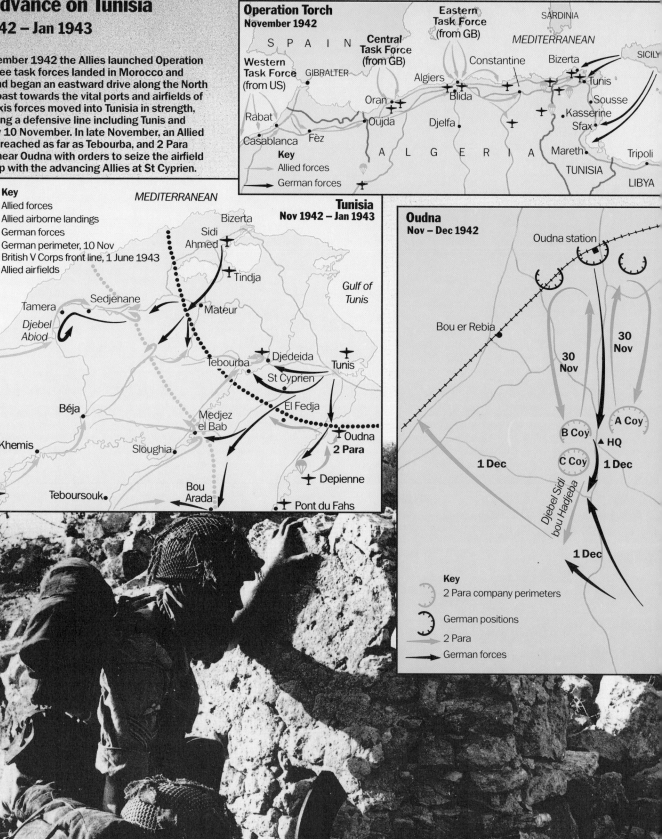

Operation Torch
November 1942

SPAIN
MEDITERRANEAN
SARDINIA
SICILY

Western Task Force (from US)
Central Task Force (from GB)
Eastern Task Force (from GB)

GIBRALTER
Constantine
Bizerta
Tunis
Algiers
Blida
Sousse
Oran
Kasserine
Rabat
Oujda
Djelfa
Sfax
Casablanca
Fèz
Mareth
Tripoli
ALGERIA
TUNISIA
LIBYA

Key
Allied forces
German forces

Tunisia
Nov 1942 – Jan 1943

Key
Allied forces
Allied airborne landings
German forces
German perimeter, 10 Nov
British V Corps front line, 1 June 1943
Allied airfields

MEDITERRANEAN
Bizerta
Sidi Ahmed
Tindja
Gulf of Tunis
Tamera
Sedjenane
Mateur
Djebel Abiod
Tabarka
Tebourba
Djedeida
Tunis
St Cyprien
Béja
El Fedja
Medjez el Bab
Oudna
2 Para
Souk el Khemis
Sloughia
Depienne
Souk el Arba
Teboursouk
Bou Arada
Pont du Fahs

Oudna
Nov – Dec 1942

Oudna station
Bou er Rebia
30 Nov
30 Nov
B Coy
A Coy
HQ
C Coy
1 Dec
1 Dec
1 Dec
Djebel Sidi bou Hadjeba

Key
2 Para company perimeters
German positions
2 Para
German forces

Battalion HQ, made its way along the high ground to the left. We must have been a brave sight, traversing the hills so far behind what the enemy considered their front line.

It seemed that nothing could stop our steady progress, when suddenly the noise of mortars and machine guns erupted from the direction of the airfield, and, with it, the bursting of bombs and the spattering of bullets among the advancing soldiers. C Company forged on, and A Company, under cover of their own weapons, reached some buildings inside the perimeter of the airfield.

It was obvious that the Luftwaffe were not using the airstrip, and I tried to send messages to the two company commanders to hold their positions. However, although I got through to the signallers where Company HQ should have been located, the only reply was: 'There's nobody here but me.'

After moving down to contact Ashford's company, I made my way towards the leading elements of C Company. As I approached, I heard heavy engines being revved up and the vicious crack of high-velocity guns. Tanks had been lurking near an old Roman viaduct, and as soon as our men left the cover of the hills this unwelcome column trundled into action. Together with a valiant few, Lieutenant P.B. Morrison wriggled towards them, intending to use grenades at close quarters. Morrison was killed and only one of his party survived the enemy hail of fire. We had come to deal with the German aircraft, and now they came to deal with us. First on the scene were the Messerschmitts, diving from every direction and firing unmercifully. Our ammunition had to be reserved for surer targets, and we could not afford to return the aircraft fire. There were 200 of us gathered in the small area, but, fortunately, the scrub provided good camouflage and when the Stuka attack followed, their bombs fell far away.

Tank and aircraft fire began to subside as the evening wore on, and just before dusk we started withdrawing to the high ground at Prise de l'Eau, with the intention of establishing an all-round defence. However, some elements of C Company had failed to receive the order for withdrawal, and, when we reached Prise de l'Eau, our effective strength had therefore been seriously depleted. The optimistic mood in which I had begun the operation was dispelled – we were outnumbered, our ammunition had been used up at an alarming rate and the biting cold of the night added to the discomfort of our wounded. Positive that the enemy would attack early the following day, I deployed a small group to set up an ambush at the foot of the hills. Contact with First Army HQ proved impossible, and we huddled together under the night sky, while streams of flak rose from Tunis. To the north, the sound of artillery

Left: Before the drop. Members of the 2nd Battalion, some wearing cushioned knee pads to prevent injuries on landing, wait for the signal to jump. Far left: Positioned in the lee of a ruined house, a Bren-gun team protects the drop zone while the rest of the battalion assembles. Above left: Major Dick Ashford, commander of A Company, during the fighting withdrawal from Oudna.

37

RETREAT FROM OUDNA

After a most gruelling scramble over very rough country, the battalion arrived at El Fedja, where it was discovered by a party of German soldiers. Major-General Frost describes the action and his battalion's subsequent breakout:

'At about 1500 hours on 2 December, mortar bombs began to land in our positions and this was soon followed by machine-gun fire. However, the ground was soft enough for reasonable slit trenches to have been built and we suffered few casualties. Two hours later, a small enemy party approached so close to A Company that there was no chance of missing them, and the whole lot were wiped out.

'The enemy was now too close for comfort, and I made a plan for withdrawal, involving parties passing through the Battalion HQ when I blew my hunting horn, forming one long column with the head organised especially to assault. It now seemed clear that if we could avoid being bounced, we should be able to get away.

'As the evening drew to a close, our hopes continued rising, for the Germans still hesitated. Once again, A Company repelled the enemy in their sector most successfully, and all were carefully obeying orders not to fire until kills were certain – we had no ammunition to waste. Just as darkness fell, the long-awaited assault came from the hill above us; this was met by a withering fire that repelled it most effectively, and, in the breathing space thus given, it was time to go.

'Steering towards a large haystack as a target and carrying our freshly wounded, we moved out. The leading parties encountered no resistance, and when we were well clear of El Fedja I sounded my horn again – this time as the signal to rendezvous. After several minutes we could only muster 110 of the 200 we had had in the farm. We formed up and set off on what we hoped would be the last lap.

'The following morning we spotted a German armoured column in the olive groves around Ksar Tyr, but the battalion had grown wary in the last few days, and it was no longer necessary to say anything when the enemy drew near. All ranks froze where they stood or lay, and absolute silence prevailed. The prowlers made off down the road to Tunis before we restarted our march.

'Two miles on, a column of armoured half-tracks approached with their machine guns covering us all the way – but they were unmistakably American. When the battalion arrived at Medjez, the AA guns and tanks that were dotted about meant that at last we could feel able to relax.'

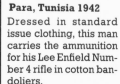

Para, Tunisia 1942
Dressed in standard issue clothing, this man carries the ammunition for his Lee Enfield Number 4 rifle in cotton bandoliers.

hampered our attempts to catch some shut eye.

No dawn was ever more welcome and after 'bully beef and biscuits' we co-ordinated our positions and began to dig deeper. Cover was sparse on the hills, and I feared that the enemy would have very little doubt as to our whereabouts when he pushed forward. As there were no aircraft on the ground for us to destroy, I had decided that our next move should be towards elements of the First Army. However, bearing in mind the armoured thrust that we were expecting, and encouraged by the contact two days before with our own armoured cars, I felt that we should hold our position for the time being and attempted to contact the First Army by wireless.

At 1000 hours on 1 December a small column of vehicles approached our position from the direction of the Oudna airstrip. There was a well-defined track leading up the valley, and soon a spearhead detached itself and came up to a well. Unfortunately, its speed took our ambush party by surprise and our original plan achieved little. The German forward party returned to where the main column had halted, and then began to shell and machine-gun our positions from a distance of 2000yds. We hit back with our mortars, and, after one bomb had landed slap in the middle of a group of vehicles and men the enemy withdrew to what they considered a safe distance.

C Company, which was holding ground behind us, facing the direction from which we hoped our own ground troops would arrive, reported that two tanks and an armoured car were approaching – displaying yellow triangles, our First Army recognition sign. A little later we were told that three of our men from an outpost had contacted the tanks and that they had climbed aboard and were now coming nearer waving their triangles. At Battalion HQ we all heaved a mighty sigh of relief. All our troubles seemed over. When John Ross of C Company came over to confirm the sighting, however, his face was grave:

> 'I thought I had better come personally,' he said. 'The tanks behind us are in fact German. They must have picked up the yellow triangles from the Depienne party. They have taken my three chaps prisoner... They have sent one in to say that they have got us completely surrounded and that there is no point in our continuing to fight. They are waiting now to hear what we have to say.'

Sickness, rage and utter weariness were my im-

mediate feelings. To plumb the depths of disillusion, while Ross had been speaking, the signallers received the only message we got during the entire operation – the armoured thrust on Tunis has been postponed. I decided that we had to move to fresh positions without delay, in order to make a clean break as soon as the darkness drew in. Having sent a warning to the companies, we set about destroying equipment that was no longer of any use. Mortar ammunition had been virtually exhausted, and we dealt with the tubes before turning our attention to the wireless sets – the sets had been in almost continuous use during the last eight hours and the batteries were finished. To show the Germans that we were in no mood to surrender, I sent a small party with Gammon bombs to get into a position from which they might have a chance of knocking out one of the tanks that was lurking outside C Company's perimeter. Lastly, and most wretchedly, we had to tell Jock McGavin, who was in charge of a section of field ambulance that had dropped with us, that the wounded would have to be left behind. As we moved off, the enemy in the valley increased their volume of fire, sending splinters from the rocks into our ranks and causing horrific wounds. I passed one man whose face had almost been sliced from his head but he held it on with both hands as he was guided along.

The sun shone down on us with full force, and after climbing for a short time we began to experience a raging thirst. Perhaps we should have realised what a problem water was going to be, given the fierce climate, but prior to our embarkation we had gleaned all we could from soldiers returning to Algiers from the front, and water had never been mentioned. Moving over the hills, heavily laden in the heat of the day, was more that we could bear and I decided to halt when we reached the northern slopes of a hill known as Sidi Bou Hadjeba. By the grace of God there was a well situated in the middle of where the new battalion area would be.

We deployed on two summits of the hill, with B Company on the right, and the remnants of C Company on the left. In reserve and looking to the left was A Company. While the units were taking up position, I lay down on a hillock to the rear in order to observe enemy activity on the plain below. This time I was under no illusions as to the identity of the armoured

Above: Advancing in extended order with fixed bayonets, paras charge across open ground under the cover of a smokescreen. Inset, far left: A mortar team goes into action. As a corporal lines up on a likely target, other paras ready the weapon's bombs. Far left: Protected by a comrade, a para lobs a grenade towards an enemy position. Below right: Casualty evacuation.

Bottom: The aftermath of a bloody encounter with the 2nd Battalion. Although short of tank-killing hardware, the paras took care of several German tanks. Here, a crewman lies on the shattered superstructure of a long-barrelled Panzer III. Below: Lieutenant-Colonel John Frost receives the DSO after Oudna from General Anderson.

cars and artillery pieces, and was pondering the most likely direction of German attack when one of A Company's officers, Keith Mountford, joined me. Asked what I was looking at, I remember saying in a nonchalant manner – which I was far from feeling – 'Just studying form Keith, studying form.'

At about 1500 hours the attack began. Infantry were carried up from the valley below in half-tracks, and light tanks were being brought up from the direction of Prise de l'Eau. Under cover of tank fire, enemy troops advanced and both sides raced for the top of the hill. I went with the Bren-gun team, but,

before we reached the crest, a burst from a German light machine gun hit our two leading men and Padre MacDonald who was behind us. I waited while the Bren was readied for action, and from my vantage point I could see several duels between our own men and the Germans, the latter armed with a similar weapon but with a higher rate of fire. Admittedly, the Germans were fresh compared to us, but there could be no doubt that their weapon handling was superior. Time and again they got into action first, and while our men were still groping for good fire positions, their opposite numbers would bring long and accurate bursts to bear. Nevertheless, we managed to prevent the Germans from staking their claim to the top of the hill, and, despite the covering fire the enemy was receiving from its tanks, we clung firmly to the reverse slope and brought a sweeping hail of fire to bear on any Germans who became too adventurous.

The paras made the most determined effort to put the enemy light tanks out of action

Meanwhile, virtually every kind of missile fell amongst our ranks, homing in on us from all points of the compass. There had been precious little time to dig in and prepare our defences, and, being so vulnerable, our casualties mounted steadily. Frank Cleaver, B Company commander, was suddenly struck down as he was consulting with his HQ. One old and battered mule remained from those we had requisitioned, and it was being used by Ronnie Gordon, the battalion medical officer, to move the badly wounded men to a collecting point. Ronnie seemed to be covered in blood from the men that he was tending, but there was not a great deal he could do. He had practically no dressings with which to staunch the wounds, nor any drugs to relieve the pain. As long as the battle lasted, it was not possible to send anyone back to McGavin.

Despite the odds being stacked against them, some of our more intrepid characters were infuriated by the proximity of the enemy light tanks, and they made the most determined efforts to put them out of action. After it was all over, various claims were made which we had no way of substantiating; nevertheless, some of the tanks were rendered unserviceable, and one in particular lay passive between the two forward companies throughout the entire battle.

Just as the enemy pressure was at its height, and we were beginning to doubt our ability to last much longer, the Luftwaffe appeared. This time the Messerschmitts seemed to take particular care to discover our exact whereabouts. We had no ammunition to spare on them and, lying doggo, we let them circle. However, when they dived and fired we were astounded to discover that we were not their targets. The Luftwaffe had made a grave mistake, and for a time our opponents lapsed into silence as the aircraft pressed home an attack on the valley where our assailants' HQ and forming-up positions must have been. This vital breathing space came just when we needed it most, and, as darkness approached, we all knew that we must use its cover to the full if the battalion was to survive to fight another day.

THE AUTHOR Major-General John Frost commanded the 2nd Battalion, The Parachute Regiment from 1940 to 1945. He retired from the army in 1968 and his books include *A Drop Too Many* and *2 Para Falklands: The Battalion at War*.

PARAS
IN THE SAHARA

Under the pitiless glare of the North African sun, Marcel Bigeard's parachute regiment fought a duel to the death with the FLN

FIVE DAYS ago, on 8 November, a convoy of the Algerian Petrol Company was ambushed near Timinoun. There's no trace of the men in the convoy, and the jeeps were burned. It looks like the perpetrators of this crime were deserters from the *Compagnie Saharienne* based at Tuat. We've got to get our hands on them ...'

In these few words, Colonel Marcel Bigeard put the captains of his 3rd Colonial Parachute Regiment (3 RPC) in the picture concerning the new mission they had been given – a mission they were hardly prepared for, having just carried out a big operation on the Moroccan frontier.

'I know,' replied Bigeard to the inevitable objections, 'Your men are dead beat. But we must do as we're ordered. And we've been given a free hand to carry out our tasks.'

'Might as well look for a needle in a haystack,' Captain Le Boudec began to grumble – but Bigeard cut him short. 'We leave at midnight.' The captains left the meeting. A free hand! They knew what that meant – they'd been told they had a free hand before. Whenever they were called in to retrieve a particularly sticky situation they were usually given a free hand. What it signified was that if they failed or they went too far and were found out, the finger of blame pointed firmly at 3 RPC.

For Bigeard himself, the mission was a particular challenge. Never before had his red berets faced such a vast expanse of the Sahara. They would be operating over an area one fifth of the size of France,

Right and above: Dropping into danger, the men of Bigeard's 3 RPC used their airmobility as a potent weapon in the wastes of the Sahara.

41

M. Flament

100,000 sq km of sand and rock. This was the Tademaït, the Sahara of literary legend, where many of the traditions of the Foreign Legion had been forged, where an endless succession of sand dunes obliterated any attempts at making roads, and where there was no water except in a few wells that might themselves be sanded up.

The trucks carrying the men of 3 RPC pulled into Timimoun on 15 November 1957. Aside from their shorts and their camouflage jackets, the men were given no extra equipment apart from anti-sand goggles and long Arab scarves. The first thing that struck them was the intensity of the light: between a brilliant blue sky and the harsh yellow of the sand, a man might easily go mad.

As soon as they arrived, the men of 3 RPC began their hunt for clues and information. Companies 1 to 3 checked all communications around the town, and investigated neighbouring oases for any signs of the political organisation of the FLN (Front de Libération

Nationale, the Algerian movement fighting against the French presence in Algeria). The old Sahara hands looked down their noses – 'No FLN here, never has been.' The paras' response was simple: if there weren't any FLN, how come a company of Algerian troops deserted as a single unit?

The 4th Company of 3 RPC remained in Timimoun. Its commander, Captain Douceur, a veteran of Indochina, didn't let himself get put off the track and soon had his hands on the first link in the chain, finding firm evidence of FLN organisation. Using their experience of Indochina and the previous year of war in Algeria, the staff of 3 RPC built up a diagram of FLN organisation in the region within five days. One of those brought in for interrogation even spilled the beans on a mutiny plot in another company of Algerian troops, after their European officers had been poisoned. Ninety-six individuals were arrested, and arms were seized. The old hands stopped sneering.

Below: Sub-machine guns and carbines at the ready, heavily laden paras move in extended line across the harsh desert landscape, searching every thorn bush and thicket for signs of the enemy. Below right, inset: Bigeard's command post. Bigeard himself hands a message to be sent out over the radio while his adjutant (centre, head to one side) follows operations on a map.

Para, 3 RPC, Timimoun 1957

Dressed for operations in the parched wastes of Algeria's desert interior, this man wears the distinctive 'Bigeard' cap, designed to protect the neck and head from sunstroke, a loose-fitting camouflage smock and sun-bleached shorts. Footwear consists of canvas and rubber-soled 'patangas', and the webbing is of French origin as are the haversack and waterbottle. His weapon is the 7.5mm MAS 36 rifle.

MARCEL BIGEARD

Born in Toul, in Lorraine, Marcel Bigeard became a legendary and controversial figure in modern French military life.

After military service in a Maginot Line fortress, and then a period working in a bank, Bigeard was a volunteer in 1939, and was captured in 1940. He tried to escape on three occasions and finally joined the Allies after the invasion of North Africa. He volunteered to be parachuted back into France and fought with the maquis.

Ending the war with the rank of captain, Bigeard went to Indochina in October 1945 and had three tours of duty there, the second leading a detachment of tribesmen and the third culminating in the siege of Dien Bien Phu, where he became one of the heroes of the doomed French resistance to the Viet Minh assaults.

After his release from captivity in North Vietnam, Bigeard was an obvious candidate for leading French forces against nationalist guerrillas in Algeria and his 3 RPC scored many notable successes, especially in Algiers during 1957 and then at Timimoun. Bigeard was prepared to countenance almost any methods to obtain the information that he felt was essential to counter insurgency, however, and this 'end justifies the means' attitude implied the widespread use of torture. As the views of President Charles de Gaulle began to swing towards granting independence for Algeria, Bigeard became implicated in the army's attempts to keep Algeria under French rule, and he ended his career under a cloud; but the success of his 3 RPC, especially during the year 1957, was undeniable.

Timimoun
3 RPC, Nov-Dec 1957

In November 1957, the men of Bigeard's 3 RPC were sent to Timimoun in the heart of the Sahara to hunt and destroy a company of FLN guerrillas. Less than a month later, the rebel forces in the area had been destroyed.

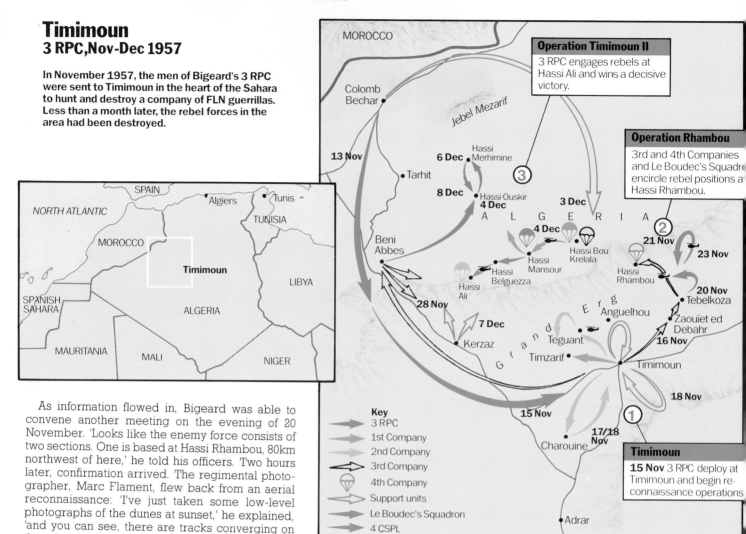

Operation Timimoun II
3 RPC engages rebels at Hassi Ali and wins a decisive victory.

Operation Rhambou
3rd and 4th Companies and Le Boudec's Squadron encircle rebel positions at Hassi Rhambou.

Timimoun
15 Nov 3 RPC deploy at Timimoun and begin reconnaissance operations

Key
→ 3 RPC
→ 1st Company
→ 2nd Company
→ 3rd Company
⛱ 4th Company
⇨ Support units
→ Le Boudec's Squadron
→ 4 CSPL

As information flowed in, Bigeard was able to convene another meeting on the evening of 20 November. 'Looks like the enemy force consists of two sections. One is based at Hassi Rhambou, 80km northwest of here,' he told his officers. Two hours later, confirmation arrived. The regimental photographer, Marc Flament, flew back from an aerial reconnaissance: 'I've just taken some low-level photographs of the dunes at sunset,' he explained, 'and you can see, there are tracks converging on these hollows...'

On the photographs that Flament had brought in, the bushes and thickets that dotted the Saharan landscape were quite clearly visible. Bigeard took a magnifying glass and could even make out the rebels themselves, camouflaged beneath the branches of the bushes. He gave his orders at once. The nearest company was the 3rd, under Captain de Lamby. These men were to move north without delay, to be heliported to their objective at dawn. Bigeard himself would head for Zaouiët ed-Dabar, halfway to Hassi Rhambou, accompanied by Le Boudec's squadron. From this small oasis, Le Boudec's force could be lifted in to help de Lamby. The 4th Company, under Captain Douceur and with Lieutenants Grillot and Roher, was to remain on the alert at the airport at Timimoun, ready to embark and parachute

in to join the fight.

Bigeard was satisfied. In order to carry out his mission properly he had demanded considerable air transport; and luckily, he had got what he needed to take his men into action.

At 0700 the following morning, Bigeard arrived at his destination, and soon made radio contact with de Lamby. De Lamby's men had marched all night through the sand and wind of the Sahara, and had reached Tabelkoza where the helicopters, under Colonel 'Felix' Brunet, made the rendezvous. At 0800 the paras embarked and within 15 minutes they were at Hassi Rhambou.

In the shelter of a dune, the paras stripped their sub-machine guns to get rid of any traces of dust or

Below left: Lieutenant Roher on the radio during the battle of Hassi Rhambou. He was killed minutes later. Below: Paras stay under cover as close-support aircraft strafe enemy positions on the other side of the dune.

and – they dare not risk a malfunction once in action. Marc Flament, the photographer, was there; he was able to capture the calmness of the troops as they studiously prepared for the battle ahead.

Sentenac's section was in the lead. Sentenac was an old non-com, whose boots had been dirtied with the mud of many fights, from the jungles of Indochina to the jebels of Algeria. He had made a spectacular escape from Dien Bien Phu and was a model for his men – and a Chevalier of the Legion of Honour.

'Forward!' The men's footsteps thudded into the soft sand. In a widely spread out line the section slowly climbed the slope leading to the crest (known as a *cif*) of a dune. As they reached the *cif* it was about 0830, and suddenly shots rang out. The leading man, Vattier, dropped his sub-machine gun and rolled back down the slope, clutching his thigh. 'Medic!' shouted Corporal Le Corre. 'They're on the other side,' explained Vattier between groans of pain, 'waiting for us to silhouette ourselves on the sky-line – ideal targets!'

Firing broke out all along the line of advance and the sound of explosions rolled over the desert

'Grenades!' shouted Sentenac. 'Throw some grenades over the crest!' Firing broke out all along the line of advancing paras. The sound of explosions rolled out over the desert. Clouds of dust obscured the sun, and the fight was on in earnest.

The paras were getting bogged down, not making much progress. But they were inching forward. Eventually, a set of grenades flew across the crest and exploded on the other side. 'Charge!' screamed Sentenac, and threw himself forward followed by his men. He reached the summit and there, as if he had run into a brick wall, he stopped, staggered and then collapsed, hit by a burst of fire that had got him in the belly. Le Corre and some others pulled him back into cover. They spread some canvas over him because the flies were already buzzing around; the

Below: Action! Two paras come under fire as they work their way forwards. In the open spaces of the desert, advancing troops could be terribly vulnerable, but the men of 3 RPC had to take risks in order to get to grips with an elusive foe.

sand was like the top of an oven. Sentenac turned on his side, supporting himself on his elbow. He grimaced and then, as if to pose for Marc Flament who was there taking pictures, he pulled himself together and closed his eyes. 'Sentenac did his best, even when he died,' was Bigeard's comment when the photograph was published.

Sentenac died at 1130, but by then his section had moved off, led by its corporals. The men stormed over the crest, pouring fire into the bushes sheltering the rebels. They gave no quarter – and they avenged their commander.

Having pinpointed the enemy, Bigeard could now bring in his other forces. Douceur's 4th Company jumped into the area at 1230, and immediately got into action, with Lieutenant Grillot taking his men into the assault. The FLN resistance did not slacken, however; on the contrary, it hardened. Encircled, the FLN knew that their only hope of survival against the paras lay in hanging on until nightfall, when they might get away.

The sun was now overhead, the implacable source of a searing heat. Sometimes the paras found a rebel's corpse, with the goat-skin water bottle, the *guerba*, empty, and a pebble in the dead man's mouth to stop the tongue swelling. But the paras suffered too. After hours in the sun, a sergeant would measure out the meagre last ration to his panting men, pinned down by enemy fire – and he would find that they would only get half a cup of warm water each, with no sign of relief before night fell, in six hours time.

Bigeard arrived. He stood there, surrounded by radio sets, co-ordinating the movements of his units, and bringing in support – notably B-26 light bombers that swept the thickets with machine-gun fire. Meanwhile, the 4th Company was advancing from dune to dune. The radios crackled as sections kept in contact. Suddenly there was a silence, and then: 'Lieutenant Roher's been killed.' Roher was lying there, his liver shattered, hands crossed on his chest, while in the sand were two long traces showing where the medic had dragged him back into cover. By now it was 1400 hours, bullets were still whistling across the desert, and the rebels were giving every bit as good as they got.

At 1500 hours, Le Boudec's squadron was heli-ported to the north of the combat zone to complete the encirclement, but the FLN still did not crack. The most fierce opposition was encountered by the 4th Company, fighting in the area where Roher had been killed. Finally, at about 1830, a few grenades finished off the last strongpoint. The silence came suddenly, almost brutally.

The dead and the wounded were flown back to Timimoun by helicopter. Bigeard, grave and strained, saluted them as they were put aboard. He told his officers: 'Now we have to seek out and destroy the rest of the rebel band. Operations continue as before.'

The very next day, with the companies re-grouped, Bigeard's men were on the hunt again. This time, it was to be a longer search. On the 24th, information reached the command post that there was a large body of rebels northeast of Timimoun, and a company was sent to the region, but at dawn a sand-storm blew up and it was not until 30 hours later that the 2nd Company could move in properly – only to find a recently abandoned camp.

Twelve days passed like this, with the paras moving from dune to dune, from well to well, some-times travelling on foot, sometimes by jeep, occa-sionally by helicopter when the machines were fit for use. The sand affected their motors terribly, and when new motors were brought out, the mechanics found that some had been sabotaged with iron filings. The paras grumbled and carried on.

Twelve days of frustration, of almost getting the rebels but finding only traces of abandoned camps, or perhaps trapping a look-out, or as the men of Le Boudec's squadron found on 4 December when they parachuted into the Hassi Mansour area, the body of one of the petrol company workers, murdered.

Bigeard's face lit up. He closed his fist and turned to his officers: 'We've got them!'

On 5 December, the 1st Company moved towards Bou Zeriba, in the Saoura valley. The paras disco-vered an abandoned camp, but aerial reconnaiss-ance indicated that there was another nearby. 'The rebels are pulling back northwards,' noted one of the intelligence officers, Lieutenant Pétot. 'We're get-ting closer.' Bigeard agreed, without adding any-thing. He wasn't impatient; he too knew that his hour would come. Up to now he had only got near to delaying forces that were protecting the bulk of the band, and, probably, the staff of Si Yacoub, the leader of the FLN in the Sahara region. For Bigeard, victory would not be complete until Si Yacoub was dead or captured – and Si Yacoub knew that too.

The 'Barnum and Bailey Circus', as Bigeard called his command post, arrived in Hassi Belguezza on 7 December, with its companies and support units deployed around. That night, a report came in that there had been a sighting near Hassi Ali. When he was told, Bigeard's face lit up. Impatiently he went to the map and pencilled in where the sighting had been made. Then he closed his fist and turned to his officers: 'We've got them!'

At dawn, 3 RPC converged on Hassi Ali. At mid-day, the 2nd Company parachuted directly onto the rebels, and engaged them at once. At 1500, another

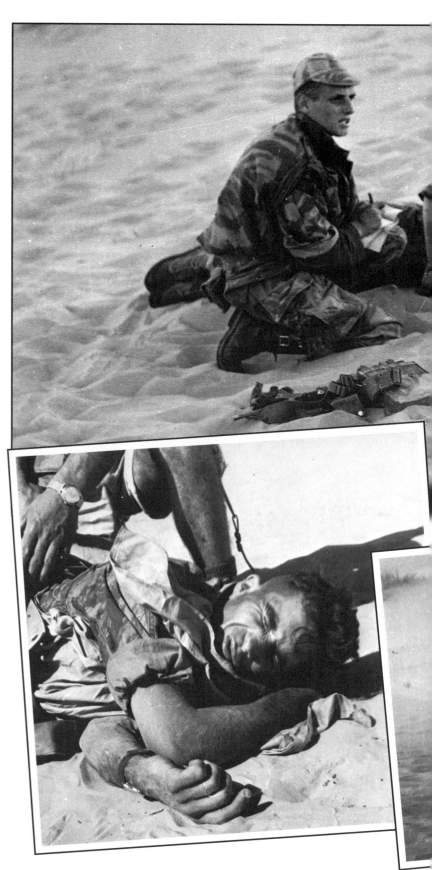

company began to be heliported to the scene of the action. In small groups, the paras of Grillot and Roher – the latter with the death of their commander to avenge – threw themselves into the assault.

At 1600 hours, the first enemy machine-gun post was taken out, and after another half hour, the second fell. With no real support weapons, the rest of the FLN could now be winkled out – a task that fell

Below: Evacuating the dead and wounded by helicopter. Airmobility was a priceless asset to 3 RPC, not only in the hunting down of guerrillas; it was also invaluable in getting men back to an operating theatre with the minimum delay. Left and left below: The death of Sergeant-Major Sentenac. Sentenac was a veteran of the Indochinese campaigns of the early 1950s, and one of the few men to escape from Dien Bien Phu. When he was shot at Hassi Rhambou, the fight was on in earnest.

3 RPC

The 3rd Colonial Parachute Regiment (3e régiment de parachutistes coloniaux – 3 RPC) landed at Bône in Algeria on 8 August 1956 when the first round of fighting in Algeria was at its peak. 3 RPC was based in Algiers from January to March 1957 during the infamous 'Battle of Algiers' that shattered the FLN organisation in the city. Then, in April, it moved to the Atlas Mountains where it fought the battle of Agounnenda. In July it was honoured in a march-past in Paris, but by September was back in action again, and in November was sent south for the operations around Timimoun.

In April 1958, Colonel Roger Trinquier replaced Bigeard and under their new commander the paras took part in many of the large-scale sweeps that were part of the Challe Offensive, including Operation Etincelles in July and August 1959.

In 1960, the unit was renamed the 3rd Marine Parachute Regiment (3e régiment de parachutistes d'infanterie de marine – 3 RPIMa) and by the end of the war in Algeria had killed or captured 3200 enemy, at a price of 76 dead and 220 wounded in its own ranks. In 1962, the regiment left Algeria for the last time and took up quarters in Carcassonne.

largely to the 2nd Company. After they had carried out the final sweep to secure the area, the men of the 2nd found the corpse of Si Yacoub. With his death, the FLN organisation in the Sahara would fall apart – and for the old Sahara hands peace would return.

As night fell, with the surrounding darkness emphasised by the fires of the bivouacs and in the hard-won silence, Bigeard noted, almost nostalgically:

'The great wind of the Sahara will cover over all traces of our footprints tomorrow. It will move the dunes, burying at random empty magazines, rusty ammunition boxes, abandoned arms, and perhaps even the memory of this battle itself.'

THE AUTHOR Jean Mabire is one of France's best-known military historians. He served on the Tunisian frontier during the Algerian war.

SHOCK TACTIC[S]

In 1940, the fortress of Eben Emael was reckoned to be impregnable, but that was before the world had seen Germany's new, revolutionary troops in action.

AT PRECISELY 0430 hours on 10 May 1940, 11 German DFS 230 gliders were towed into the air by Ju 52 tugs from the Cologne-Ostheim airfield, about 120km east of the Dutch border. The gliders held Assault Section 'Granite', which consisted of two officers and 83 men, all of whom were crack paratroop engineers drawn from the Luftwaffe's 7th Airborne Division.

The gliders were on route for the supposedly impregnable Belgian fortress of Eben Emael and, if everything went according to plan, they would be towed for 25 minutes before being released high over the Dutch border to glide down to their target. Their task on arrival was the destruction of the guns and fortifications of Eben Emael before they could be used to delay the advance of the German land forces over the nearby bridges on the Albert Canal, a major defence line that threatened to block Hitler's planned invasion of the Low Countries in May 1940. If the German Sixth Army was to break through as planned, between Roermund and Liège, Eben Emael had to be taken.

The fortress had only been completed in 1935, and had been carefully sited on a rocky outcrop that dominated the most important section of the Albert Canal. Between 1932 and 1935, the Belgians had built an installation that stretched over 700m from east to west and 900m north to south. On the northeast face, a steep slope dropped 40m to the Albert Canal while on the northwest side, the floodplain of the Jeker river had been raised and the defences improved by a trench with steep embankments. In the east and south, where the surrounding countryside was on the same level as the defences, Belgian engineers had constructed a wide trench and a wall 4m high.

The fortress was built on several levels with a total of 64 strongpoints housing a variety of artillery pieces including 12cm revolving cannon, anti-tank and anti-aircraft guns. All the guns were protected by heavy steel cupolas, some of which had walls 30cm thick. The Belgians were convinced that these were impervious to all but the heaviest and most prolonged of artillery bombardments or air attacks. Extensive minefields and stretches of barbed wire had been sited to channel any attacker toward pillboxes bristling with machine guns. The fortress entrance was on the reverse slope of the hill and was protected by a water-filled moat. The Germans were unsure as to the strength of the Belgian garrison, but believed that the senior officer at Eben Emael, Major Jottrand, had 1200 men under his command. For their part, the Belgians assumed that their defences would force any attacker to deploy a major force to undertake a lengthy siege, by which time the important bridges over the canal would have been destroyed and reinforcements brought up to continue the de[fence]

Above: DFS 230 gliders on a training mission before the assault on the Belgian fortress of Eben Emael. In the mission proper, Ju 52s, and not Stukas, were used to tow the 11 gliders that held the 85 men of Assault Section Granite to the Dutch border, from where they swooped onto their target. As part of the mission, three other sections were to capture vital bridges over the Albert Canal in preparation for the German Army's advance into the Low Countries.

laying action.

The men of Assault Section Granite were the key element in a plan devised by Hitler and General Kurt Student, commander of the German paratroop corps, to overcome this formidable obstacle to the German conquest of France and the Low Countries. They formed part of the larger *Sturmabteilung* (Assault Group) *Koch* whose overall objectives were the Kanne, Vroenhaven and Veltwezelt bridges over the Albert Canal. Surprise was to be achieved by landing airborne troops by glider at each objective, a few hours ahead of the main invasion force. As it was essential for the German force to secure all of its objectives simultaneously, Hauptmann (Captain) Koch divided his command into four self-contained elements, each with its own specific duty to perform.

Three Assault Sections were to capture the vital bridges: 'Iron' under Leutnant (Second Lieutenant) Schachter was to take the crossing at Kanne; 'Concrete', led by Leutnant Schacht, was detailed to seize the concrete bridge over the canal at Vroenhaven and the third section, 'Steel', under Oberleutnant (Lieutenant) Altman, had to secure the steel bridge at Veltwezelt. Assault Section Granite was commanded by Oberleutnant Rudolf Witzig, a 25-year-old engineer with a reputation as a dedicated and professional officer. From November 1939, Koch's men had trained for their task in the utmost secrecy and had practised glider assaults on the captured Polish fortifications at Gleiwitz.

Every paratrooper carried either a rifle or a sub-machine gun, as well as 50kg of explosives

On 10 May each glider contained an impressive arsenal of weapons; every paratroop engineer carried either a rifle or a sub-machine gun, as well as 50kg of explosives or other vital equipment. There were special explosive charges secured to long poles to push through gun embrasures, the equivalent of Bangalore torpedoes to blow openings through barbed wire, and flamethrowers to burn out resistance. The most important munitions, however, were 20 50kg and 28 12.5kg *Hohlladung* (hollow charges). It was with these hollow charges that Witzig's men intended to blast their way into the fortifications of Eben Emael.

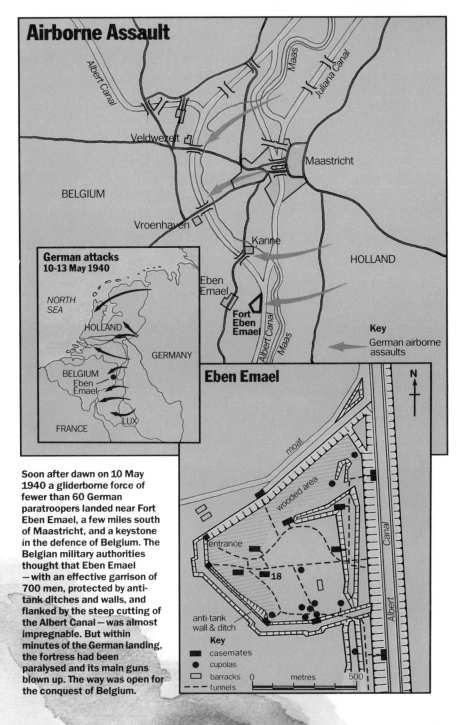

Soon after dawn on 10 May 1940 a gliderborne force of fewer than 60 German paratroopers landed near Fort Eben Emael, a few miles south of Maastricht, and a keystone in the defence of Belgium. The Belgian military authorities thought that Eben Emael —with an effective garrison of 700 men, protected by anti-tank ditches and walls, and flanked by the steep cutting of the Albert Canal — was almost impregnable. But within minutes of the German landing, the fortress had been paralysed and its main guns blown up. The way was open for the conquest of Belgium.

On route to Eben Emael, Assault Section Granit lost two of its gliders. One, containing Leutna Witzig, had its tow-rope broken and the pilot only ju managed to steer the glider down to a bump landing in a German field. A second glider was als forced to turn back and land near Düren after one the engines of its Ju 52 tug failed.

Because of these unforeseen problems, only nir gliders of Assault Section Granite successfully land ed on the Eben Emael plateau at 0520 hours; addition, two of these gliders had difficult landing which prevented their paratroopers from makir any real contribution to the attack. Nevertheless, th Belgian garrison was caught by surprise and re mained in a state of considerable confusion throug out the battle, despite the fact that they had been p on alert since 0030, following warnings of Germa troop movements along the frontier. However, ther had been three similar alarms over the previou month that had come to nothing and, initially, ther seemed little urgency to respond. To make matte worse, although Eben Emael was supposed to have garrison of 1200 men, on the day of the attack, ther were only some 700 on duty. The remainder wer either on leave, or had been assigned quarte nearby, in villages and farmhouses. The absence these 500 men proved to be a serious handicap fc the Belgians.

By nightfall, most of the main defences had been bombed and blasted into ruins

The garrison was not expecting a German attack an also delayed their response because they thoug the gliders were either British or French. Indeed some Belgian defenders said later that they thoug the gliders were nothing more than disabled enem reconnaissance planes. The Belgians, howeve soon realised their mistake and when the 55 men Witzig's command who reached the fortress leap from their gliders, they were greeted by wailin sirens, flares and bursts of tracer. Nevertheless, the began to carry out their carefully-rehearsed tasks

In the absence of Witzig, Oberfeldwebe (Sergeant-Major) Helmut Wenzel assumed overa command, and he must be given the credit fc directing the early and crucial stage of the Germa attack; for it was in the first 20 minutes that th Germans successfully paralysed the fortress. As th Germans attacked the steel cupolas with their ho low charges, they were staggered to see the devas tating effect these explosions produced. Until the the paratroopers had only practised with them fc reasons of secrecy, and had never seen them used their full effect.

One squad, led by Feldwebel (Senior Sergean Niedermeier, attacked Casemate 18 on the souther side of the fortress. With one 50kg hollow charge Niedermeier destroyed its steel observation cupol and then two of his men fixed a 12.5kg charge again a steel door below the barrel of one of the 35mm gur in the casemate. The size of the explosion, the effec of its shock waves, and the hole blown in th armoured cupola amazed Niedermeier. Inside, th Belgian gunners had been blown from their sea and the rest of the crew had been thrown against th walls of the casemate. Niedermeier then led hi squad through the gaping hole and, with alacrit pursued the surviving Belgian defenders, who ha abandoned the cupola and retreated into the tunne system that ran beneath the fortress.

Left, top to bottom: The second stage of the German assault on Eben Emael involved the crossing of the Albert Canal to the east of the fortress, where it flowed through a 40m-deep cutting. First across were men of the 1st Engineer Battalion under the command of Sergeant Portsteffen. Their rubber dinghies came under fire from two Belgian positions during the crossing.

Above left: The devastating effect of a hollow charge.

Elsewhere on Eben Emael, other German squads were also using their hollow charges with ruinous effect. With these explosives, Assault Section Granite were able to penetrate the steel cupolas of Eben Emael and the fearsome explosions devastated the fortress's interior.

Oberfeldwebel Peter Arent, the commander of No. 3 Squad, was a key figure in the initial stages of the attack. His glider landed less than 50m from the casement wall of Eben Emael, and immediately came under smallarms fire. Arent and his men, carrying their packs of explosives, began to run across open ground, swept by a murderous barrage of tracer bullets, towards the shelter of the concrete walls and their assigned target. Arent then planted a 50kg hollow charge against the side of the cupola which exploded with an almighty roar and blew in a great hole. Leading his squad, firing a sub-machine gun, he quickly subdued the defenders, and then set about preparing to hold the cupola against an expected Belgian counter-attack.

Arent, however, was then ordered by Wenzel to attack another strongpoint and destroy its two anti-aircraft guns which were threatening to upset the paratroopers' timetable for securing the fortress. Arent and his squad approached the strongpoint by edging along the concrete wall, safe from the heavy fire of Belgian machine guns located in the main casements above their heads. He planted charges against a cupola housing two machine guns and the resulting explosion destroyed the position.

Major Jottrand, the Belgian commander of Eben Emael, had lost the initiative during the early phase of the German assault and was unable to organise a co-ordinated resistance. Although he was able to order artillery fire to be brought down from neighbouring field batteries against the fortress in a last-ditch attempt to dislodge the Germans, he had no clear idea of the strength of the enemy force and was dismayed by the rapid loss of so many of his strongpoints. From his command post deep in the centre of Eben Emael, the noise and shock waves from the hollow charges must have seemed terrifying; a feeling made worse by his belief that the fortress was able to withstand the blast of any conventional explosive charge.

At 0830 hours a lone German glider sailed through heavy Belgian anti-aircraft fire and successfully landed on Eben Emael. Oberleutnant Witzig had rejoined his command. After his glider had been forced to land in Germany, he had quickly organised another Ju 52 tug and, after a few false starts, had succeeded in taking off. As soon as he had received a report from Wenzel, Witzig ordered his men to attack and destroy those areas of Eben Emael still

The German attack on Eben Emael was one of the most audacious aerial operations of World War II and its success depended on the paratroopers reaching their objective in total secrecy and then landing with pin-point accuracy. To achieve these aims they had to rely on an entirely untried weapon of war: the assault glider.

The DFS 230 was designed by Hans Jacobs and was put through its first test flights in late 1937. Senior German officers were particularly impressed by these early experiments and one, Ernst Udet, reported to his senior officer on the glider's abilities, stating that with suitable modification it would be capable of dropping troops behind enemy lines. Within a few weeks of this conversation, orders were issued for the construction of a military version able to carry a pilot and 10 fully-equipped paratroopers.

Although the DFS 230 was little more than a scaled-up version of a conventional sailplane, it performed admirably when used to land small-scale raiding parties. It was capable of carrying 272kg of freight in addition to the troops and could glide for 20km when released at 2000m.

Experience, however, showed that the DFS 230 was extremely vulnerable to enemy ground fire during its slow, shallow landing approach. Later variants incorporated the means to overcome these problems: the DFS 230B variant was provided with an external parachute pack to reduce landing distances and a 7.9mm MG15 machine gun was fitted to the rear of the cockpit for suppressive fire. Some gliders also carried a pair of fixed MG34s in the nose.

The DFS 230, however, did have one major weakness: a relatively small load capacity which made it of limited use in large-scale airborne operations. Nevertheless, production of the glider continued until April 1942, by which time 1022 had been built.

Hollow charge

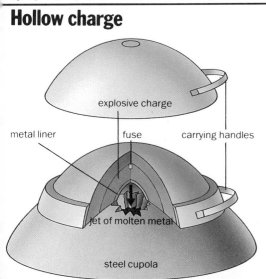

explosive charge

metal liner fuse carrying handles

jet of molten metal

steel cupola

INTENSIVE TRAINING

The capture of Eben Emael was crucial to the success of the German offensive against the Low Countries in May 1940 and, in the six months before their operation, the men of *Sturmabteilung Koch* were put through a rigorous and highly secret training programme. Oberleutnant (Lieutenant) Rudolf Witzig, the commander of 'Assault Section Granite', was one of those present during the programme which was to prepare the men for their revolutionary parachute assault on the fortress:

'Security was vital, since our success – indeed our survival – depended on taking the enemy by surprise. We were all made aware of this and drastic measures sometimes had to be taken; our training and details of equipment, tactics and objectives had to be kept completely secret, and even among ourselves the name of the fortress was not generally known until after its capture. No leave was granted, nor were we allowed out or to mix with

Above: Oberleutnant Rudolf Witzig, who commanded the German assault force that stormed the fortress of Eben Emael.

men from other units.

'Even glider practice in the Hildesheim area was carried out on the smallest possible scale: the gliders were then dismantled, moved to Köln in a furniture van and reassembled in hangars surrounded by wire entanglements guarded by our own men.

'After the fullest use had been made of the training facilities in Hildesheim, the detachment practised attacking strongly defended fortifications in the Sudetenland and also carried out trial demolitions at Polish installations near Gleiwitz. Lectures at the sapper school at Karlshorst introduced us to the principles of fortress construction. Finally, deserters from Belgian fortifications were interrogated and we were able to check what we had been learning against the information they supplied.

'Thus the picture became complete, and the sappers acquired confidence in their weapons: none of us would have changed places with anyone, not even with men in armoured forts.'

held by the Belgians. The Germans, however, immediately came under heavy fire and were forced to withdraw to the shelter of several captured casemates. The Belgians had recovered enough to launch a single infantry counter-attack.

During the afternoon Stuka dive-bombers attacked specific targets on and around Eben Emael and silenced several pockets of resistance. By nightfall, most of the main defences of the fortress had been bombed and blasted into ruins but, although the Belgians had retreated into the interior of the fortress, Witzig feared a night attack against his scattered force. He therefore ordered his men to evacuate a number of the captured strongpoints and oncentrate in a few safe areas. The abandoned rongpoints were blown up.

Although Witzig expected the Belgians to launch a ounter-attack during the night of 10/11 May, he emembered being surprised by their infantry's ck of aggressive spirit:

'That night was uneventful. After the hard fighting during the day, the detachment lay, exhausted and parched, under scattered fire from Belgian artillery and infantry outside the fortification; every burst of fire might have signalled the beginning of the counter-attack we expected, and our nerves were tense. For the most part, however, the enemy lacked the will to fight.'

t 0700 hours on the morning of 11 May, a detachment German engineers from the 51st Engineer Batta-on, under the command of Unterfeldwebel ergeant) Portsteffen, reached Eben Emael and ade contact with Witzig after a hair-raising cros-ng of the canal in a flimsy rubber dinghy. By id-morning, troops of a German infantry regiment ad joined them, and Witzig's men withdrew from e battle. After another two hours of difficult fighting, uch of it underground, the Germans were sur-rised to hear the sound of a lone trumpet, and then ee a white flag which suggested that Major Jottrand ished to capitulate. The battle was over.

Over 700 Belgian soldiers had been defeated by a few dozen German paratroop engineers

ver 700 Belgian soldiers, defending what had been onsidered the strongest fortress in Europe, had een defeated by a few dozen German paratroop ngineers, armed with 56 hollow-charged explo-ves. Witzig's unit lost six killed and 20 wounded, a ird of its original strength, in the day-long battle but ad succeeded in knocking out most of Eben Emael's asemates. Assault Section Granite had played a key ole in enabling the rest of Assault Group Koch to apture most of the Albert Canal bridges intact and us allow German ground forces to move unhin-ered into Belgium. Only the Kanne bridge was estroyed by the Belgians, who managed to touch off everal demolition charges as the paratroopers ere landing.

Witzig, who was awarded the *Ritterkreuz* Knight's Cross) and promoted to Hauptmann (Cap-in) for his exploits, later said that his success had een due to his section achieving surprise, the hattering effect of the hollow charges on the morale f the Belgians, and the lack of outside support for the arrison. But the success was also the result of very iethodical training and planning which had pre-eded the attack, since every one of Witzig's men ad known exactly what to do, was at the peak of hysical fitness, and was capable of showing the idividual initiative that had enabled Oberfeld-vebel Wenzel to take temporary command in the bsence of Witzig during the first crucial hour of the peration.

The capture of Eben Emael was, perhaps, the nest example of a daring airborne operation in Vorld War II. Despite the loss of two gliders, the German paratroops carried out their tasks with grim etermination and paved the way for their army to onquer western Europe.

HE AUTHOR Keith Simpson is senior lecturer in War tudies and International Affairs at Sandhurst. He is urrently writing a book on the German Army.

Left: Two men cover one of Assault Section Granite's engineers as his flamethrower squirts a deadly stream of fire into a concrete emplacement. The speed of the German assault assured that the Belgians lost control of the fortress 30 minutes after the paratroopers had landed. Above: Tired and dirty but still able to raise a smile, a group of paratroopers takes a break after their capture of Eben Emael.

Lieutenant, Paratroops, Eben Emael 1940

This paratroop officer at the award ceremony for the vic-tors of Eben Emael is kitted out with the jump smock specially designed for parachute opera-tions, which became the trademark of German para-troops during World War II. Underneath the smock he wears field grey trousers and a Luftwaffe flying blouse. Other paratroop features are the cut-down helmet, 'camouflaged' with mud, and side-lacing boots. On the leather waist belt is a pistol holster holding the Luger 08 pistol. The yellow pa-ratroop arm-of-service forms the background to the rank badges worn on the jacket col-lar. A highly decorated soldier, he has been awarded both 1st and 2nd classes of the Iron Cross as well as the Knight's Cross which hangs at his throat.

The 6e Bataillon de Parachutistes Coloniaux (6th Colonial Parachute Batalion – 6BPC) had its origins in the 6e Bataillon Colonial de Commandos Parachutistes (6th Colonial Para-Commando Battalion – 6 BCCP), which was formed in May 1948 to help meet the growing challenge of the war in French Indochina. 6 BCCP was redesignated 6 BPC in March 1951, but the following August the formation was temporarily disbanded.

The task of reforming 6 BPC fell to Major Marcel Bigeard. Officially established on 1 November 1951 at St Brieuc in Brittany, the 'Bataillon Bigeard', as it was soon known, underwent eight months of rigorous training before setting sail for Indochina. Arriving at Haiphong at the end of July 1952, the two French components of the battalion, designated 11 Company and 12 Company, were joined by two units of Vietnamese troops, the 6e Compagnie Indochinoise Parachutiste (6 CIP) and 26 CIP. Along with a Command Company, these made up the full complement of 6 BPC. After some initial operations in Phuc Yen in September, the battalion was dropped into the path of a Viet Minh advance at Tu-Le on 16 October. The fighting retreat from Tu-Le earned both Bigeard and his battalion considerable fame. After Tu-Le, 6 BPC was soon back in action. In December 1952 the battalion encircled and virtually wiped out two Viet Minh companies at Luc Dien.

The following February, they returned to the Black river area, this time taking the offensive in a series of bold counter-attacks. The remainder of 1953 was spent in operations in Laos.

On 16 March 1954, the battalion was dropped into Dien Bien Phu. Despite heroic efforts, the French positions were overrun by the Viet Minh on 7 May and the whole force was either killed or, like Bigeard, captured. 6 BPC officially ceased to exist on 1 June, when remaining base camp personnel were transferred to other units.

Struggling through jungle and across raging mountain torrents, the paras of 6 BPC fought a grim withdrawal from the outpost at Tu-Le

AT 1230 HOURS on 16 October 1952, the sky over Tu-Le, a remote village in the Thai mountains of northern Vietnam, filled with billowing parachutes as the first wave of Major Marcel Bigeard's 6e Bataillon de Parachutistes Coloniaux (6th Colonial Parachute Battalion – 6 BPC) drifted down towards their drop zone. As the paras rolled up their parachutes and took stock of their surroundings, they were struck by an overwhelming sense of isolation and solitude. The village lay in a small valley two kilometres wide, surrounded by mountain tops thickly covered with tropical forest and bamboo. Somewhere in that wilderness, the paras knew, a powerful force of their Viet Minh enemies was assembled and preparing to advance in their direction. No-one expected an easy time at Tu-Le, but the reality was to outstrip their worst fears.

Bigeard's 6 BPC was an elite component of the French forces that had been fighting General Vo Nguyen Giap's Viet Minh guerrillas in French Indochina since 1946. The French had proved capable of defeating the guerrillas whenever they were able to bring their superior firepower into play, so by 1952 Giap had decided to concentrate his efforts in the northern mountains, where the colonial power could not deploy heavy artillery and frequent low cloud reduced the effectiveness of air support. Three Viet Minh divisions, the 308th, 312th and 316th, were ordered to push southwest across the mountains from the Red river to the Black river and on into Laos. The French would be forced either to abandon their outposts in the region or to reinforce and defend

Below right: Marcel Bigeard, CO of 6 BPC.
Below left: A French para in Indochina.

em, risking a major military disaster by fighting on nfavourable terms, far from their main bases.

In early October 1952, aware of an unusually high vel of Viet Minh activity, the French reinforced eir garrison at Nghia Lo, which they considered e key outpost between the Red and Black rivers – ut they still had no idea of the scale of the offensive ey were facing. On 14 October, Giap finally un- eashed his three divisions and, within 24 hours, all e small garrisons between Nghia Lo and the Red ver had been wiped out or forced to withdraw.

At 2200 hours on 15 October, 6 BPC was ordered to repare for action. General Raoul Salan, comman- er of the French forces in Indochina, was at that oment visiting Saigon, leaving his deputy, General e Linarès, in command in Hanoi. De Linarès im- ediately decided to commit 6 BPC to Tu-Le, 30km om Nghia Lo. From there he hoped the paras could ount counter-attacks against the enemy's lines of ommunication, as well as blocking the path to the lack river.

By the early evening of 16 October, all of Bigeard's

ight: As orders come through on the radio, a rench para machine-gun section sets up in a ocky position prior to a Viet Minh assault.

RETREAT
FROM TU-LE

57

Ordered to reinforce the French garrison at Tu-Le, the paras of 6 BPC were attacked by vastly superior Viet Minh forces and had to make a fighting withdrawal through the mountains of northwest Vietnam. Harried by the enemy all the way, the paras suffered heavy losses, but finally reached safety.

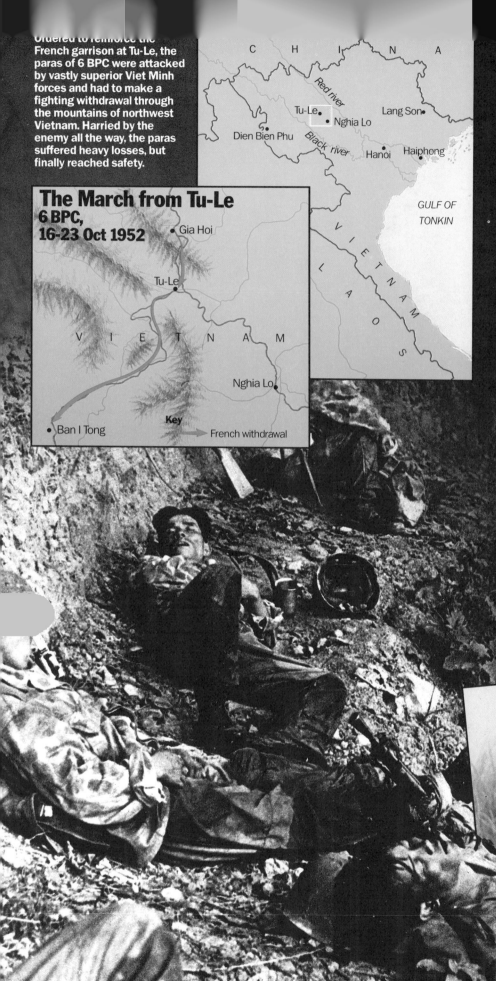

The March from Tu-Le
6 BPC, 16-23 Oct 1952

Gia Hoi

Tu-Le

V I E T N A M

Nghia Lo

Ban I Tong

Key

→ French withdrawal

C H I N A

Red river

Tu-Le
Nghia Lo
Lang Son

Dien Bien Phu

Black river

Hanoi
Haiphong

GULF OF TONKIN

V I E T N A M

L A O S

000 officers and men had landed safely – apart fro few sprains and bruises – and assembled to rece orders. Realising that the post at Tu-Le itself, oc pied by a small garrison of local Thai troops, was readily defensible, Bigeard deployed the bulk o force on high points in the surrounding mountain form a set of mutually supporting positions. His French companies, Lieutenant Le Roy's 11 Comp and 12 Company commanded by Lieutenant Tra dug in on hilltops about one kilometre to the eas Tu-Le. Lieutenant Magnillat's 6e Compagnie dochinoise Parachutiste (6 CIP), one of the Fren officered Vietnamese parachute companies of 6BPC, took up position to the south, while the oth 26 CIP commanded by Lieutenant de Wilde, joir Command Company in defence of the post its Patrols were sent out on the mountain tracks to g advance warning of any approaching enemy for

For 24 hours, all was quiet. Then, at dusk or October, Bigeard's men heard a sound like dist thunder rolling across the mountains from the eas was the opening barrage of mortars and recoill rifles as the Viet Minh began their attack on Nghia By 0900 hours the following morning, outnumbe 15 to one, the French force at Nghia Lo had be wiped out. When the news reached General Sala headquarters, he immediately sent orders Bigeard to withdraw his battalion and the garriso of the other small outposts in the area back to Black river. If the battalion did not pull out in time would, like Nghia Lo, be surrounded and destroy

But there was an ambiguity to the orders Bigeard was to save the outlying garrisons, particularly that at Gia Hoi some 15km to the north would have to wait for them to reach Tu-Le bef beginning his own withdrawal. Never a man to av risks, Bigeard took the bold but dangerous decis to stay at Tu-Le until the evening of the 19th, giv the local Thai troops at Gia Hoi time to get there.

At dawn on the 19th, Bigeard despatched a c tachment of 26 CIP to hold the pass at Kao Pha, t hours' march to the south on the escape route to Black river, and 6 CIP was sent out on reconnai ance to the southeast, towards Nghia Lo. At midd six kilometres out from Tu-Le, the reconnaissar force spotted a column of infantry advancing acros broad plateau: it was the enemy at last. 6 CIP stealthily took up position on a mountain side overlooking the plateau and waited. Magnillat described what followed:

'At 1630 hours, as the Viet Minh lead company started up the winding path 200m below us, 6 CIP opened up with its machine gun and 10 automatics simultaneously. The 60mm mortar and 57mm gun joined in. Stretching over more than a kilometre, the Viet Minh column broke apart, scattering

After a gruelling struggle through the jungle (below) members of 6 BPC lie exhausted on the trail (far left). Below left: Bigeard oversees the carrying of a wounded para. Bottom: Lieutenant de Wilde (centre) with his 26 CIP

across the dry paddyfields. We could see shells exploding in the middle of that ants' nest; bodies lay everywhere...'

This onslaught lasted only a few minutes. Then 6 CIP headed back to Tu-Le, expecting to arrive just in time to join the withdrawal. However, when they arrived back, the news was that the Gia Hoi garrison had still not arrived. 'Bruno', as Bigeard was known to his men, had decided they must wait another night. This would certainly mean holding off an attack.

As night fell, the men occupied their carefully prepared positions and nervously kept watch. At 2300 hours, the pitch darkness was pierced by a column of lights snaking down a hillside to the northeast. The Gia Hoi garrison had finally arrived, Thai men, women and children advancing by the light of bamboo torches down to Tu-Le. The Viet Minh must already have been in position around the valley, but they held their fire. Presumably their plan of attack was already decided.

At 0200 hours, a para on watch at 12 Company's position east of Tu-Le spotted the silhouette of a man struggling to free himself from the barbed wire that provided the outermost line of defence. With a sharp burst of automatic fire, the para gunned him down. Within seconds, 12 Company's position was deluged with enemy fire and a second Viet Minh force opened up against the command post at Tu-Le itself. The guerrillas had moved in close under cover of darkness, and from the outset fighting was at close quarters. But the Viet Minh had clearly underestimated the strength of the paras' defences, prepared and reinforced over the previous three days. The human-wave tactics that had overcome Nghia Lo would not work again. Bodies piled up outside the barbed wire as the paras maintained a merciless rate of fire.

The brunt of the assault was borne by 11 Company, ambushed from both sides half-way along the valley

The battalion's 12 Company suffered worst in the night's fighting. At one point, the Viet Minh got into an outlying section of the company's defences and from there swept the area with automatic fire, pinning down the defenders behind any cover they could find. An NCO, Sergeant Guérin, decided that the enemy must be driven back. Leaping from cover, he stood bolt upright in front of the Viet Minh-occupied position and poured sub-machine gun fire down onto the guerrillas. No-one could survive long in the open, and Guérin was soon cut down, but the enemy were forced to move back to safer ground.

By 0630 hours, when the Viet Minh withdrew from Tu-Le pursued by French mortar fire, the paras had lost two dead and 10 were badly wounded. They counted 96 enemy corpses outside the wire. But Bigeard's men knew that they had only won a breathing-space. If they were encircled by the Viet Minh, then in the long run their fate would be sealed. But still Bigeard held on at Tu-Le, this time to see if the clouds that hung low over the mountain tops would lift sufficiently to allow a Morane aircraft to land at the small airstrip and take out the wounded. At 1200 hours the weather had cleared sufficiently for two B-26 Invaders to bomb and strafe Viet Minh concentrations on the mountainsides around Tu-Le, but no Morane appeared. Even Bigeard could wait no longer. At 1300 hours the battalion finally began to withdraw. First to set off were the Thai troops from Tu-Le and the garrison that had come in from Gia Hoi.

Top: Exhausted from numerous savage engagements with the Viet Minh, the paras of 6 BPC trudge towards the Black river. Above: Defeated in Indochina but with head held high, Bigeard leads the 3e Régiment de Parachutistes down the Champs Elysées on Bastille Day, 1957.

They were followed by 26 CIP (part of which was already stationed at Kao Pha pass), Command Company, 11 Company and, bringing up the rear, 12 Company. 6 CIP was positioned at the crest of the first line of mountains behind Tu-Le. The retreating troops would pass through 6 CIP, which would then join the rear of the withdrawal. The main body of the battalion, carrying the wounded on stretchers and accompanied by the Thai families, progressed without incident into the next valley, and marched on towards Kao Pha. But as 12 Company passed through 6 CIP, a column of Viet Minh infantry was spotted moving up the hill a few hundred metres behind them, helmets covered in palm leaves, a traditional jungle camouflage. The French rearguard opened fire, hoping to delay the enemy advance, while the company commanders radioed orders to speed up the withdrawal across the valley to Kao Pha. Soon Viet Minh troops were appearing on all sides on the forested slopes. Fighting had also started down in the valley, as the Viet Minh attempted to cut the parachute battalion in two. The brunt of the assault was borne by 11 Company, ambushed from both sides half-way along the valley track. As 12 Company and 6 CIP also began to withdraw, they quickly split up into small units, each struggling to force a way through as best it could.

Everywhere among the dried-out rice-paddies of the valley floor, men faced one another in brutal close-range combat, playing a deadly game of hide-and-seek around the earthen banks that divided up the paddyfields. Lieutenant Magnillat was in the thick of the action:

'European and Vietnamese paras supported one another, leaping from bank to bank during lulls in the fighting, then diving down and opening fire as soon as they saw the enemy, behind, in front, to the left, to the right... I followed the line of the track, already strewn with the dead and dying... There was nothing I could do, and, like the others, I emptied my magazines to carve a way through...'

Night was falling by the time the last of the paras, bloodstained, supporting wounded comrades and dragging the dead behind them, reached the forest path that led up to Kao Pha. The Viet Minh made a dispirited attempt to follow, but were easily driven off. They had had enough for the day. Regrouped at the top of the pass, Bigeard's men could count their losses: 83 dead or missing, 34 of them from 11 Company and 22 from 6 CIP.

By now Bigeard's men were suffering from physical and nervous exhaustion, but he knew they must move on immediately. Three-quarters of their ammunition was gone; they could not afford another major encounter with the Viet Minh. At 0200 hours on 21 October, the battalion set out once more on the 70km march to the Black river, the Thais in front with the wounded, then the badly mauled 6 CIP and 11 Company, while Bigeard himself with the other companies brought up the rear. Progress was painfully slow in the pitch darkness of the mountain jungle; at the worst points, each soldier held on to the back of the tunic of the man in front, to avoid blundering off the path.

Daybreak eased the problems of movement, but brought renewed Viet Minh attacks. First, Bigeard's

Major Marcel Bigeard 6 BPC, Indochina

Major Bigeard wears a retailored version of British camouflage windproofs with brown leather para boots and gaiters. His hat is the large-brimmed fatigue or utility windproof cap favoured by many paratroopers.

Command Company turned to face the enemy attacking from the rear and drove them off with concentrated fire. Then the other companies in turn took on the task of covering the retreat, halting for a while to confront the Viet Minh, and then hurrying to rejoin the column. In this wearing fashion the battalion safely reached the valley of Muong Chen around midday, which was occupied by another small garrison of Thai troops. As his men washed off the dirt and blood of the last two days in the Nam Chang river, Bigeard radioed Salan for an immediate airdrop of supplies, and for air attacks on the pursuing Viet Minh. Both requests were fulfilled in the course of the afternoon, B-26 strikes holding up the enemy advance while the men rested and re-equipped. By nightfall, the battalion was ready to move on.

For Bigeard's battalion, the night journey that followed was sheer torture. The exhausted men, almost every one carrying a piece of heavy equipment as well as his own pack and rifle, struggled along the ravine cut through the mountains by the Nam Chang river, working their way across perilously steep slopes in the darkness. A false step, a slip in the wet mud, could bring a fall of 10m onto bare rock. One pair of stretcher-bearers, losing their footing, tipped a wounded man down into the ravine, never to be seen again. Fighting their way across swift mountain torrents, soldiers formed human chains to avoid being swept away. As exhaustion took hold during this third consecutive night without sleep, some simply lay down beside the track, hoping to be left to die rather than go on, but officers and NCOs beat them mercilessly with bamboo sticks until they got to their feet to continue the march.

Mud-stained, pale and haggard, the paras looked like ghosts being ferried from the land of the dead. In all, 91 men had been left behind

The following morning, 22 October, the battalion saw the first sign that its ordeal might soon be over. From 1000 hours onwards, the paras passed a long column of the 56th Vietnamese Battalion, marching in the opposite direction to take over the task of stemming the Viet Minh advance. Bigeard's men were visibly heartened, and by 1830 hours the whole force had reached the post of Ban I Tong where, it seemed, they would at last be able to rest. But only two hours later, a message came through that the Vietnamese battalion was in full retreat; the paras would not be safe until were over the Black river.

The prospect of yet another night-march was almost too much for the men to face, but the terrain was easier this time and somehow they dredged up the reserves of energy and willpower to make it. There were some difficult moments crossing swollen tributaries, but by dawn the advance units were boarding Thai canoes, sent to ferry them across the Black river. Mud-stained, pale and haggard, the paras looked like ghosts being ferried from the land of the dead. In all, 91 men had been left behind.

The paratroopers had shown such courage and endurance that they were greeted like victors. Over 400 officers and men – two-thirds of the entire force – were decorated for bravery. Bigeard told his men: 'You have suffered appallingly... Do not regret it... Let us prepare for our battles of the future.'

THE AUTHOR R.G. Grant graduated in Modern History from Trinity College, Oxford. He has written extensively on the military campaigns of the 20th century.

The daring exploits of German paratroopers in the Low Countries during 1940 so impressed Prime Minister Winston Churchill that he recommended the formation of an elite British airborne force. Their first parachute jump took place in June 1940 and volunteers came forward to join the units that on 1 August 1942 became The Parachute Regiment.

Parachute troops were used successfully on several occasions in the early years of the war, but it was not until September 1944 that they mounted their biggest operation. Over 10,000 men of the 1st Airborne Division were dropped on Arnhem to seize a vital bridge. The assault failed but the courage and tough fighting skills of the paras won them the admiration of the enemy. After World War II the value of maintaining a small but highly motivated airborne force was recognised and the paras went on to fight in Britain's wars of decolonisation; while in recent years the regiment has served in Northern Ireland and been a vital part of Britain's NATO commitment.

Although still trained for airborne assaults, The Parachute Regiment has been used in an infantry capacity: of its three battalions only one acts in a paradrop role while the other two are employed more conventionally. The paras maintain a fiercely guarded reputation for battle efficiency that has made them one of the finest units in the British Army. The paras were in the thick of the action to regain the Falklands in 1982. After spearheading the landings at San Carlos on 21 May, 2 and 3 Para were to encounter some of the fiercest fighting of the conflict.

2 PARA:
READY FOR ANYTHING

The first and bloodiest action of the land war in the Falklands was fought by 2 Para, when they assaulted Darwin and Goose Green. In an epic attack, 450 men of the battalion smashed into 1500 Argentinians

A FLASH of light in the sky to the west, followed by the report of the 4.5in gun of HMS *Arrow*, told the men of 2 Para that it was 0630 hours on 28 May 1982 and that the battle for Goose Green was under way. 2 Para had been ordered south from its positions on Sussex Mountain – guarding the beach-head at San Carlos – to take out the Argentinian forces around Goose Green and to secure the important airfield there. Reconnaissance reports had suggested that the Argentinians were only at battalion strength but, as events were to prove, this was far from the case and 2 Para's resources were to be stretched to the limit. The British troops, or 'Toms' as they called themselves, had a real fight on their hands.

Outnumbered and lightly-armed, 2 Para's real strength lay in the professionalism and determination of its soldiers; each man – whether officer or other rank – was a volunteer and had undergone an exceptionally tough training and selection procedure before being allowed to wear the coveted red beret of a paratrooper. During the course of his training and subsequent life in 2 Para each man developed a personal confidence that contributed to the creation of a fighting machine that recognised few limitations. The bond between officer and soldier was far closer than usual in the rest of the Army. The close physical trust necessary before parachute drops – each man checking the equipment of the man in front – helped create a mutual respect rarely experienced in other regiments.

The battle, from the outset, contained all the ingredients that could lead to disaster. Despite the rigour of the paras' training they were, nonetheless, inexperienced troops whose introduction to infantry fighting was to be a night assault. They faced an unknown and untried enemy; had little accurate intelligence of his location and strength, and were to conduct an attack over 25km from any friendly forces, with little supporting fire.

Major Dair Farrar-Hockley, commander of A Company, opened the land battle at 0635 hours and, after a brief fight, his company took Burntside House, a large building to the left of the battalion's axis of advance. The attack

steadily southwards down the isthmus.

The paras of B Company moved forward at 0710. Fired on by Argentinians dug in to their left, they launched an attack in which white phosphorus grenades proved a deadly weapon when lobbed into a trench, for the burns caused by the phosphorus were horrific. B Company made rapid progress.

At the centre of the advance D Company had caught up with Battalion Tactical HQ and the CO, Colonel 'H' Jones. Earlier, D Company had lost its way but had regained contact when B Company began its move. The overall attack was falling behind schedule, however, due to fierce Argentinian resistance, difficulties of navigation and the very poor visibility. Consequently, 'H' was insistent that D Company should get ahead as quickly as possible.

D Company went forward when, suddenly, it came under intensive smallarms fire from the right. Battalion HQ was also in the line of fire and took cover

boosted the confidence of the company, although their enthusiasm was such that, under the assault from tracer, 84mm Carl Gustav anti-tank weapons and, particularly, white phosphorus grenades, the house caught fire and was subsequently gutted. The attack on Burntside House was the signal to B Company, commanded by Major John Crosland, to begin its attack on Argentinian defences on the right of the battalion's route. D Company (under Major Phil Neame) acted as the reserve at this stage and was held in the centre of the battalion's line of advance. C Company acted as the armed reconnaissance team for 2 Para and as such had led the advance down from Sussex Mountain and prepared the way forward for the main assault on Darwin and Goose Green. C Company, about half the size of the 100-man strong rifle companies, A, B and D, was held back in the initial stages, ready either to exploit tactical advantages as they occurred or to repulse any Argentinian counter-attacks. The Support Company – armed with snipers' rifles, machine guns, mortars and Milan anti-tank missiles – was deployed on the far side of Camilla Creek and brought round to give direct support to the rifle companies as the battalion moved

Above: The opposition – one of the well-concealed Argentinian 120mm heavy mortars that threatened to blunt 2 Para's advance. Goose Green can be seen in the distance. Top: Sergeants Hunt and Squires fix a night sight to a 7.62mm L42A1 sniper rifle during the voyage to the South Atlantic. Note the camouflaged stock and barrel. Left: Paras tab their way to victory.

as best it could by lying in wheel depressions in a track. While D Company dealt with the enemy, HMS *Arrow*, providing the bulk of the fire support and illumination, radioed Battalion HQ and reported that her 4.5in gun had jammed. The only other support came from the light guns and two mortars deployed at Camilla Creek House, all of which had little ammunition.

Three paras were killed and others suffered gunshot wounds. Any casualties were left where they fell

Argentinian artillery fire was now raining down on the British positions with considerable accuracy, but, fortunately for the paras, the damp peaty ground of the battlefield absorbed the impact of the Argentinian shells and reduced the killing power of the splinters. It was this, above all, that accounted for the relatively low casualties suffered by 2 Para.

D Company pressed home its attack, although the proximity of B Company – some distance ahead – made it necessary for considerable constraint to be shown in returning the enemy's fire. During this assault three paras were killed (the first of the battle) while others suffered gunshot wounds and white phosphorus burns. Any casualties were left where they fell until circumstances permitted them to be treated. The reason was simple: if one man went down, the battalion would lose a second man if someone stopped to help. This was not a callous practice: it was the only way that a light force such as

a parachute unit could hope to survive on the battlefield. In the event, one man, Private Fletcher, did stop to help an injured colleague Corporal Cork and the same machine gun that had knocked down his friend killed him. He was found with an open field dressing in his hand.

At about 0900 the rain stopped, though the sky was still overcast and remained so throughout the day. D Company finished mopping up the enemy and A Company was instructed to pass alongside them and push on towards Darwin, over a kilometre further on and screened from view by a low hill. The Argentinian artillery fire became more intense and soldiers took whatever cover they could, either in captured Argentinian trenches or simply by lying out in the open in natural hollows. One shell landed directly between the CO and his adjutant, but failed to explode: 'Lucky they're using such lousy ammunition,' was 'H's' laconic comment.

Over to the right, B Company advanced down the side of a shallow valley towards the gorse line, above which were the ruins of Boca House. As they moved down the featureless slope the platoons of B Company came under fire all at the same time. Each platoon attempted to pull back behind the crest of the hill they had just left or to take cover in whatever dead ground they could find.

By now, A Company was also in trouble. As they approached Darwin Hill, figures were seen moving on the slopes. At first it was thought they might be Falklanders but when a soldier's call was answered in Spanish, recognition dawned on both sides simultaneously. The leading platoon of paras, followed by the remainder of the company, ran towards the hill in an attempt to take the position by surprise. They came under heavy fire from well-placed bunkers along the top of the hill. Five paras went down before the company found shelter in a gorse-filled gully that ran up the hillside. A Company was now well and truly pinned down and attempts to smash the enemy bunkers using grenades and 66mm LAW rockets all

Far left, below: A Royal Marine of the Blowpipe team that fought with the paras takes cover under heavy enemy fire. Centre: The reverse slope of Darwin Hill, photographed by the author, during a lull in the fighting. Officers, armed with 7.62mm SLR rifles, plan the final stages of the battle amidst the clutter of war. Stretchers are close at hand. Below: Men of A Company wait for the order to advance on Goose Green. The rough moorland is typical of the ground over which battle was joined.

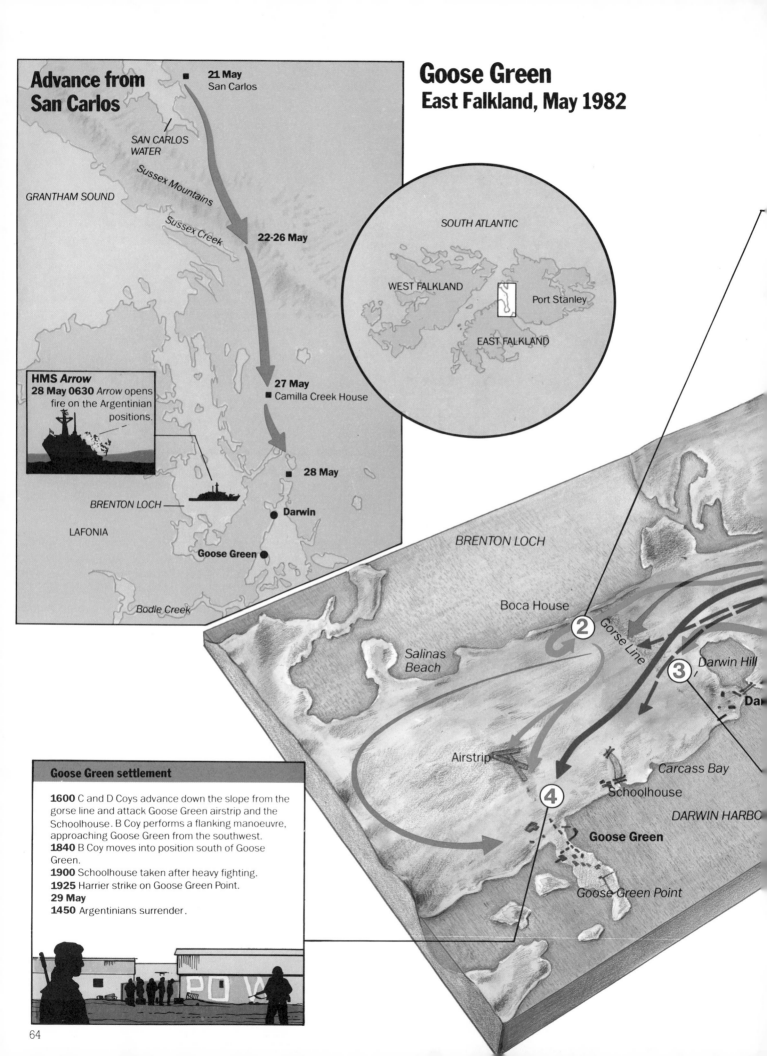

Goose Green
East Falkland, May 1982

Advance from San Carlos

21 May
San Carlos

SAN CARLOS WATER

GRANTHAM SOUND

Sussex Mountains

Sussex Creek

22-26 May

HMS Arrow
28 May 0630 Arrow opens fire on the Argentinian positions.

27 May
Camilla Creek House

28 May

BRENTON LOCH

LAFONIA

Darwin

Goose Green

Bodie Creek

SOUTH ATLANTIC

WEST FALKLAND

Port Stanley

EAST FALKLAND

BRENTON LOCH

Boca House

②

Gorse Line

③ Darwin Hill

Da

Salinas Beach

Airstrip

Carcass Bay

④

Schoolhouse

DARWIN HARBO

Goose Green

Goose Green Point

Goose Green settlement

1600 C and D Coys advance down the slope from the gorse line and attack Goose Green airstrip and the Schoolhouse. B Coy performs a flanking manoeuvre, approaching Goose Green from the southwest.
1840 B Coy moves into position south of Goose Green.
1900 Schoolhouse taken after heavy fighting.
1925 Harrier strike on Goose Green Point.
29 May
1450 Argentinians surrender.

Boca House

1030 B Coy crosses the gorse line near Boca House and comes under heavy fire.
1400 D Coy advances to the west of Boca House. Support Coy brings Milan into action against enemy bunkers.
1530 D Coy moves up the slope from the beach behind Boca House. The Argentinians surrender.

Burntside House

0200 2 Para 'tabs off' from Camilla Creek.
0630 A and B Coys cross the start line near Burntside House.
0635 A Coy attacks the forward platoon of Argentinians in Burntside House, overwhelming them with superior firepower.

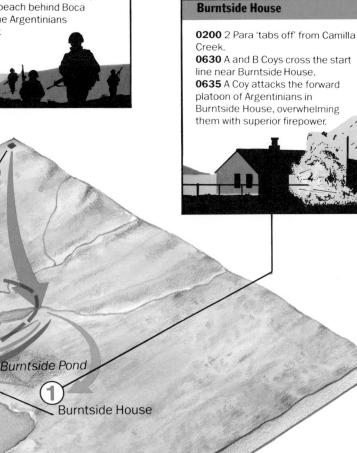

Camilla Creek House

Creek

Burntside Pond

① Burntside House

onation
it

Darwin Hill

1030 A Coy attacks Darwin Hill. After confused fighting they are brought to a standstill in the gorse gully below the hill. A left-flank attack is halted by Argentinian fire.
1125 Major Farrar-Hockley's call for a Harrier strike refused due to bad weather. A Coy joined by Col 'H' Jones and Battalion Tac HQ.
1300 Farrar-Hockley leads a mortar party onto a ledge bearing on enemy trenches, but the party is repulsed. 'H' Jones falls while leading a second attack.
1330 Jones dies, but A Coy renews the assault and breaks through the Argentinian lines. Darwin Hill is taken.

Key
2 Para
A Coy
B Coy
C Coy
D Coy
Support Coy

failed. The paras, crouching in the gulley with machine-gun bullets whistling above them, were hardly able to move.

Both A and B Companies were now in serious trouble, but since the neck of land, on which Goose Green and Darwin stood, was so narrow, there seemed to be no opportunity of using D Company to try to outflank the Argentinian positions. D Company, therefore, was told to hold itself in reserve. It was clear that time was in favour of the Argentinians. The paras' ammunition was running low and there was little chance of any being brought forward, casualties were increasing, artillery support had virtually ceased to exist and air support could not be provided because bad weather at sea prevented the Harriers from flying. The Argentinians were able to mount air operations and the rear areas of 2 Para were attacked by three Pucara ground-attack aircraft at 1155.

While the enemy was engaging A Company the Colonel made his own assault and was mortally wounded

Colonel Jones and his Tac HQ inched forward under heavy fire to A Company's position. The CO knew that the momentum of the attack had to be regained, but another attempt on the hill cost the lives of two officers and a corporal, and under a storm of fire the men of A Company were forced back to the point from which he had started. It was during this attack that H and his party moved round to the right, and while the enemy troops were engaging A Company the Colonel made his own assault, was shot and mortally wounded. Far from lowering the paras' morale, H Jones' sacrifice gave his men new determination; grimly A Company attacked again and this time forced its way through the Argentinian lines, capturing the entire position.

When the CO was killed the battalion second-in-command, Major Chris Keeble, took over. He made his way to Darwin Hill and over the radio spoke to Major Neame to establish what D Company thought it could do. Neame had noticed a low cliff face along the shore by Boca House and as the tide was not at full flood he thought he could get his company along the slope under cover of the cliff face to outflank the Argentinian positions without being seen. Keeble told him to get on with this plan while B Company kept the Argentinians occupied with smallarms fire.

An important asset had now reached B Company from the Support Company, Milan anti-tank missiles. They were set up and several firing posts began to engage the enemy positions. The Milan's effectiveness was amazing: missile after missile crashed into the enemy bunkers and Argentinian fire began to slacken, so B company could again begin to move forward into positions from where they could directly assault the enemy.

One unfortunate Argentinian was seen to leave a bunker that had been struck by a missile, run a few yards and jump into another. As he leapt, this bunker too was hit by a missile and disintegrated in a cloud of dust and flying stones. 'Bet that took the edge off his day,' remarked a Tom with some satisfaction. The end came quickly: as D Company stormed from the beach and B Company continued to pour fire into the trenches, the Argentinians decided they'd had enough. White flags began to appear and the position was taken.

Barely pausing, D Company pressed on and moved left along a shallow valley, sufficiently deep to screen it from enemy forces on the airfield. Their objective was the Goose Green schoolhouse and eventually the airfield. This would leave the paras in a position on the outskirts of the settlement. B Company set off in a wide sweep southwards that would take them to the right of the airfield, and then on for some distance when they would swing left and in a semi-circle move across the isthmus until they were on the southern outskirts of the settlement.

Back on Darwin Hill, A Company had secured the position and cleared Darwin settlement. While the bulk of the company set about consolidating its defence and other troops rounded up prisoners, one platoon was detached to join C Company, which then advanced down the long, gentle gradient towards the airfield and Goose Green. To the Toms it resembled a World War I scene, with an extended line of soldiers advancing across ground that seemed as smooth as a billiard table.

Then came the ear-splitting crashing and lines of tracer as anti-aircraft guns on the airfield poured a stream of fire onto the British

Suddenly, some of the paras noticed Argentinians running across the airfield. The Toms realised helplessly, what weapons the enemy troops were racing for – and then came the ear-splitting crashing and lines of tracer as anti-aircraft guns on the airfield poured a stream of heavy-calibre fire onto the British. The 20mm double-barrelled automatic Rheinmetal cannons from the airfield were soon joined by 35mm weapons in Goose Green itself. The men at Keeble's command post behind the gorse hedge on Darwin Hill frantically hit the deck as the high-explosive rounds raked along the hedge.

The men of D Company, screened from the airfield, were relatively safe from the anti-aircraft guns, but as they approached the schoolhouse they came under heavy fire from both the school and the edge of the airfield. A brisk firefight was soon in progress and C Company joined in. The schoolhouse caught fire and as it contained a considerable quantity of munitions it burned well. At this point Lieutenant Barry, having seen a white flag in the area of the schoolhouse, went forward to take a surrender but in the process was shot and killed. The result was

Paratrooper, 2 Para Goose Green 1982

Basic uniform consists of a windproof jacket and trousers in DPM (disruptive pattern material) alongside which are worn black combat gloves and 1958-pattern web equipment. Other features include short cloth puttees and a face-net veil worn as a scarf. This soldier wears the cut-down para-trooper model of the glass-reinforced-plastic helmet fitted with a DPM cover. He is armed with the 7.62mm L1A1 SLR, a semi-automatic rifle, fitted with a 20-round maga-zine, capable of a rate-of-fire of 40rpm to a maximum effective range of 600m. Despite the fact that the SLR was a develop-ment of the Belgian FN FAL, British paratroops were impressed by the FN FALs carried by their Argentinian opponents which had a superior gas-recoil system and, in many cases, had folding stocks.

Above: Testament to the ~~f~~rocity of the battle to ~~r~~capture Goose Green – the ~~P~~aras bury their dead. They ~~lo~~st 15 men killed and 30 ~~w~~ounded. Many of the dead ~~w~~ere officers and senior ~~N~~COs, who made the ultimate ~~sa~~crifice leading from the ~~fr~~ont. Far left: An abandoned ~~3~~5mm Oerlikon AA gun. This ~~g~~un was used against the ~~P~~aras as they attacked the ~~ai~~rfield on the edge of Goose ~~G~~reen. A well-aimed cluster ~~b~~omb dropped by a Sea ~~H~~arrier silenced it for good.

BOCA HOUSE

'At first light, as we approached our objective, we were caught in a difficult position as we were subjected to over-fire from Darwin Hill. The only thing to do was to move forward, so I ordered the two leading platoons, 4 and 6, to move ahead with Company HQ into the gulley in front of Boca House. We then started to fight our way down this gulley into the bottom and up the other side towards a sort of gorse line which gave some cover from the enemy's fairly dominant position at Boca House. As the light increased, so did the accuracy of their fire. I had two options, either withdraw completely or get forward. I certainly wasn't going to withdraw so I ordered my two forward platoons ahead with my own HQ. I left my reserve, 5 Platoon, on the crest line to protect the whole of the high ground in case we had to beat a hasty retreat; it was that platoon which took a battering. We also got fairly well larded with artillery and mortars but 5 Platoon were taking a lot of long-range fire from machine guns and snipers and were taking casualties. I said to them over the net:'Right, once we get down into the gulley you withdraw onto the hill line and just hold the ridge line position.' It was during this action that we lost young Stephen Illingsworth. He had rescued Private Hall, who had been shot, and then, because we were short of ammunition, had gone back for Hall's kit and while doing this, was killed. It was a

very brave act, no doubt about it, a classic young soldier's act, extremely brave, totally unselfish and one can only give the highest praise for him. He was my first death in the campaign. Street was also wounded. He is very much the old company soldier but I heard him scream when he got two shots in his left leg.'

Major John Crosland, B Company Commander, seen above in the Falklands.

inevitable: the Toms in that area took no chances and gave no quarter.

With an end to the fighting around the schoolhouse and the completion of B Company's move to the south of the settlement, the men of 2 Para could breathe more easily. The Argentinian artillery was still in action, however, as was the Argentinian Air Force. Two A-4 Skyhawks made fast runs using cannon against B and D Companies, although one was shot down by smallarms fire. A second attack was made by Pucara aircraft, one of which was shot down by a Royal Marine Blowpipe detachment which had been seconded to 2 Para.

Another Pucara made a run over the battlefield dropping napalm

At last a Harrier attack was possible and for the first time that day the men of 2 Para felt there were others on their side. At about 1930 – with the light fading – three Harriers attacked the enemy positions with cluster bombs, and as the explosions echoed over the battlefield a cheer went up from the men of 2 Para. Just before dark, firing lessened although another Pucara made a run over the battlefield, dropping napalm on D Company. It was an ill-judged attack; every single gun was turned on the aircraft, which immediately went out of control and crashed, showering B Company with fuel.

In a final effort to defeat 2 Para, the enemy flew in reinforcements by helicopter and began to put them down about a kilometre south of the settlement. B Company moved to prevent this while artillery fire from the gun line at Camilla Creek House soon scattered the Argentinians.

As night fell, on the evening of the 28th, so the gunfire died down across the battlefield. Major Keeble ordered no aggressive patrolling and no firing unless necessary. His aim was to give the Argentinians time to think about a diplomatically-worded ultimatum of surrender he had sent to them via two prisoners, who were to return under a white flag no later than 0830 local time the next day. It was a cold night. The men of 2 Para went about their various tasks and sentry duties in the hope that morning would not bring renewed fighting.

At 0825 the prisoners returned under a white flag, the surrender accepted. For the loss of 15 men killed and 30 wounded 2 Para took prisoner or killed about 1300 Argentinian servicemen. Captured hardware included four 105mm pack howitzers, two 35mm anti-aircraft guns, six 20mm anti-aircraft guns, six 120mm mortars and two Pucara aircraft.

The most significant result, however, was the re-assertion of an old truth: war, for the infantry, is a battle of will. He whose will breaks first loses. And 2 Para had not broken, during over 12 hours of the most intense fighting.

THE AUTHOR Captain (now Major) The Reverend David Cooper served as padre to 2 Para. A weapons expert and Bisley shot, he was present at Goose Green and was mentioned in despatches after playing a major role in casualty evacuation.

'THE PHILISTINES'

Within the South African Defence Force (SADF) in the early 1980s, a number of British, Rhodesian and American troops were jocularly known as 'the Philistines' on account of their cavalier attitude to counter-insurgency warfare. These former members of the Rhodesian Army had joined the SADF following the creation of Zimbabwe in April 1980. Some were absorbed into 32 Battalion, a unit containing ex-FNLA guerrillas. In addition, Colonel Carpenter, commander of the SADF's 44 Parachute Brigade, had recruited a force of, mainly Rhodesian, professional soldiers to act as a new fighting arm of the brigade. Its name was the Pathfinder Company.

The role of the Pathfinder Company was to conduct mobile, fighting patrols deep inside Angola. Already highly trained in counter-terrorist operations, the pathfinders were totally self-sufficient and independent of the rest of the SADF.

After passing a selection course, the company's volunteers underwent further training in bush warfare and conventional pathfinding techniques, and then moved to their permanent base at Ondangwa in South West Africa (Namibia). From there the pathfinders launched operations against SWAPO, sometimes on foot, but more usually utilising a convoy of Landcruisers, Land Rovers and Unimog trucks. Led by Colonel Carpenter, the force was highly successful throughout its short and controversial history.

The Pathfinder Company was disbanded when Colonel Carpenter left 44 Parachute Brigade in early 1982. Above: The silver wings worn by SADF paras who have completed 50 jumps.

BUSH PATHFINDERS

Battle-hardened veterans from all over the world, the men of the Pathfinder Company, 44th Parachute Brigade acted as a spearhead in a raid against guerrillas in Angola

THE PATHFINDER Company of 44 Parachute Brigade, South African Defence Force (SADF), was activated in early 1980, and, along with many other foreign troops, I was recruited direct from service in Support Commando of the Rhodesian Light Infantry. During 1980, 44 Para Brigade had been fully reorganised. Based at Bloemfontein, 1 Parachute Battalion (1 Parabat) consisted of national servicemen doing their two-year call-up, and one company was permanently based at Ondangwa in South West Africa (Namibia). Two and 3 Parabats comprised Citizen Force personnel who had completed national service but were still required to attend a yearly camp, often for active duty in South West Africa (Namibia) or Angola. The permanent headquarters of the three parabats was 44 Para Brigade.

By early 1981, two pathfinder selection courses had produced sufficient personnel to be deployed on active service and a convoy of vehicles was being prepared for their use in the workshops of the South African Department of Scientific and Industrial Research. The convoy consisted of three Toyota Landcruisers, two mounting 0.5in Browning machine guns and one with a 20mm cannon bartered from the South African Air Force (SAAF); three Land Rovers which would carry twin FN MAG light machine guns mounted at the rear, plus a single machine gun for the commander, and three Unimog trucks were to carry

Left: A 'Philistine' in the flesh – an ex-Rhodesian Army pathfinder in FAPLA uniform and carrying a Soviet 7.62mm AK assault rifle. Above: An SADF Unimog, armed with a captured Soviet 14.5mm machine gun, and (top) a Unimog after the short, sharp shock of a SWAPO landmine.

the fuel, rations and ammunition needed for long-range patrols. All the vehicles were fitted with smoke dischargers and winches, as well as foam-filled tyres as a precaution against puncturing from thorns.

The convoy was delivered to Murrayhill, the path-finders' permanent base, only days before we set off

JOINING THE PATHFINDERS

Every volunteer for the Pathfinder Company, 44 Parachute Brigade, was required to turn up at the SADF headquarters in Pretoria for preliminary vetting and medical examination. Successful candidates were issued with kit and sent to the unit's South African base at Murrayhill, an abandoned farm at Hammanskraal on the Pretoria highway. Training commenced immediately under Captain Botha and Company Sergeant Major McDonald (an ex-member of the British SAS who had commanded mercenaries in the FNLA after the capture of the infamous 'Colonel' Callan). The men then transferred to the para brigade's bush camp at Mabilique on the Limpopo river. There, bush-craft, infantry skills and pathfinding were taught, with continual emphasis on the development of peak physical fitness. For instance, a full ammunition box was carried on every run, and a 5-10km run rounded off every day's training. All fire practice was conducted with live rounds.
The determination and endurance of the men under selection were put to the test in the Drakensburg mountains in Natal. They had to cover a fixed distance of mountainous terrain within a time limit, carrying measured weights and the heavy ammo box. Each leg of the route had its own time limit and weight loading, and failure to complete any section on time meant an immediate end to the candidate's hopes of inclusion in the Pathfinder Company. However, such was the calibre of the men volunteering for the unit that only a few were defeated by the high standards of entry. Above: The beret badge of the South African paras.

for Sector 10, the operational area in South West Africa (Namibia) that borders Angola. The pathfinders took two weeks moving up through the Kalahari Desert along the Botswana border, trying out ambush and anti-ambush drills, patrol formations and types of laagers along the way. It was decided that two-vehicle sections worked best, the commander riding in a Landcruiser and the second-in-command in a Land Rover. This combination also provided a satisfactory blend of firepower. For communication between vehicles, VHF radios were carried, and contact with base camp was maintained with HF sets.

Our first operation in Angola turned out to be a dawn attack on a known SWAPO (South West Africa Peoples' Organisation) base. Following a preliminary SAAF air strike, the camp was to be assaulted by 32 Battalion with the pathfinders providing close support with machine guns.

The company received its orders and prepared kit. There was no standard dress, and South African brown uniform mingled with Rhodesian camouflage and any other uniform available. Webbing was also left to individual preference. Personal armament consisted of the South African version of the Israeli Galil, the R-4 rifle. This weapon was not as popular with the men as the old Rhodesian issue FN FAL, however, as most disliked its smaller calibre and 'tinny' feel. Some of us took along hand guns, both privately-owned models and the issue 9mm Star automatic. Each vehicle carried a quantity of M79 grenade launchers and an RPG-7 rocket launcher.

The day before the attack, the company crossed the 'cut line' (the border with Angola). Aided by aerial photographs, we struck north, seeking a route through the scrub. When the bush became dense, hampering progress, a Unimog was called to the fore and this marvellous workhorse would crash, bend and batter a road through for the others to follow. At last light we linked up with 32 Battalion.

Before dawn the next day, the terrorist camp began to buzz with activity. The enemy had discovered that something was up and soon speculative

fire was being laid on likely approach routes with BM-21 multiple-barrel rocket launchers. The air strike went in on schedule, and met anti-aircraft fire from several points around the camp. The ground forces then commenced their advance into the camp area. A well-disciplined sweep-line was formed by 32 Battalion, with the pathfinder vehicles spaced at intervals along it. We moved forward, firing into likely enemy cover. There was no return fire, however, and it soon became apparent that apart from the anti-aircraft gunners, everyone else had fled.

While 32 Battalion dealt with two unexploded bombs which had been dropped by Mirages on the initial strike, the Pathfinder Company moved out to clear the anti-aircraft positions. Supporting helicopters had reported seeing terrorists wheeling of heavy machine guns, but we managed to locate one position with three 14.5mm machine guns still intact. When we arrived a guerrilla, wounded in one leg and unable to escape, chose to shoot himself in the head. After checking for booby traps, the guns were lifted out by Puma helicopter. (Later Colonel Carpenter, commander of 44 Para Brigade, managed to retrieve one and it was mounted in a Unimog for our own use.)

Because the element of surprise had been lost, the attack was only a partial success, but we were satisfied that the pathfinders had done well on this our first operation.

In total secrecy an invasion force was being gathered and formed into battle groups and task forces

During the summer of 1981, the Pathfinder Company mounted ceaseless combat patrols into Angola, but all the time the men were waiting for 'the big one'. This was to be a large-scale invasion of Angola that would destroy SWAPO's ability to mount incursions into South West Africa (Namibia), as well as give FAPLA (Popular Armed Forces for the Liberation of Angola) such a bloody nose that they would have to reconsider the support they gave SWAPO. Unknown

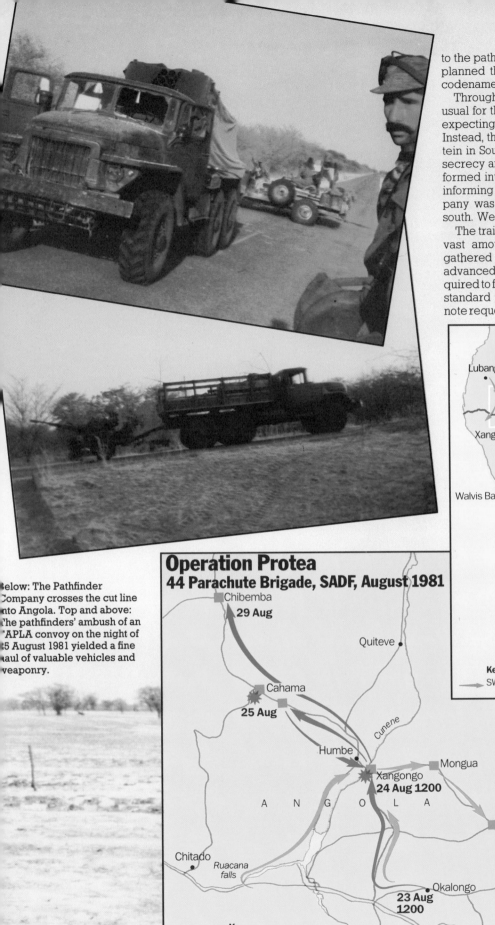

to the pathfinders, the SADF hierarchy had already planned the op and was putting it into action. Its codename was Operation Protea.

Throughout South Africa men were reporting as usual for their annual camps and boarding aircraft, expecting to be flown to various training areas. Instead, they found themselves landing at Grootfontein in South West Africa (Namibia), where in total secrecy an invasion force was being gathered and formed into battle groups and task forces. Without informing us of the operation, the Pathfinder Company was ordered to leave Ondangwa and head south. We departed at 0800 hours on 19 August.

The training area was bushland near Omuthiya. A vast amount of men and equipment had been gathered and rehearsals had already reached an advanced stage. Upon arrival, the men were required to fill out medical and next-of-kin forms. It was standard practice for the pathfinders to include a note requesting that next of kin be notified only in the

Below: The Pathfinder Company crosses the cut line into Angola. Top and above: the pathfinders' ambush of an APLA convoy on the night of 25 August 1981 yielded a fine haul of valuable vehicles and weaponry.

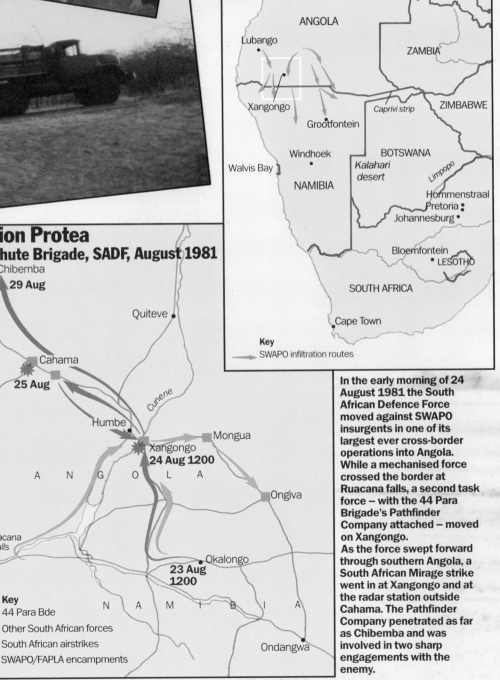

Operation Protea
44 Parachute Brigade, SADF, August 1981

Key
- 44 Para Bde
- Other South African forces
- ✳ South African airstrikes
- ▪ SWAPO/FAPLA encampments

Key
- → SWAPO infiltration routes

In the early morning of 24 August 1981 the South African Defence Force moved against SWAPO insurgents in one of its largest ever cross-border operations into Angola. While a mechanised force crossed the border at Ruacana falls, a second task force – with the 44 Para Brigade's Pathfinder Company attached – moved on Xangongo.

As the force swept forward through southern Angola, a South African Mirage strike went in at Xangongo and at the radar station outside Cahama. The Pathfinder Company penetrated as far as Chibemba and was involved in two sharp engagements with the enemy.

Left: The Pathfinder Company rejected heavy armoured vehicles in favour of fast, light, adaptable platforms for a formidable range of offensive armament. The Landcruiser in the foreground carries a 0.5in Browning machine gun, with a light machine gun for the commander, while the Unimog has a 60mm mortar mounted on its flat-bed. Bottom left: A pathfinder foot patrol in Angola. No man is dressed alike, and their weapons come from both Western and Communist sources. Bottom right: Amongst the early casualties of Operation Protea was this Soviet-made BRDM-2 scout car. Below: This guerrilla, wounded in a raid on a SWAPO base, chose to finish himself off rather than surrender to the South Africans.

event of death. Nobody wanted their families worried unnecessarily.

The next day the company began practising camp attacks with Task Force Alpha. We were to specialise in tank hunting, and for this our RPG-7s were replaced by French 89mm rocket launchers. Men of 32 Battalion made up a prominent part of the attack force and many of our old Rhodesian friends came over. At night, many of us who had been recruited from outside South Africa would gather around a blazing fire and, with the help of a few beers and lusty singing, celebrate the coming events. The South Africans, who could not understand our enthusiasm, had already nicknamed us 'the Philistines'. It was a name everyone quickly took to their hearts.

On 21 August we were ordered to be ready to move any time after 1700 hours. The following day, at 1100 hours, the company was given its final briefing: Task Force Alpha would attack target 'Yankee', which was the town of Xangongo, and the FAPLA armoured brigade positioned there. As tank hunters, the Pathfinder Company would remain uncommitted, but ready to be deployed as required. By 1745 the task force was heading for its form-up point (FUP), and at midday on 23 August, it had reached Okalongo, 30km from the cut line, where a major refuelling programme was carried out. The FUP was reached shortly afterwards.

The move from the FUP to the target started at 0230 on the next morning. Crossing the cut line, a Unimog carrying a multiple rocket launcher detonated a mine and became the first casualty of Operation Protea. Then, at exactly 1200 the SAAF Mirages struck Xangongo. The ground forces, including the pathfinders, were already on the outskirts and 32 Battalion provided the assault troops, supported by artillery fire from 155mm G-5 guns. By 1900 the town was firmly in South African hands.

All was quiet by midday on the 25th, so Colonel Carpenter arranged for his men to become attached to Battle Group 30. Joining up with Ratel infantry combat vehicles, the Pathfinders hared along the tarmac road towards an FAPLA camp, 80km north-west of Xangongo, but the camp was already deserted by the time the column reached it.

At last light the battle group units dispersed for the night, one Ratel company remaining on the road to halt any FAPLA vehicles coming down from Cahama in the north. The pathfinders camped 200m off the road, about a kilometre down from the Ratels.

Corporal David Beam was the gunner on Colonel Carpenter's Landcruiser. Due to his wealth of knowledge gained serving in US Marine helicopters in Vietnam, Beam was responsible for all our heavy machine guns. At 2200 hours he was on guard when a convoy of petrol-driven trucks passed by, heading north. As all the friendly forces had diesel engines, Beam quickly woke the sleeping crews. By now the convoy had reached the Ratels blocking the road and a sharp engagement was heard to take place, lasting between five and 10 minutes. It was followed by a silence, broken only by the sound of the FAPLA convoy now driving back the way they had come. By chance they stopped again, right next to the pathfinders who were now stood-to at their vehicles.

At a command from Colonel Carpenter, all the vehicles on the side nearest the road opened fire. Men from the far side assisted with rocket launchers and their 60mm mortar. An incredible amount of red and green tracer streaked across the sky, while a nearby artillery unit added to the surreal scene by firing illumination shells.

Both lorries exploded, hit by 89mm rockets, and after only a few minutes Botha's men ceased firing

The FAPLA stopped firing and all was quiet again. The pathfinders had suffered no casualties or damage, but noises coming from the far side of the road indicated that the terrorists could now be setting up mortars. A patrol, under Captain Botha, was quickly formed and, armed with 89mm rocket launchers, the men silently inched their way towards the sounds.

On the other side of the road they saw two Russian GAZ lorries and several FAPLA soldiers setting up mortars. Unseen, the pathfinders crossed the road and formed a firing line. At a signal from Captain Botha they opened fire. It was dramatically effective. Both lorries exploded, hit by 89mm rockets, and after only a few minutes Captain Botha's men ceased firing. There was neither sight nor sound of the enemy, but recognising the dangers of sweeping a contact area in the dark, the patrol returned to the camp. With the action over for the night, sentries were posted while the rest caught up on some long overdue sleep. Exploding ammunition in the burning vehicles made a din for some time to come.

By early morning the Pathfinder Company was up and ready to move. To everyone's great satisfaction, the entire FAPLA convoy was found deserted and almost intact on the road. It consisted of a fully equipped radio jeep, two BTR armoured cars, two BM-21 multiple rocket launchers and four other GAZ trucks, each with twin 23mm anti-aircraft machine guns mounted on the back. These nine vehicles captured, plus the two lorries destroyed, made a successful night's work. Although no enemy bodies were found, trails of blood showed that casualties had been removed.

After returning to Xangongo for a quick clean-up, the company set off on an independent mission,

The camps had been empty for a number of days.

By 29 August all possible enemy positions outside Chibemba had been checked and found deserted, so it was decided to enter the town itself. As one of our Land Rovers had broken down, Colonel Carpenter elected to leave the mechanics behind, protected by two other vehicles, while he approached the town with seven vehicles and 26 men. The column had got no further than the kraals on the town outskirts before the colonel's Landcruiser was destroyed by a landmine. Two crewmen, myself and Corporal Beam, had to be casevaced by helicopter. The former US Marine later had to have both legs amputated. The colonel and his American driver were shaken, but able to carry on. However, when our helicopters reported at least 1000 SWAPO and FAPLA guerrillas in Chibemba, the colonel made a tactical withdrawal in order to reorganise.

The pathfinders continued their checks on suspected enemy camps, but fought only one engagement. This occurred when the leading vehicle emerged from the bush right onto a group of resting guerrillas. Taking the only course of action possible, it charged straight into them, shooting on all sides. In a moment all the terrorists were dead, either shot or run down. For the pathfinders this marked the end of Operation Protea, and they returned home to Murrayhill and leave.

In October the Pathfinder Company joined a 2 Parabat force in an operational parachute jump into Angola as part of a camp attack. This was to be their last action as a unit. Changes were taking place at 44 Para Brigade and Colonel Carpenter was moving on to Military Intelligence. After his departure the pathfinders found themselves involved in giving instruction to the Citizen Force paras. Upon completion of their one-year contracts some men chose to leave the army, while others, the majority, transferred to 32 Battalion. Thus the Pathfinder Company was disbanded.

THE AUTHOR Graham Gillmore served in the Grenadier Guards and the Rhodesian Light Infantry. He was an SNCO in the Pathfinder Company, 44 Parachute Brigade, until he was wounded during Operation Protea in 1981. He now works for a London security firm. All names used in this article, have been altered to protect those still involved in sensitive work in Africa.

Above: A pathfinder patrol north of Xangongo unleashes a hail of fire into a suspected SWAPO encampment. Below: The author (with sergeant's stripes) and a Landcruiser fitted with twin 0.5in Brownings. The vehicle was later destroyed during a raid in Angola.

heading north to the town of Chibemba where reports indicated an FAPLA force of unknown size. Deliberately making our presence known in the town area, we then lay in ambush along the road, hoping to catch any patrols reckless enough to come after us. This tactic showed no results, so it was decided to visit known SWAPO and FAPLA camps. Before entering a camp area we called over helicopter gunships, but no enemy force was encountered.

CASSINO

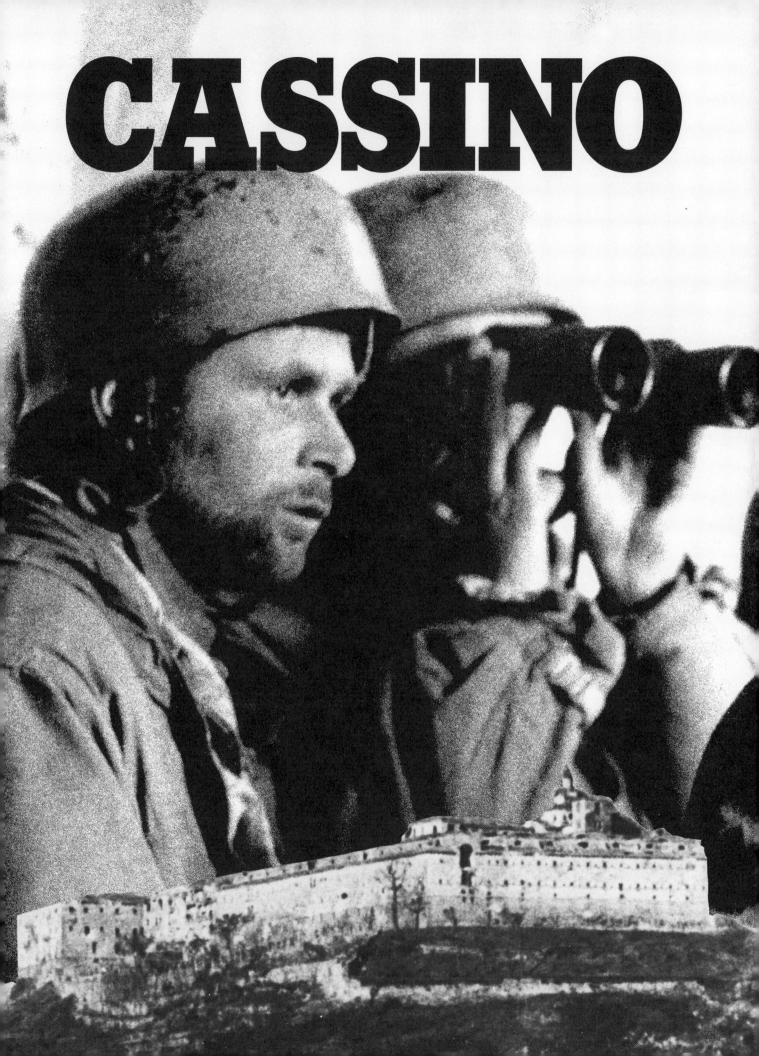

By 1943 Russia was pressing her allies to create a major new front in Europe to draw German forces from the east. After the conquest of North Africa, Britain was eager to prosecute a Mediterranean campaign and oust Italy from the war. The USA wished to open the western front in France, but preparations for an invasion from Britain were far from complete. It was thus decided in January 1943 that Allied troops in Africa should be transferred to do battle for the Mediterranean: the immediate objective became the conquest of Sicily.

On 17 August 1943 US troops took Messina, completing the campaign in Sicily. Hitler, aware that Italy was secretly prepared to capitulate, sent troops to 'reinforce' the Italians south of Rome and build up lines of defence.

The British Eighth Army crossed from Messina to Reggio on the 'toe' of Italy on 3 September. Six days later there followed landings by the US Fifth Army at Salerno, and the British 1st Airborne Division at Taranto at the 'heel' of Italy. Allied progress northwards was slowed by well-prepared German defences and at the end of 1943 it was finally halted by the Gustav Line, a heavily fortified chain of positions straddling the mountains south of Rome.

On 22 January an Allied force landed at Anzio, 120km to the north, in order to attack the line from the rear. Instead, it was contained at the beachhead and forced to fight a prolonged defensive battle for survival. To relieve this force, the Allies in the south had to gain access to the Liri valley, but this was blocked by the German stronghold of Cassino. Shielded from the full use of armour by the flooded Rapido river, Cassino became witness to some of the bloodiest fighting of the Italian campaign.

Fighting in the ruins of a town almost destroyed by Allied bombardment, the German paras showed that they could conduct a tenacious and ruthless defence

ON 15 FEBRUARY 1944, a large force of American bombers, comprising 142 B-17 Flying Fortresses, 47 B-25 Mitchells and 40 B-26 Marauders, took off for Cassino, a town strategically placed on the road to Rome in the Gustav Line, a major German defensive front across Italy. Their objective was the magnificent Benedictine abbey of Monte Cassino, one of the finest ecclesiastical monuments in Europe. By nightfall all the monastery except the thickest outer walls had been blasted to rubble.

The destruction of Monte Cassino had been ordered in the belief that it was occupied by German forces. In fact, Generalfeldmarschall (Field Marshal) Kesselring, C-in-C South, had prohibited his troops from entering the building and not one German was within its walls. However, the shattered ruin was soon to become the indomitable fortress of the battle-hardened paratroops of Germany's 1st Para-

chute Division.

On the slopes below the monastery were the positions of men from Kampfgruppe (battle group) Schulz, recently rushed to Cassino from Anzio. The battle group consisted of the 1st Parachute Regiment, the 1st Parachute Machine Gun Battalion, and the 3rd Battalion of the 3rd Parachute Regiment. Of these, the machine-gun battalion held the slopes of Monte Cassino, and the 3rd Battalion was defending Calvary Hill (Point 593). Their commander was Oberstleutnant (Lieutenant-Colonel) Karl-Lothar Schulz, a tough, experienced paratrooper who had won the Knight's Cross for his bravery at Rotterdam in 1940. For 10 days his men had resisted assaults by the US II Corps, finally forcing them to admit defeat.

In the lull following the bombing of the abbey, Kampfgruppe Schulz received substantial reinforcement from the 1st Parachute Division, commanded by Generalleutnant (Lieutenant-General) Richard Heidrich. Heidrich carefully positioned his three regiments: the 3rd covered the monastery and

Previous page: Elite German paratroopers and (below) the doomed monastery of Monte Cassino. Above: View of the road to Rome. Below: A lethal MG42 nest.

Defending Cassino
German 1st Parachute Division, Feb-March 1944

The US Fifth Army reached the Gustav Line along the Garigliano and Rapido rivers early in 1943. The offensive against the section of the line at Cassino, which dominated the route to Rome, began late in January with an assault by the US VI Corps. The troops advanced to within 400 yards of the monastery but were repulsed. The 2nd New Zealand Division and 4th Indian Division attacked in mid-February without success. On 15 March they attacked again, and the Third Battle of Cassino began.

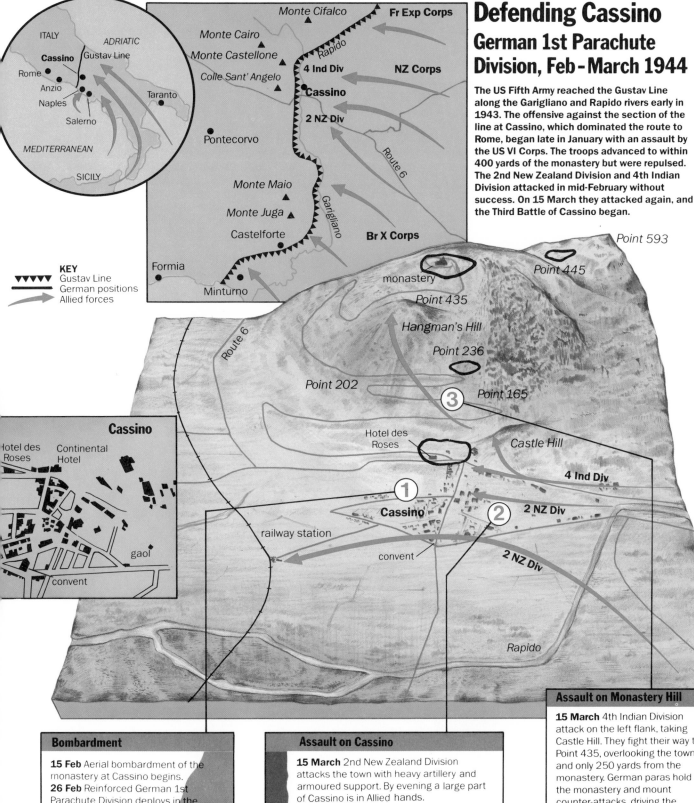

Inset map labels:
ITALY · ADRIATIC · Cassino · Gustav Line · Rome · Anzio · Naples · Salerno · Taranto · Pontecorvo · MEDITERRANEAN · SICILY

Monte Cifalco · Fr Exp Corps · Monte Cairo · Monte Castellone · Rapido · 4 Ind Div · NZ Corps · Colle Sant' Angelo · Cassino · 2 NZ Div · Route 6 · Monte Maio · Monte Juga · Garigliano · Br X Corps · Castelforte · Formia · Minturno

KEY
- ▼▼▼▼▼ Gustav Line
- ——— German positions
- ➤ Allied forces

Terrain map labels:
Point 593 · Point 445 · monastery · Point 435 · Hangman's Hill · Point 236 · Point 202 · Point 165 · ③ · Hotel des Roses · Castle Hill · 4 Ind Div · ① · ② · 2 NZ Div · Cassino · railway station · convent · 2 NZ Div · Rapido · Route 6

Cassino (inset)
Hotel des Roses · Continental Hotel · gaol · convent

Bombardment

15 Feb Aerial bombardment of the monastery at Cassino begins.
26 Feb Reinforced German 1st Parachute Division deploys in the monastery, town and surrounding hills.
15 March 0830 Aerial and artillery bombardment of Cassino commences. 1st Parachute Division strength in the town is halved, but the survivors remain at their posts.

Assault on Cassino

15 March 2nd New Zealand Division attacks the town with heavy artillery and armoured support. By evening a large part of Cassino is in Allied hands.
16 March German paras establish a defensible perimeter around the Hotel des Roses and the Continental Hotel. Heavy fighting continues from house to house.

Assault on Monastery Hill

15 March 4th Indian Division attack on the left flank, taking Castle Hill. They fight their way to Point 435, overlooking the town and only 250 yards from the monastery. German paras hold the monastery and mount counter-attacks, driving the Indians back. Castle Hill lost by the Allies.
19 March Allies recapture Castle Hill.
22 March Allies call the offensive off.

the town, the 4th the massif, and the 1st the area around Monte Castellone and the lower slopes of Monte Cairo. The men held a 13km divisional front which included several valuable natural obstacles. Beneath the monastery itself were innumerable passages and cellars which provided cover from enemy aerial observation and artillery fire. Although the building's rubble was unstable, it provided opportunities for very effective defensive fighting. The main entrance could not be used, as artillery bombardments from three sides were being maintained in spite of the lull. The chalk slopes of Monte Cassino and Monte Castellone were exposed to artillery fire and thus many of the defensive preparations undertaken by the paratroopers had to be carried out under cover of darkness.

The work that was now necessary would have seemed formidable for two divisions, let alone one that was under strength. The 1st Parachute Division had been formed in the spring of 1943 from the remnants of the old 7th Air Division. When the Allies invaded Sicily in July 1943 it had a strength of 15,000 men, but seven months of attritional warfare had reduced it to barely half that strength by February 1944. Many of the parachute battalions were down to less than 300 men, and companies were reduced to between 30 and 40 men. The division had been in action without a rest since Salerno, and the survivors were very tired, with many suffering from malaria. Nevertheless, the paratroopers of the 1st Parachute Division knew themselves to be an elite force that had been given a tough job because other divisions were not up to it, and they were determined to confirm their reputation.

In the years since their heroic but costly air drop on Crete in 1941, German airborne forces had evolved into elite ground formations which Hitler used as part of his Feuerwehr (fire brigade). After 1943 the 1st Parachute Division had been equipped with more effective weapons, including the 7.5cm anti-tank gun and the light 7.5cm and 10cm field guns. The paratroopers wore a mixture of tropical and European theatre uniforms, including the camouflage jump smock. In the absence of cloth helmet covers, parachute helmets were often covered with string foliage netting. Despite the demise of their airborne role, the paratroopers of the 1st Parachute Division retained the right to carry a holstered Luger or Walther pistol as a personal weapon.

They had shared the dangers of parachute jumps and learned to rely upon each other's skill and courage

On the eve of the third battle of Cassino, the morale and the *esprit de corps* of the 1st Parachute Division were very high. Not only were the men united by their belief in Nazism, but also a particularly close bond had been established between all ranks while they had shared the dangers of parachute jumps and learned to rely upon each other's skill and courage. The young paratroopers of 1944 were very conscious of being members of an elite formation that demanded the very highest fighting abilities in its men. Many of the officers and NCOs were veterans of the campaigns in Holland, Belgium, Crete and Russia; and there was a tradition of personal leadership from the front, especially by senior officers. Fighting spirit and physical toughness alone were not what made the 1st Parachute Division an elite formation, however. Experience and training had been made the basis for courage, initiative and determination.

The division's high level of training and flexibility at all levels was due to the driving force of Heidrich, the divisional commander. Heidrich was a professional soldier who had won the Knight's Cross as commander of the 3rd Parachute Regiment on Crete, and then the Oak Leaves on 5 February 1944 for his command of the division during the fighting in southern Italy. He was to be awarded the Swords to the Knight's Cross on 25 March 1944 for his defence of Monte Cassino. Heidrich believed in imaginative and realistic training. Field training of individuals and units with live ammunition had been his speciality. He trained his soldiers to be individualists who were tough and self-reliant. Each paratrooper was expected to become a complete soldier, an infantryman, an engineer and an anti-tank gunner all in one. Heidrich tolerated no slackness or weakness, and was known as a hard man. He never tired of telling his men that 75 per cent of success in battle was achieved on manoeuvres. But Heidrich was no simple martinet; he enjoyed the respect and genuine affection of his men, and his attention to training was to reap benefits in the 1st Parachute Division's defensive battle for Monte Cassino.

Whole streets were destroyed and the ensuing rubble blown up and ploughed over time and time again

The third battle of Cassino, timed to begin on 15 March, was to take the form of a frontal attack on the town itself by the 2nd New Zealand Division, and an attack by the 4th Indian Division on Monastery Hill. Before the ground attack began, a massive air bombardment was mounted against the German positions in Cassino to obliterate the paratroopers and bury them in the town's cellars and bunkers. About 5 tonnes of explosive had been provided for every German soldier in Cassino. The Allied forces had been pulled back in secret and they now waited for the rare spectacle of an entire Italian town being blown to pieces by concentrated carpet-bombing. From 0830 hours on the 15th, wave after wave of Allied bombers dropped their loads over the paratroopers of the 3rd Parachute Regiment in Cassino. Over the next four hours whole streets were destroyed, and the ensuing rubble blown up and ploughed over time and time again. Some 500 American bombers dropped 1000 tonnes of bombs on Cassino and, as soon as the bombing ended, an eight-hour artillery barrage from 746 guns unleashed nearly 200,000 shells into the town.

Leutnant (Lieutenant) Schuster, the commander of No. 7 Company, 2nd Battalion, 3rd Parachute Regiment, was in the town during the bombardment:

'Tensely, we waited in our holes for the bombs to drop. Then they came. The whining scream of their approach, the roar of their explosions and the noise of the aircraft themselves mingled with echoes flung back from the hills to produce an indescribable and infernal bedlam of noise. The whole earth quaked and shuddered under the impact. Then – a sudden silence. Hardly had the dust settled a little than I dashed out to visit the other two strongpoints. I stumbled blindly about in a welter of craters. From somewhere a voice shouted: "All's well!" and the next great wave of air hulks loomed into view above me. I could not go back. I remained where I was, and the flood-gates of hell opened once again. We could no longer see each other, all we could do was to touch and feel the next man. The blackness of night en-

Top left: Behind an emplacement improvised from a table and heavy rubble, a paratrooper of the 1st Parachute Division waits for the next Allied assault on Cassino. Resting on the box of 'potato masher' grenades is his 7.92mm paratroop rifle 42 (FG42), a weapon that was issued exclusively to airborne troops; its bipod stand lies folded alongside the barrel. To his right is an MP40 sub-machine gun. Centre left: A paratrooper with grenades watches the ruins of Cassino for enemy movement. Bottom left: Hidden from the air by a network of broken wood, a paratrooper waits behind his MG42.

veloped us, and on our tongues was the taste of burnt earth. Rubble and dust came pouring down into our hole. Breathing became a desperate and urgent business. At all costs we had to avoid being suffocated, buried alive. Crouching in silence, we waited for the pitiless hail to end.'

Leutnant Jamrowski, commanding Nos. 5 and 8 Companies, was trapped in the cellar that constituted his battle headquarters, and had to dig his way out:

'We lost all sense of time, and how long we worked I don't know; but we seemed to be making no impression, and it looked as though we would never get out; some of the men began to lose heart, and I, too, was hard put to overcome an inner feeling of hopelessness. At last we seemed to be making progress, and then the rubble and earth outside came sliding down and undid all we

German Paratrooper, Monte Cassino 1944

Although fighting in an infantry role, German paratroopers still wore their distinctive uniform; here Luftwaffe blue-grey trousers, para smock in splinter-pattern camouflage and para helmet painted blue-grey. Slung over his shoulders is a canvas small-arms bandolier, each pocket holding a clip of 7.92mm ammunition for the Mauser 98k rifle. Despite the fact that this German rifle was a less effective weapon in most situations than the FG42 or MP40 it was still issued in large quantities to all German troops. Tucked inside his standard Army belt are two stick grenades.

RICHARD HEIDRICH

Richard Heidrich was a powerful formative influence on Germany's emergent airborne arm. When Hermann Göring formed the 1st Parachute Regiment on 1 January 1939 it consisted of just two battalions. The 1st Battalion had grown out of a detachment of police parachute troops which had become part of the Luftwaffe. The 2nd Battalion, on the other hand, developed from a German Army parachute unit formed in 1936 at Stendal, a new parachute school 100km west of Berlin. Volunteers from the army were equipped with machine guns and mortars and were known as the Heavy Parachute Infantry Company. The task of expanding this unit into a battalion was given to the then Major Heidrich, who had been serving under Rommel as a tactics instructor at the Potsdam Military School. He was appointed commander of the battalion and it became 'das Bataillon Heidrich'.

During the invasion of Crete, in which he commanded the 3rd Parachute Regiment in its assault on Canea and Suda Bay, he earned the Knight's Cross.

By 1943, at the age of 47, he had become commander of the 1st Parachute Division with the rank of major-general. His division was heavily involved in the fights for Sicily and southern Italy, and he was awarded the Oak Leaves for his leadership. He is seen below in the uniform of colonel, the rank he held at Crete.

had done. "Never mind – stick it!" I shouted. "We're not going to die here, like rats in a sewer!" Once again we started to claw away, and after hours of labour we cleared a small cleft. We cleared the entrance, and after being buried alive for 12 hours, we squeezed our way out into the open. Darkness had now fallen. Cassino was unrecognisable in the tangled mess of ruins and rubble that confronted us.'

General von Senger und Etterlin, commander of XIV Panzer Corps, who visited Heidrich the next day, was reminded by the devastation at Cassino of the Somme where he had fought as a young officer during World War I. Before the bombardment, the 2nd Battalion had a strength of 300 men and five guns. After the bombardment it had been reduced to 140 men and one gun. Schuster's No. 7 Company had been reduced to a handful of paratroopers, and Nos. 5 and 8 had no more than 30 men each. Hauptmann (Captain) Foltin's No. 6 Company, however, having sheltered in a rock cavern at the foot of Monastery Hill, had survived intact.

Although Heidrich had positioned himself at the battle headquarters of his 3rd Parachute Regiment during the early morning, he had no contact with the 2nd Battalion, nor with XIV Panzer Corps for that matter, as all telephone and wireless communications had been disrupted. The defence of Monte Cassino was in the hands of those scattered groups of paratroopers who had managed to scramble out of the rubble after the bombardment. For the Allies, the effect of the massive bombardment was disappointing. Although it had killed, wounded or buried half the paratroopers defending the town, it had not broken their spirit. Few were disorientated for very long, and if anything the bombardment and the waiting had made them furious and desperate for a fight. The bombardment was also a tactical failure because it had turned the whole area into a moonscape of rubble and craters which made the task of the advancing Allied troops very difficult.

The mountains of debris caused by the bombardment not only slowed down the New Zealanders' advance, but also separated them from their supporting armour, and the attack became an unco-

Below: Exhausted German troops snatch a moment's respite from the nightmare of Cassino. Above right: Paratroopers carry a casualty to cover. Right: Mortar crews prepare to fire in a bombed-out courtyard.

THE ALLIES AT CASSINO

The fight around Cassino and in the Liri valley brought together a greater number of disparate Allied forces than any other in World War II. The final reckoning of their casualties in the drive to Rome, about 105,000 killed or wounded, included men from nearly all the countries involved in the Allied war effort.

In January 1944 the US II Corps attacked Cassino, flanked by the British X Corps and the French Expeditionary Corps, the latter comprising largely Moroccan and Algerian units, but also including some Tunisian troops. In February, General Harold Alexander, C-in-C Allied Forces in Italy, saw that an impasse had been reached and sent in the New Zealand Corps; of its three divisions only one actually came from New Zealand, and it included a Maori battalion. The remaining divisions were British and Indian, a notable element of the latter being its three battalions of Nepalese Gurkha Rifles. Despite gallant efforts this combined force was beaten back and Alexander called off frontal assaults on Cassino on 22 March.

On 11 May the reorganised 15th Army Group, which now included the US Fifth Army and the British Eighth Army, renewed the attack in force. Taking the brunt of the German fire was the recently-arrived Polish Corps, comprising two infantry divisions and an armoured brigade. Flanking the Poles were the British X Corps and XIII Corps, while on their far left was the French Expeditionary Corps, now reinforced by French motorised infantry, a Moroccan mountain division, and Moroccan goumiers.

In the event, the French outflanked the Gustav Line, forcing the Germans into a fighting retreat, and it became the turn of the Canadians. Their I Corps broke through the Germans' secondary defence, the Adolf Hitler Line, on 22 May.

AFTER CASSINO

Fallschirm-Jäger Rgt.1

By 1945 Germany's airborne arm, which in January 1939 had comprised only the 1st Parachute Regiment (whose cuff-title is shown above), stood at a strength of 10 divisions.

In early 1944 the 4th Parachute Division was formed, and it performed very well at Anzio. Thereafter, the creation of new 'parachute' divisions became a standing priority. Thus, one third of each of the 1st Parachute Division's three regiments at Cassino was sent to France to become the nucleus of II Parachute Corps, which came to comprise the 2nd, 3rd and 5th Parachute Divisions.

When the Allies invaded Normandy, the 3rd Parachute Division was rushed to St. Lô, where it delayed the Americans for a full month. The 5th Parachute Division was deployed at Caen. In August, the defence of Brest was entrusted to the 2nd Parachute Division. Despite shelling by the 15in guns of HMS *Warspite*, the paratroopers held the port until 18 September.

On 4 September 1944 General Student's First Parachute Army was formed, actually a hotchpotch of Luftwaffe personnel and lightly wounded paratroopers. It supported the SS panzer units in Holland and fought at Arnhem.

In December 1944, Hitler's Ardennes offensive saw the last German airborne operation of the war.

---

ordinated crawl forward, allowing the battered paratroopers good opportunities to fight short, sharp delaying actions. Equally important was the fact that junior officers of the 2nd Battalion took the initiative and secured strategically valuable positions overlooking the routes of the Allied advance. Thus, Leutnant Jamrowski organised the surviving members of his two companies and occupied the houses on the slopes of Castle Hill (Point 193) that dominated the whole of the northern sector of Cassino.

Although Heidrich had lost contact with the 2nd Battalion and could not co-ordinate the defence of the town directly, he was able to bring devastating artillery fire down onto the advancing New Zealanders. In particular, the fire of his 71st Mortar Regiment gave the defenders noisy and effective support, and the shrieking salvoes and plunging fire of the mortars had the same effect as carpet bombing. Heidrich directed the firepower of every artillery piece, mortar and anti-aircraft gun in the area against the New Zealanders. Throughout the ensuing battle for Monte Cassino, this very effective and sustained artillery fire support was crucial in enabling the German paratroopers to hold their positions.

Despite the heroic efforts of the paratroopers in Cassino and the supporting artillery fire, by the evening of 15 March two-thirds of the town had been captured by the New Zealanders. Lieutenant-General Freyberg, the commander of the New Zealanders, decided to continue the attack on the town and to make a direct assault on the monastery itself using the 4th Indian Division. Although the Indians captured Hangman's Hill (Point 435), they were unable to dislodge the paratroopers from the monastery itself, and they quickly became subject to counter-attacks.

A tank was built into the entrance lobby of the Continental Hotel

For the next six days, the third battle for Cassino became a slogging match between the Allies and the paratroopers. At one point Allied forces from the south and the west surrounded the monastery, but the paratroopers fought on. However, Heidrich recognised that it was impossible to defend every sector of the perimeter, and on 16 March he established a shorter defensive line in the town. Two positions, the Continental Hotel and the Hotel des Roses, commanded both the New Zealand advance down Route 6 and the Indian access points to the massif beyond Castle Hill. Both hotels were turned into strongpoints, and a tank was built into the entrance lobby of the Continental. The paratroopers dug in amongst the surrounding buildings, constructing weapon-pits and bunkers. Heidrich then slowly infiltrated reinforcements under the cover of darkness.

For the paratroopers in the town the battle went on 24 hours a day, with little time for rest. Later, Leutnant Jamrowski remembered:

'The night was our friend. By night we were able to move. But there wasn't a hope of any rest. First, we had to rebuild and improve our positions, establish communication between various strongpoints, get the wounded away and bring up ammunition, food and water. When you consider

against which he was to operate. The general impression in the battalion was that Chinese Farm was held by small forces of Egyptian infantry who were harassing the Israeli convoys as they attempted to get through. Expecting a limited engagement, the paras went to do battle without a supporting tank force, and even their mortars and other heavy weapons were left behind.

Occasional illumination flares fired by the Egyptians forced the paratroopers to drop to the ground

Thus, carrying only their personal weapons and RPG bazookas, the paratroops helicoptered out to their jumping-off point at the beginning of the Akavish road. At 2330 hours on the 16th, with Mordecai's battalion in the lead and brigade headquarters following, the paras began their advance towards the Akavish-Poton junction. Only 200yds down the road they came under heavy fire – from tense and nervous Israeli tank crews who were expecting an Egyptian attack. Only after shouts, signals and frantic arm-waving did the firing stop. The battalion reached the junction without further incident and then spread out as arranged.

At first, movement was slow. From time to time the officers swept the area with their binoculars and night-vision instruments. Suspicious objects were examined slowly and carefully. Communications were difficult, and no company wanted to open fire on another. Occasional illumination flares fired by the Egyptians forced the paratroopers to drop to the ground, slowing their progress even further. The brigade commander, Colonel Uzi Ya'iri, ordered Mordecai to step up the pace. Suddenly a company commander reported: 'I see something suspicious. A white shape on the dunes.' The men held their fire; it

On 6 October 1973, while Israel observed the Jewish fast day of Yom Kippur, Egyptian forces crossed the Suez Canal into the Sinai. In the north, Syria invaded the Golan Heights. The Arab world, seeing little hope of a peace settlement being secured from Israel by diplomatic means, had once again decided to resort to war.

Taken off guard, at first the Israelis could do little to stem the tide, and Egypt soon established a long but shallow perimeter on the east bank of the canal. Following successes against the Syrians in the north, however, Israel was able to rally greater forces in the Sinai. Anticipating a broad Egyptian offensive, the Israelis prepared for a mobile defensive battle. On 14 October the Egyptian forces, pressurised by Syria to abandon their strong defensive line and to mount an offensive in Sinai, began their advance. By evening, 300 of Egypt's 800 tanks had been lost and the remainder were in retreat. The next day, Israel decided to cross the canal in the vicinity of Deversoir, north of the Great Bitter Lake. Commanded by Major-General Sharon, the action was codenamed Operation Stout Hearted Men. Sharon's aim was to reach the canal through a gap that Israeli intelligence had identified between the Egyptian Second and Third Armies. By the early hours of 16 October, the 243rd Paratroop Brigade was crossing the canal in small rubber boats and establishing a bridgehead on the west bank. Tanks of the 421st Armoured Brigade soon followed, ferried over in small boats.

At last realising the importance of the bridgehead, the Egyptians made frantic efforts to capture it. It was subjected to a constant artillery barrage, and the section of the Egyptian perimeter that separated it from Israeli-held Sinai, an area known as 'Chinese Farm', became the scene of one of the most bitterly contested battles of the Yom Kippur War.

CHINESE FARM

Chinese Farm, the area lying athwart Israeli routes to their bridgehead at Deversoir, was in fact neither Chinese nor a farm. It was an abandoned agricultural settlement, built by the Egyptians in the early 1960s with the aid of Japanese advisers. Israeli troops who had reached the position in the war of 1967 had assumed the Japanese writing on the deserted buildings to be Chinese, and the place had become known as Chinese Farm. After crossing the Suez Canal on 6 October 1973, the Egyptians recaptured the settlement. Criss-crossed by irrigation canals and sand dunes, it was an excellent defensive position, and by the time of Operation Stout Hearted Men it was well defended, housing tanks and infantry armed with missiles and RPG bazookas. The battle of Chinese Farm was fought in a roughly triangular area, the base of which ran for 25 miles along the Suez Canal and the Great Bitter Lake south of Ismailia. The vertex of this triangle was at Tasa, with one arm extending west for 18 miles to the canal and the other arm extending southwest to the junction of the Great and Little Bitter Lakes.

There were four main axes in this triangle: east of, and parallel to, the canal was the Lexicon axis, which linked all the outposts of the Israeli defensive Bar Lev Line.

Slightly to the east of Lexicon was a second axis known as the Artillery Road.

Roughly bisecting the triangle, running southwest from Tasa to join Lexicon, was another axis named Akavish. Last, to the west of the Akavish and Artillery Road junction was Tirtur, a route built before the war to bring heavy bridging equipment to the canal.

It was on these axes that the outcome of the Chinese Farm battle and, by extension, the whole Israeli canal-crossing operation, hinged.

could be Israeli tank crewmen who had managed to escape from their burning tanks during the day. The Israelis were then fired on. It was 0100 hours on 17 October.

B Company, commanded by Yakov Levy, was on the battalion's northern flank, leading the advance. The company stormed the source of fire, and Levy was wounded. He bandaged himself, led another charge, and was hit a second time. After three unsuccessful attempts to storm the source of fire, he reported to Mordecai: 'There's no point in even talking about attacking. It's impossible with the force at my disposal.' Mordecai did not know the size of the enemy force attacking Levy. He tried to get this information from the company commander, but was told that Levy was dead. Eyal Raz, Levy's deputy, had been badly wounded. The company's third in command, Jacky Hakim, was dead as well. None of those still alive was talking about assaults, only about rescue.

Within minutes of being fired upon, two of the battalion's four companies were trapped under fire

Mordecai positioned reinforced holding forces to aid in the rescue of B Company, and then ordered Aharon Margal's C Company to attack the Egyptian position from the left. This attack was greeted by heavy machine-gun fire. Margal saw his men cut down and then took a bullet in the throat, later dying on his way to hospital.

Thus, within minutes of being fired upon, two of the battalion's four companies were trapped under fire, with many soldiers either dead or wounded and without the ability to attack the source of fire. Soldiers from B Company were unable even to reach their wounded comrades. (Later it was discovered that 10 Goryanov machine guns, two tank platoons, and two infantry companies armed with anti-tank missiles were in the small sector from which the fire was coming. Behind this position was another, and behind that another, and so on, right up to the actual buildings of Chinese Farm.)

Mordecai ordered his E Company – the battalion's reserve company then located at Tirtur – to move towards B Company, to see if it was possible to launch a further assault, and if not, to rescue the wounded. E Company rushed north, came under immediate fire and suffered many casualties. A second attempt succeeded in making contact with B Company. E Company's men began evacuating the wounded, moving them behind a small hillock 200yds away. This carried on all night, under heavy Egyptian fire and with the greatest possible speed. By morning, 60 wounded were concentrated behind the hillock,

Far left: An exhausted soldier snatches a few moments' sleep. Left: A para sights along his FN LMG. Both tank personnel (below left) and the hard-pressed para medics (below right) took heavy casualties. Bottom right: A wounded soldier is evacuated.

which became known as 'Wounded Hill'. C Company's survivors, by now on the battalion's flank, began evacuating their own wounded to the battalion aid station, while at the same time firing at the Egyptians with every weapon at their disposal.

By this stage – 0300 – Mordecai realised he was up against a large enemy concentration. Each further assault would bring more casualties. It was clear that the paratroopers could not dislodge the Egyptians from their positions. All they could do was wait to be rescued. Mordecai ordered his men to dig in, find cover and return the enemy's fire. 'Don't let them even raise their heads,' he ordered, 'We're going to hold on at all costs.'

Dawn was at the most two hours away. Major-General Adan, whose division had assumed control of the Chinese Farm battles, knew that if the Israeli bridge was not in the water by morning, another day would pass without it being possible to place it over the canal. Thus, while the 35th Brigade was fighting it out at Chinese Farm, tanks and APCs streamed along Akavish towards the Israeli crossing point. The convoy's progress was at this stage the main pre-

87

occupation of the front commanders, who were as yet unaware of the plight of the paratroopers. Only at 0400 did Adan inform his superiors that the paratroop attack had run into serious difficulties.

When the paratroop commander had contacted Adan and asked for permission to evacuate and regroup, Adan hesitated, not wishing to give his permission without the approval of Major-General Shmuel Gonen, the GOC Southern Command, and Lieutenant-General Chaim Bar Lev, the former Chief-of-Staff who had been appointed 'Front Commander' (thus in effect superseding Gonen). Gonen, when he heard of the request, replied that only the wounded could be evacuated. What was not realised by the Israeli command was that the request was not to abandon the battle but to be relieved.

Throughout the night, paras left their positions to run and pull to safety those who had been hit

Mordecai requested a reinforcement of tanks and rescue forces. His main worry at that stage was that Egyptian tanks would arrive on the scene and destroy what was left of his battalion. Israeli APCs sent to him evacuated some of the wounded and promised to return. They didn't. Mordecai ordered the wounded to be evacuated on stretchers. Each rescue attempt drew a hail of heavy fire from the Egyptian positions. Throughout the night, paratroopers left their positions to run and pull to safety those who had been hit. If the rescuers themselves were hit – and many were – others would rush up and take their place. And so it went on, throughout the battle.

As the moon rose, so did the Egyptian fire intensify. Tank fire was coming from the Egyptian flanks, while machine-gun fire from the centre of their positions swept the area. Egyptian artillery located the Israeli positions and began spitting shells. Egyptian infantry were even firing Sagger missiles at the Israelis who were dug in opposite them. In response, Mordecai set up a defensive line opposite the Egyptians, between 70 and 100yds from their positions. He ordered his men to conserve their ammunition and

only shoot at clearly defined targets.

A tank battalion of the Israeli 460th Armoured Brigade, commanded by Lieutenant-Colonel Ehud, himself a former paratroop officer, was sent to rescue the trapped battalion. The tank crews, many of them experiencing their first day of war, entered unfamiliar territory without knowing the precise locations of either the Egyptians or Mordecai's men. The early morning mist did not make their task any easier and Ehud reported that he could not succeed. Later on, another attempt was made to link up with the trapped paratroopers. Mordecai told Ehud he would let off a coloured smoke grenade, but he said afterwards: 'I knew that the moment I opened the grenade I would draw enemy fire and this, of course, is what hap-

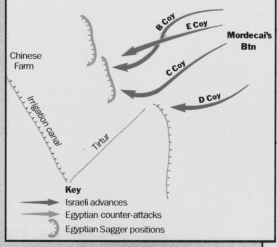

Chinese Farm

On the night of 15 October 1973, Israeli forces on the east bank of the Suez Canal counter-attacked, advancing across to the west bank and beginning an attempt to isolate the Egyptian bridgeheads in Sinai. The narrow Israeli corridor was threatened by an Egyptian attack concentrated at Chinese Farm. On 18 October, the farm fell to the Israelis.

Chinese Farm

B Coy
E Coy
Mordecai's Btn
C Coy
D Coy

Irrigation canal
Tirtur

Key
→ Israeli advances
→ Egyptian counter-attacks
⟩ Egyptian Sagger positions

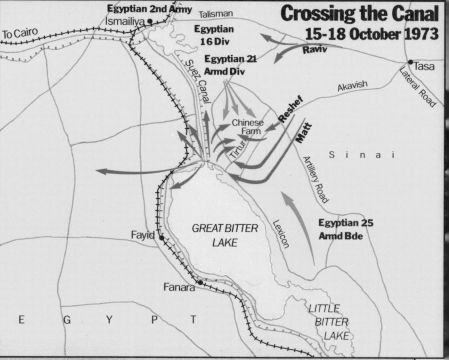

Crossing the Canal
15-18 October 1973

Egyptian 2nd Army
Ismailiya
To Cairo
Talisman
Egyptian 16 Div
Egyptian 21 Armd Div
Raviv
Tasa
Suez Canal
Akavish
Lateral Road
Chinese Farm
Reshef
Matt
Tirtur
Sinai
Artillery Road
Fayid
GREAT BITTER LAKE
Lexicon
Egyptian 25 Armd Bde
E G Y P T
Fanara
LITTLE BITTER LAKE

pened. The Egyptians attacked my position with everything they had.' Nevertheless, the idea worked, for Ehud managed to reach the trapped battalion. Mordecai ordered his men to prepare for a joint assault with the tanks. Ehud's tanks moved towards the Egyptians, but within two minutes three of them were on fire, the result of direct hits by Egyptian missiles. The paratroopers were now called on to rescue the rescue force.

A survivor of this desperate plight, Sasson Gur Ariyeh, later recalled:

'At 0730, Zeldas arrived to rescue us, together with seven Pattons. The Egyptians fired missiles at them and within half an hour all the tanks were burning. One tank caught alight close to my position. Three crewmen got out, one of them on fire. We rushed to roll him in the sand to smother the flames.'

'His crewmates yelled for us to get away since the tank was about to explode. There were many wounded lying nearby and we ran like hell to get

Top left: Troops look on as an Israeli M48 tank rumbles across one of the pontoon bridges spanning the Suez Canal. The establishment of these vital crossing points was made possible by the bravery and persistence of the 35th Paratroop Brigade in the face of heavy casualties during the prolonged and bitter fighting at the Chinese Farm. Once the Egyptian line east of the canal had been breached, the way was clear for the rapid and uninterrupted advance of Israeli armour and troops (centre) and the final push southwards towards Suez (bottom).

them clear. We didn't make it. Seven paras were killed when the tank blew up. I was seriously wounded in the stomach. My friend Shlomo had his leg blown off. I told the two medics to leave me and attend to him. One medic crawled to him but caught a bullet in the head. The other medic was hit a few seconds later.

'A wounded officer told us to hold on, he was going for help. I learned later he crawled for five hours until he reached our boys.'

Gur Ariyeh would lie until afternoon before he was rescued, watching as those around him slowly died. Shlomo regained consciousness long enough to say, 'See that leg lying over there? It's mine,' before he too died. Ehud's battalion was forced to withdraw.

'We ran out of ammunition and our chances of getting out alive became slimmer with each passing minute'

Despite their losses, the paratroop battalion fought for 14 hours before it was finally evacuated. Egyptian attempts to bring about the collapse of the paratroop position, through heavy machine-gun, artillery and tank fire, all failed. Yitzhak Mordecai later commented:

'I don't know where my men got their stamina from. We ran out of ammunition and our chances of getting out alive became slimmer with each passing minute. Yet during the entire battle, I never once heard anyone say, "Let's get the hell out of here."'

The paratroopers, in fact, refused to break off the engagement without an official order to do so. The order came early that afternoon, but the men were still in exposed positions and could not move until APCs came to rescue them, squad by squad: they were replaced by tanks. Mordecai was among the last to leave. That evening, he received the first accurate account of his losses – 40 dead and approximately 100 wounded.

The paratroopers were still recovering from their ordeal when they received word to prepare themselves for another attack on Chinese Farm. Mordecai was told that the attack would take place that very evening. Unlike Arnhem – if the legend is to be believed – no paratrooper said anything about being happy to go in again. They made few, if any, protests when Mordecai was later told that fresh forces were attacking Chinese Farm, and he and his men were no longer needed.

The 35th Paratroop Brigade's assault on Chinese Farm did not succeed in its objectives of clearing the enemy from the area – that would be done only after more bitter fighting, mainly by tank brigades. Nonetheless, apart from adding to their own already enviable legend, the Israeli paratroopers who fought the action did succeed in engaging the Egyptians long enough for much-needed men and supplies to travel along the temporarily opened routes to the Suez Canal. When the Egyptians at Chinese Farm broke, the Israeli bridgehead was no longer a small-scale, daring raid, but an established fact, and by the time of the final ceasefire the focus of the war in the south had shifted to Egypt, where the initiative was now resting firmly in the hands of the Israel Defence Forces.

THE AUTHOR Jeffrey Abrams is a freelance editor and writer based in Israel. He is a former associate editor of *The IDF Journal*, the quarterly English language review of the Israel Defence Forces.

THE PARAS GO IN

Suez crisis, November 1956: the men of 3 Para jumped into the teeth of fierce Egyptian resistance on the narrow airfield at Gamil

'PREPARE FOR ACTION! Stand up, fit equipment! Check equipment! Tell off for equipment check!' The orders came in sequence as the men went through their final pre-jump drills, checking their helmets, their 120lb equipment containers, each man checking the parachute of the one in front. Then came the warning, 'Red on! Stand in the door!'

THE BRITISH PARAS AT SUEZ

After World War II, the parachute formations of the British Army were gradually whittled down until all had been disbanded except the 16th Independent Parachute Brigade Group. This group, formed in 1948 with a nucleus from the old 2nd Parachute Brigade, had been named the 16th in honour of the wartime 1st and 6th Divisions which had fought at Arnhem and Normandy.

The British government's intention to deploy an airborne force at Suez caught the military establishment off guard. When the crisis began, the 1st and 3rd Battalions of The Parachute Regiment were serving in Cyprus in counter-terrorist operations against Colonel Grivas and his EOKA organisation. In this role their parachute training had lapsed, and as soon as the 2nd Battalion arrived in Cyprus with the brigade's supporting arms, both battalions were returned to England for urgent practice. Still unaware that an air assault was in the offing, the paras returned to Cyprus and resumed operations which continued right up to the end of October.

The battalion selected for the initial assault, 3 Para, had been welded into a tight, purposeful unit by the hard campaigns in Cyprus. It contained a number of veterans of The Parachute Regiment's historic battles, including the Rhine crossings and Arnhem, and these men had created a strong esprit de corps among the battalion's national servicemen. Brought up to standard by their rushed refresher course in England, 3 Para gained the distinction of making the last combat jump conducted by the regiment to date.

Above: Para wings awarded to qualified men in the early 1950s.

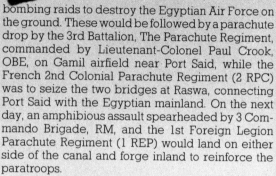

The sticks of men squeezed together, lining up behind Number One, who stood at the port trooping door of the Valetta transport. The joint British and French fighting force raised for Operation Musketeer was about to go into combat.

The British paras had taken off at 0415 hours from Nicosia airfield in Cyprus on 5 November 1956. Their operation was designed to gain control of the Suez Canal, owned by the Anglo-French Suez Canal Company, but recently nationalised by Egypt's head of state, President Gamal Abdel Nasser.

Operation Musketeer involved about 80,000 men, spearheaded by the British 16th Independent Parachute Brigade, commanded by Brigadier M.A.H. Butler, DSO, MC, and 3 Commando Brigade, Royal Marines; leading the French forces were their 10th Parachute Division and 7th Mechanised Division, both of which were fresh from service in Algeria. The operational plan entailed a series of preliminary bombing raids to destroy the Egyptian Air Force on the ground. These would be followed by a parachute drop by the 3rd Battalion, The Parachute Regiment, commanded by Lieutenant-Colonel Paul Crook, OBE, on Gamil airfield near Port Said, while the French 2nd Colonial Parachute Regiment (2 RPC) was to seize the two bridges at Raswa, connecting Port Said with the Egyptian mainland. On the next day, an amphibious assault spearheaded by 3 Commando Brigade, RM, and the 1st Foreign Legion Parachute Regiment (1 REP) would land on either side of the canal and forge inland to reinforce the paratroops.

Perhaps Lieutenant-Colonel Crook's greatest problem was the drop zone (DZ) on which the 3rd Battalion (3 Para) would land. Gamil airfield lay on a narrow spit of land between the Mediterranean Sea

Suez
3rd Battalion, The Parachute Regiment 5-6 Nov 1956

Spearheading the Anglo-French effort to reopen the Suez Canal after its closure by President Nasser of Egypt, 3 Para carried out a successful assault on Gamil airfield, to the west of Port Said, early on 5 November 1956. As the amphibious assault on Port Said was launched the following day, 3 Para provided vital covering fire from its positions to the west and was heavily engaged throughout the day's fighting.

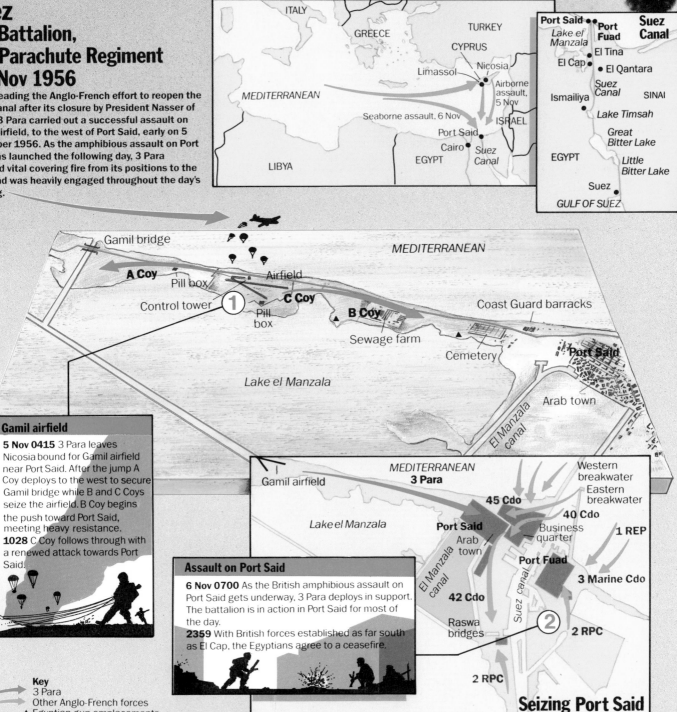

Gamil airfield

5 Nov 0415 3 Para leaves Nicosia bound for Gamil airfield near Port Said. After the jump A Coy deploys to the west to secure Gamil bridge while B and C Coys seize the airfield. B Coy begins the push toward Port Said, meeting heavy resistance.
1028 C Coy follows through with a renewed attack towards Port Said.

Assault on Port Said

6 Nov 0700 As the British amphibious assault on Port Said gets underway, 3 Para deploys in support. The battalion is in action in Port Said for most of the day.
2359 With British forces established as far south as El Cap, the Egyptians agree to a ceasefire.

Key
3 Para
Other Anglo-French forces
▲ Egyptian gun emplacements

Seizing Port Said

---

and Lake el Manzala. It was less than a mile long, and the paras would have to drop in tight sticks of about 20 men from each aircraft run over it. Cross-winds would mean men dropping into the sea or the lake, while an overshoot would land men on an Egyptian-held sewage farm at the airfield's eastern end. In addition, the beaches on the spit were strewn with mines, and well-sited machine guns covered the whole area. Crook decided to drop A Company at the western end to seal it off. C Company was to seize the southern perimeter, and B Company was to gain control in the east in preparation for an advance into Port Said itself. In support of the companies, Crook had elements of the 33rd Parachute Light Regiment, Royal Artillery, and the 9th Parachute Squadron, Royal Engineers, with a field surgical team and an

Page 91 : A member of 3 Para, armed with a Sten sub-machine gun, on the battle-torn Gamil airstrip. Inset: Lieutenant-Colonel Paul Crook, accompanied by Rupert, the Regimental mascot, waits with paratroopers to be airlifted to Cyprus. Above: An outmoded Hastings transport drops equipment over Gamil. Left: British paratroopers en route from Cyprus to Egypt.

RAF forward air control team. Defending the airstrip was a battalion of Egyptian troops and an unknown number of National Guardsmen with four SU-100 self-propelled guns.

In the British Valetta transports, nervously fingering the quick-release boxes of their X-type parachutes, the men of 3 Para waited for the signal to jump. There ahead of them was the airfield. A Canberra had just dropped a smoke flare to mark the jump point of the paratroops, and a gentle breeze was blowing it out to sea. The paras moved rapidly down the aircraft and, to prevent themselves being thrown against the side of the fuselage by the slipstream, each threw himself in a strong dive, chest leading, from the door. For the paras the world briefly became a kaleidoscope of blue sky, sand and

OUTMODED EQUIPMENT

The Suez crisis in 1956 clearly demonstrated how unprepared the British were for a full-scale airborne assault. Unlike the French parachute regiment which landed on Port Fuad from modern Noratlas aircraft, the British were obliged to use obsolescent Hastings and Valettas, both old designs with tail wheels and side cargo doors. The French could drop 17 men in 10 seconds from their tail ramps, while the British were limited to 15 men over 20 seconds.

Expecting eventual delivery of Beverley and Argosy planes, the British had already adapted their ancillary gear in readiness for the new transports. Their Austin Champ vehicles, designed to be carried by the Beverley, were too big for the Hastings, and World War II jeeps and trailers had to be sought out all over Cyprus. The dropping-beams to which the underslung jeep crash-pans were attached also had to be found, and one was actually collected from an airborne forces museum.

For use against the Egyptian T-34 tanks and SU-100 self-propelled guns the paras had only six 106mm recoilless rifles. Much of their armament predated even such World War II innovations as the Sterling sub-machine gun, and included .303in No. 4 Lee-Enfield rifles, Sten guns, Bren light machine guns and even .303in Vickers medium machine guns.

The weapons, ammunition and other supplies were all dropped in containers, meaning that, unlike the French paras who had guns with folding stocks for use as they came down, the British were defenceless until they reached the ground.

trailing khaki parachutes, until at last all the canopies had billowed open. Below them they could hear the hammer of anti-aircraft fire. The light battery beside the Gamil bridge, A Company's first objective, was hacking at the aircraft as they roared over, and soon the machine guns of the pillboxes at each end were spitting hot metal at the aircraft and the vulnerable men dangling under their canopies.

Captain Sandy Cavenagh, 3 Para's medical officer, took a splinter in the left eye when a shell came through the equipment container hanging below him, severing its suspension cord. Major Geoff Norton, commander of the paras' Support Company, found himself all but entangled in severed rigging

lines as machine-gun fire slashed through his canopy. One sapper's 'chute was shredded by an anti-aircraft round and he broke both legs on landing. Private Neal from the Medical Section landed in the sewage farm. Private Lamph landed in the sea and managed to gain the rare distinction of making a parachute assault and yet also being the first amphibious soldier ashore, all in about 10 minutes and in both cases under heavy fire. Another soldier landed in one of the minefields.

The fire was murderous, and for the first 30 seconds or so, until they could retrieve their containers, the paras had no weapons with which to fight

ed the Egyptian back into his hole just in time for the British soldier to land on top of him.

While B Company cleared the buildings and the water tower at the eastern end, smashing the pillbox on the southeastern perimeter which had caused so many casualties at the start of the drop, A Company went for the control tower and the airport buildings. They were captured quickly and with few casualties, much to the relief of one soldier, Private Pugsley: the drop had been almost too accurate in his case and he landed in one of the palm trees just outside the tower itself, giving him a grandstand view of his comrades firing past him with their rifles and machine guns at the defenders inside. These buildings cleared, A Company went on to tackle the second pillbox, the one at the western end of the airfield. The OC, Major Mike Walsh, gave this difficult job to 1 Platoon; there was a strong possibility that they would take heavy casualties in the process as between them and their objective was a 400yd stretch of open sand.

Lieutenant Peter Coates led two sections forward in a series of tactical bounds, using whatever folds in the ground offered cover, while the third section gave supporting fire and then, about 100yds from the pillbox, Coates called in the heavy artillery. Private Clements crawled forward with his 3.5in rocket launcher and put a round through the

back. Once they did, however, the battle began in earnest. B Company had suffered worst from the warm reception, for within seconds they had lost nearly 10 per cent of their strength to machine-gun fire and mortars. The officer commanding (OC) the company, Major Dick Stevens, rallied the men and they launched an immediate assault on the Egyptian positions. Private Looker had reached them first: jumping near the end of his stick he had drifted dangerously close to the Egyptians, and one particularly keen defender had climbed out of his slit trench to get a better shot at the helpless paratrooper as he swung below his canopy. Looker was saved as his container, oscillating like a 120lb pendulum, knock-

gun port. The platoon surged forward and overran the pillbox: two defenders were killed, nine were captured, and there were no British casualties.

The south side of the airfield was cleared by C Company, while Headquarters and D Companies (the latter an assortment of cooks, clerks and storemen who had been formed into a fighting reserve

British Para, Suez 1956

Typical kit for the fighting paratrooper at Suez: denim trousers, camouflaged Denison smock and face veil, '44 pattern web equipment, and the familiar red beret. Armament comprises the old British .303in No.4 Lee-Enfield rifle with bayonet.

Top left: Lieutenant-Colonel Crook (centre) and members of 3 Para move into the airport buildings after the drop. The para to his left replaces his steel helmet with the legendary red beret. Above left: A Soviet-built SU-100 self-propelled gun stands abandoned. Left: Paras release one of the jeeps dropped in the first wave over Gamil. Background picture: Sweeping resistance from their path, men of A Company move in on the central complex of the airport.

force, in accordance with the regiment's insistence that every man in the battalion should be a trained paratrooper) collected the heavy drop equipment and set up both Lieutenant-Colonel Crook's headquarters and a rudimentary HQ for Brigadier Butler, who had also jumped with the battalion. Then a problem presented itself: the DZ was so soft that the crash-pans to which the jeeps were fitted had not worked properly. On impact these were supposed to crumple, cutting the canopies free automatically and releasing the vehicles so that they could be driven off immediately. Sweating and swearing under a growing volume of mortar fire, now interspersed with salvoes from Russian-built Stalin Organs – multi-barrelled rocket launchers – which the Egyptians had deployed, they struggled to free the vehicles, while others rushed to the containers nearby which held their 106mm recoilless rifles, machine guns and mortars, and the precious ammunition.

With the sun glinting on their bayonets and winged cap badges, the men were ready to move

The loads carried by the men made fast movement impossible. The men actually had too much to carry, a common problem in the British Army, but always an unavoidable part of airborne operations when each man has to carry all his kit on his back. Once they reached their initial rendezvous (RVs), however, they could ditch their bergens and join the battle in earnest.

With the initial objectives secured, it was now the task of B Company to exploit forward. Their decimation in the earliest stage of the battle had been sudden and brutal and, while Crook was happy with Dick Stevens' progress, he nevertheless went up to

offer the men some moral support, accompanied by Brigadier Butler. The two men arrived, looking like directing staff on an exercise in their maroon berets, and the effect they had on the men was very positive. Steel helmets were still being worn because there had been no time to take them off, but soon the paras' berets appeared and, with the sun glinting on their bayonets and winged cap badges, the men were ready to move. The mortar fire had not slackened, however, and Dick Stevens was wounded minutes after Crook's arrival.

The battalion's mortars were in operation and a short vicious 'stonk' preceded the assault

His second-in-command, Karl Beale, assumed command of B Company and sent Sergeant Norman down the road to the north of the sewage farm, with a section from that NCO's platoon, to blast out another pillbox which had been giving trouble. The battalion's mortars were in operation now, and a short, vicious 'stonk' preceded Norman's assault, leaving the way clear for another platoon, led by Lieutenant Chris Hogg, to probe forward under the watchful eyes of the anti-tank platoon, who were ready with their recoilless guns. As Hogg led his men through the sewage farm to the empty buildings at the far end, the 106mm guns destroyed a self-propelled gun, a success which cheered the paras. Meanwhile, Francois Collet and his staff were calling down air strikes from the carriers offshore, and one of these was nearly Hogg's undoing. Ordered only to make contact with the enemy and then report back, he and his men came under fire from the cemetery beyond the sewage farm and withdrew to the concrete troughs of the sewage farm. Two French Mystères saw them below and made a strafing run which had the platoon diving into the troughs for cover. A thick crust on the sewage supported their weight – just – and they made it into the dense reeds in front of B Company's position. A terse message from Collet to his airborne compatriots informed them that, yes, 3 Para had got beyond the sewage farm already, and targets were to be engaged when ordered, not before!

C Company now took over from B Company: at 1028 hours a massive air strike, supported by the battalion's mortars, medium machine guns and recoilless rifles, pulverised the enemy position that Hogg had found in the cemetery and, at 1030 precisely, the company rose as one man from its shell scrapes and advanced steadily across the 300yds of low sand dunes to the cemetery wall. The Egyptian positions were in a shambles, but many of the defenders were still entrenched and the fighting was savage, with few prisoners taken on either side.

Below: Following the initial assault, helicopters were used in a full-scale troop drop.

It seemed to take an age for the cemetery to be cleared. Fighting at close quarters with their grenades and Sten guns, the younger soldiers had to summon immense nerve and provide mutual support to get through. C company's commander, Major Ron Norman, MBE, MC, had fought on Crete against the invading German paratroopers in World War II, and he couldn't help feeling a grudging respect for those Egyptians who stood and fought so hard against the intimidating parachute assault.

Finally the defenders retreated, many of them joining the women and children who were fleeing from Port Said on the *feluccas* which plied the El Manzala Canal between Port Said and Gamil. As C Company consolidated, many of the men threw away their Stens, which had proved unreliable in many cases, and replaced them with Egyptian Berettas, Schmeissers, Russian-made SKS Simonov rifles and PPSh sub-machine guns which had been left behind. Back at the airfield's control tower, despite the attention of an SU-100 self-propelled gun in Port Said which had found the range, the Headquarters staff were organising the next stage of the assault. Naval helicopters had already flown casualties out of the airfield and 9 Parachute Squadron had cleared the runways of the empty oil drums used by the Egyptians to block them. Colonel de Fouquieres, the French commander's liaison officer, now arrived in a Dakota, ignoring the mortar and machine-gun fire which periodically raked the airfield, and after a short conference with Brigadier Butler, took off again for Akrotiri bearing eight more casualties and 3 Para's medical officer, Sandy Cavenagh, who had been ordered to leave.

As C Company fought eastwards it came under fire from a block of flats on the outskirts of Port Said. However, continual air strikes had eroded Egyptian morale, and the four SU-100 self-propelled guns in the defended apartment block had been abandoned. Machine-gun fire from the flats was holding up the company's advance when Lieutenant Mike Newall, OC Machine Gun Platoon, spotted both the guns in the ground-floor flats and an abandoned Bren-gun carrier lying in no-man's land. Leaving his platoon, for whom he had been scouting out better fire positions, he ran to the carrier through a storm of fire and, assisted by a C Company sergeant, got the thing working. The two men drove straight at the machine-gun post, overran it and returned in triumph to what they thought was the front line. The company had been under sniper fire for some time and knew that there was no British armour for miles; on hearing the carrier coming down the road, B Company's anti-tank detachment prepared for action, the first ranging shot from their spotting rifle hitting fair and square. Only a quick-witted NCO prevented the loss of the two men.

As D-day came to an end, C Company pulled back to the airfield, leaving B Company to hold any Egyptian attacks at the sewage farm. Next day the paras expected to see a major naval bombardment to mark the beginning of the second stage of the operation, the amphibious assault on Port Said. All the 3rd Battalion's objectives had been secured, and their comrades in the French 2nd Colonial Parachute Regiment had completed their tasks at Port Fuad with typical panache. Their commander, Colonel Conan, had made telephone contact with the Egyptian commander and he was confident that a surrender could be negotiated without further military action: Conan, therefore, ordered all air strikes to cease at 1700 hours. Brigadier Butler took a helicopter to join Conan in the French positions, and from 1800 to about 2030 hours an uneasy peace reigned.

As night fell, the 2nd Battalion came ashore with a squadron of Centurion tanks

A quick peace settlement was too much to hope for, however, and after a fairly quiet night 3 Para was deployed on 6 November in support of the amphibious invasion of the port. Following a series of air strikes and a naval bombardment of the beach-head, 40 and 42 Commandos, Royal Marines, hit the beaches just before 0700 hours, with 3 Para's medium machine guns helping to give them a clear run from their craft. A little later, 45 Commando, RM, was landed by helicopter in the town, and the 1st Foreign Legion Parachute Regiment was coming ashore alongside Port Said's eastern breakwater. Elements of 3 Para were in action throughout the day, and, as night fell, the 2nd Battalion (2 Para) came ashore with a squadron of Centurion tanks. Joined by the brigadier, 2 Para forged out to El Cap, 19 miles down the Suez Canal, and at 2359 hours the Egyptians agreed to a ceasefire.

The 3rd Battalion, The Parachute Regiment, came out of Suez quite well. In military terms, the operation was an outstanding success, and for 3 Para to have done so well with so little support or specialised equipment against an enemy strong in numbers and armour, especially in the confusion of an airborne assault, was no mean feat. Operation Musketeer taught a great many lessons: one of the most important was that a parachute battalion is more than the sum of its parts – and, if given the right support, it is nearly invincible.

THE AUTHOR Gregor Ferguson is the editor of *Defence Africa and the Middle East* and has contributed to several other publications. His most recent work is a short history of The Parachute Regiment in which he served in the 10th (Volunteer) Battalion.

Above: British paras consolidate the Canal road leading into Port Said. Top: Members of the assault force wait to be airlifted out of Egypt following the ceasefire agreement.

RADFAN FIREFIGHT

In the harsh terrain and blazing heat of Aden the men of 3 Para fought a merciless campaign against Radfani rebel tribesmen

IN LATE APRIL 1964, British Army trucks were rumbling up the Dhala road towards the village of Thumier, situated in the foothills of the Radfan mountains north of Aden. By the end of the month the strike force was assembled. The men of 45 Commando, Royal Marines, already based in Aden under the command of Lieutenant-Colonel Paddy Stevens, had established a camp just east of the road, and on the eve of the operation they were joined by the paras of B Company, 3rd Battalion, The Parachute Regiment (3 Para). Four rifle platoons with a section of 3in mortars, all under Major Peter Walter, were also brought up in support.

The operational plan formulated by Brigadier Louis Hargroves, overall commander of the force, had called for a parachute drop on the night of 30 April. The paras were to drop onto a key feature codenamed Cap Badge, occupying it until 45 Commando completed a sweep towards it from Wadi Boran. Unfortunately, the troop from 22 SAS which was detailed to mark the drop zone in the boulder-strewn landscape became embroiled in a fight for survival and was forced to withdraw. Also, the intensity of fire attracted by low-flying British aircraft in the area showed that the paras would be embattled immediately upon landing. The drop was therefore cancelled; instead, it was decided to undertake the operation entirely by night march.

On the night of 30 April, the marines and paras set out into the darkness. All were heavily laden, principally with ammunition and water. It was one of those marches which demand much of the infantryman.

For the officers navigating, there was the problem of maintaining direction across steep and

The campaign in the Radfan mountains was marked by a lot of foot-slogging under a blazing sun, and it proved a severe test of the paras' physical endurance. Support weapons such as the GPMG (below) and the rocket launcher (left) had to be carried long distances into battle, and GPMG ammunition was shared out amongst those armed with lighter weapons (below left). The principal threat to the paras was the Radfanis' highly accurate sniper fire (far left) and, as all these photographs show, the paras soon developed a healthy respect for the tribesmen's marksmanship. Bottom left: In the baking heat of the Radfan, the water-bottle constituted a vital piece of equipment.

THE RADFAN CAMPAIGN

The British Army, brought in by the Aden Federal government in April 1964 to curb tribal insurrection in the Radfan, was to see action in the region until the end of August.

The military campaign proceeded in three distinct stages, each marked by a new commander. The first British force, known as Radforce, was led by Brigadier Hargroves and comprised 45 Commando Royal Marines, B Company of 3 Para, two regiments of the Federal Regular Army, the 1st Battalion, of the East Anglian Brigade, an SAS troop and support units. Operations began on 29 April, Radforce gaining control of the northern sector of the Radfan by 5 May, but it was clear that a larger force was needed to tackle the tribes in the massif to the south.

On 18 May Brigadier Blacker, who succeeded Hargroves, led a much larger force, including seven infantry battalions, armoured cars, Centurion tanks, artillery and air support, against the Bakri ridge and into the Wadi Misrah, the stronghold of the predominant Quteibi tribe. Fighting in searing heat over hard terrain, Blacker's force finally defeated the Quteibis while taking the Jebel Huriyah on 10 June. On 14 June Brigadier Blair took over from Blacker and proceeded to consolidate the British victory. His troops were much in demand elsewhere in Aden, however, and by 24 August most of the force had been withdrawn. The Radfani tribesmen were never completely brought to account, therefore, and they continued to plague the British until their final withdrawal from Aden in 1967.

broken country. For every hundred yards of advance they were forced to climb or descend three hundred. Bearings were lost in the darkness and had to be rediscovered. If one of the heavily laden men fell, there was a constant fear that he had broken a limb, raising the question of whether he should be carried, which would entail abandoning important loads, or be left behind, perhaps to be found by a band of merciless tribesmen. They knew that they were marching against the clock, and that daylight would expose them to fire from all around.

As the sun rose, Major Walter saw that they were still far from their objective. Skirting crests and resting in shadows, he avoided an encounter on the line of march and at last he saw the village and the stone watch-towers which were his target. He had hoped to surprise the towers' garrisons by night, but now he had to close on them in daylight. Still half-a-mile distant, Radfani riflemen began firing, and as bullets ricocheted among the rocks the paratroopers were forced down.

Under cover, the men were neither safe nor pursuing their objective, so Major Walter led a dash with the majority of the leading platoon to clear the positions surrounding the central watch-towers. Two other platoons were deployed to clear the village. No sooner had the leading parties moved off than a group of tribesmen, believing them to be the entire force, came in to attack them from behind. The fourth platoon with supporting elements had yet to close up and its commander, Captain Barry Jewkes, saw what was happening. He quickly laid an ambush and the Radfani were killed.

The noise of this action, combined with that of

Below: The RAF Bristol Belvedere short-range tactical transport helicopter was of great value in the Radfan. However, the paras mostly relied on the smaller Scout helicopter as the Belvederes were frequently unavailable.

Left: A typical 3 Para combat section, armed with rifles and a GPMG, and linked by radio to a senior officer at their headquarters (below left). Below: A para returns Radfani fire as a radio operator reports back to base.

REBELLION IN THE RADFAN

The Radfan is a wild, mountainous region, scored by deep ravines, situated some 70 miles by road from the town of Aden. It is inhabited by the Quteibi, Ibdali and Bakri tribes, fierce and hardy people who have traditionally supplemented their meagre income with raids on travellers on the Dhala road, which connects Aden with the Yemen.

In the early 1960s, Aden and the small independent states surrounding it were becoming increasingly influenced by Arab nationalist movements. The Radfan peoples, already incensed by the establishment of a customs authority which was denying them their income from the highway, eagerly accepted arms from Yemeni sympathisers and began to mine the Dhala road and snipe at passers-by. In addition, they mounted a nightly fusillade on the Federal Guard fort at Thumier.

In January 1964 a limited punitive action was ordered by the Federal government of Aden. Codenamed Operation Nutcracker, an assault on the Radfan was carried out by the Federal Regular Army (FRA) of Aden, supported by RAF aircraft and a British artillery unit. Although it succeeded as a show of strength, capturing several known agitators, the withdrawal of the force was immediately followed by renewed tribal activity. Moreover, the tribesmen were now receiving assistance from trained members of the Aden National Liberation Front (NLF) which was determined to gain complete independence for Aden.

By April the government had lost control in the Radfan, and with the FRA now under pressure from rebels throughout the Federation, it saw no option but to call in the British Army to restore law in the mountains.

clearing the watch-towers and the village, drew the entire weight of the local forces down on the paratroopers. A prolonged struggle ensued for possession of the battleground. The British force had the valuable support of two mortars, but ammunition for these weapons was limited. Although the artillery at Thumier was out of range, the radio was used to bring RAF Hawker Hunters in to strike at Radfanis positioned in caves and sangars in the rocks. The aircraft were also able to suppress the fire from snipers spread out on the overhanging heights.

Late in the afternoon the paras were relieved to see the marines of 45 Commando driving the Radfani snipers from the heights. Soon 3 Para's padre appeared in a Belvedere helicopter, and the wounded were airlifted to the military hospital in Aden. The area was then secured by an infantry battalion and the marines and paratroopers withdrew to Aden.

The anti-tank platoon armed with rifles and machine guns, advanced to the deserted village of Shab Tem

Still, no-one in Aden believed that a day of warm skirmishing had conquered the Radfani, and a brigade headquarters was brought from Northern Ireland to continue the campaign of pacification. It was commanded by Brigadier C.H. Blacker. The rest of 3 Para, commanded by Lieutenant-Colonel A.H. Farrar-Hockley, was brought to Aden from the Persian Gulf to lend its strength to the campaign, leaving only the regimental band at their station to show the flag, the men taking up rifles in place of their musical instruments. Major Walter's B Company returned to the Gulf to support them.

The group which assembled in the Wadi Rabwa close to Thumier comprised 3 Para less B Company, I Parachute Light Battery, Royal Horse Artillery, with its four 105mm guns, 3 Para Engineer Troop, transport and medical elements, and a rifle platoon formed by the Royal Army Ordnance Corps detachment which normally looked after the platforms on which the paras dropped their heavy equipment. This force was to clear the ridge on which the Bakri villages lay. None of the big Belvedere helicopters of the RAF was available to carry heavy loads forward; at best there would be two Scout helicopters of 653 Squadron, Army Air Corps, to carry a few light loads and make reconnaissance flights. There was just a chance that Land Rovers might be able to crawl up the track leading out of the Wadi Rabwa. Otherwise,

PARA ARTILLERY

The guns deployed by I Parachute Light Battery in support of 3 Para in the Radfan mountains were 105mm Model 56 pack howitzers, known to the British as the 105mm L5. This field gun had been developed on behalf of the Italian Army, by OTO Melara at La Spezia in northern Italy, to replace their British 25-pounders and US 105mm howitzers, and it entered production in 1957. The weapon was well received worldwide, and the British Army imported considerable numbers to replace its own 25-pounders. Eventually, the 105mm Model 56 could be found in virtually all Royal Artillery batteries other than those based in West Germany.

At 1290kg it was a lightweight artillery piece, an important factor in hard country where equipment has to be manhandled. Its weight made it ideal for airborne units (a Belvedere could carry it in one load) and it was widely distributed among mountain units which were able to dismantle it into 11 components for pack transport by animal (hence the term 'pack howitzer').

Since the weight specification determined a short barrel, the range of the gun, using standard US 105mm M1-series ammunition, was only 10,575m. The three-section trail could be folded, and when weight was crucial one section could be removed, along with the shield. One attraction of the Model 56 was its great versatility. The gun could be set high for use as a howitzer, or cranked into a low-profile anti-tank position which also served to improve its stability when fired.

everything had to be backpacked from the start. The 105s had to remain in the wadi, considerably shortening any cover they might be able to offer forward.

On the night of 16/17 May, Farrar-Hockley advanced the anti-tank platoon, armed with rifles and machine guns, to the deserted village of Shab Tem, and from this outpost he took forward three patrols in bright moonlight to seek routes up to the far ridge. They discovered only one, and even this involved crossing several ravines with steep sides. Next day it became evident that the track out of the Wadi Rabwa was so poor that it could not be used by laden vehicles moving up to Shab Tem. The quartermaster and the mechanical transport officers, therefore, sent several empty vehicles across the worst break in the track and organised the manhandling of loads over to them: ammunition, water and food. If there should be a severe battle, these would be their sole source of replenishment.

On the night of 17/18 May, with the stocking up of supplies still in process, the column set off. A Company led, supported by the machine-gun and mortar platoons. C Company and the Royal Engineers were deployed as fighting porters, each officer and soldier carrying about 180lb and a personal weapon for self-defence. It was very hot, and progress was slow, only about half-a-mile an hour, up and down the precipitous slopes. Just before dawn, Farrar-Hockley halted on a knoll surmounted by two deserted houses. The porters shed their loads and returned to Shab Tem. As the remainder made camp, there was a brief flurry of fire from a flank, sending bullets

whistling over them. Two of the battalion's mortars fired a random response onto the flashes and, as the moon came up, all fell quiet.

Next day, the Army Air Corps Scout helicopters flew a series of loads forward from Shab Tem, while the paras watched the silent and apparently deserted landscape from five concealed observation posts. At nightfall, C Company reappeared to take on the role of an advanced guard, while A Company and the engineers humped the loads. A fighting patrol was despatched, and then the column set off, wending its way through the deep ravines, and finally securing its objective on the top of Hajib escarpment as dawn approached.

The Bakri fighting bands were uncertain as to what to do next. They did not like operating at night, preferring to use darkness to regroup and rest. All of them crack marksmen, they preferred to wage guerrilla war by day among the rocks and caverns with which they were familiar, sniping and closing in when any British position looked vulnerable. They had now lost a good deal of territory. Moreover, less than two miles from 3 Para's position was the Wadi Dhubsan, an area never previously penetrated by government forces, in which lay the Radfanis' principal grain stores. When the battalion group began to expand their positions, at first on the flank and then towards the height overlooking the Wadi Dhubsan, the Radfani resistance hardened.

When A Company began to advance towards this height, its left protected by the anti-tank platoon, groups of tribesmen opened fire from two villages ahead. C Company was drawn in, and the British artillery, firing at extreme range, dropped shells onto the Radfanis as the two companies advanced

Beyond the villages and a little to one side lay a saddle of ground, beyond which stood stone watch-towers. They were beyond the guns' range, and too robustly constructed to be destroyed by mortars. The RAF Hunters were called down, and they ran in on the structures with bombs and 30mm Aden guns. The watch-towers fell silent: when the paras checked them later on, they found a 12ft bloodstain in one room.

The British force now looked down into the Wadi Dhubsan. This area, hitherto a safe base for Radfani operations, was to be entered as a demonstration of power, and the grain stocks held there were to be destroyed. Brigadier Blacker told Lieutenant-Colonel Farrar-Hockley, 'The aim is not to slaughter tribesmen, but to teach them that we will come

Cap Badge and Bakri Ridge
3 Para, May 1964

The mountains of the Radfan, in the north of the Federation of South Arabia, were the scene of a Yemen-backed revolt in the early 1960s. In January 1964 a joint British/Federal Government operation was launched in the Radfan to restore order, and late in the following April a force of marines and paras moved into the Radfan and commenced operations in the Bakri Ridge area. On 5 May, the Cap Badge feature was seized, and on 26 May 3 Para began their sweep along the Bakri Ridge.

The Radfan

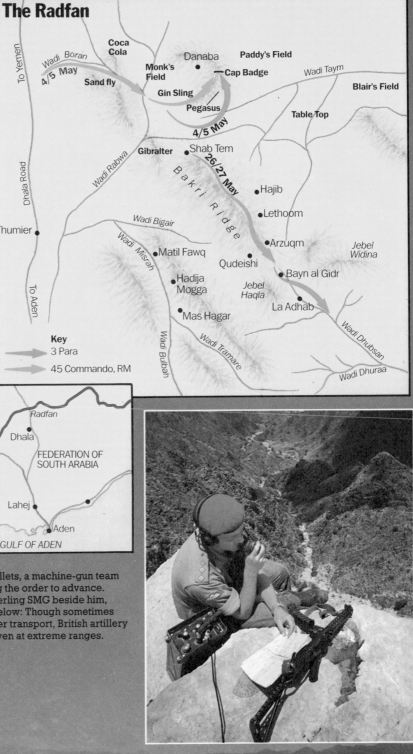

Key
→ 3 Para
→ 45 Commando, RM

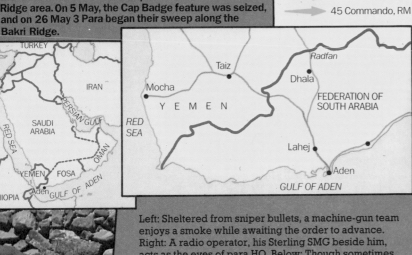

Left: Sheltered from sniper bullets, a machine-gun team enjoys a smoke while awaiting the order to advance. Right: A radio operator, his Sterling SMG beside him, acts as the eyes of para HQ. Below: Though sometimes marooned by lack of helicopter transport, British artillery provided effective support, even at extreme ranges.

wherever we need to if they misbehave.' In the event, the final assault was delayed by rainstorms. Stores remaining in the Wadi Rabwa were forwarded to a new dump on the Hajib escarpment, and the engineers worked round the clock to extend the track from Shab Tem in order to bring forward the guns of I Parachute Light Battery.

There were two tracks into the Wadi Dhubsan, one fair and one poor, which wound 3200ft down the mountain into the valley. Reckoning that there would be ambushes laid on both tracks, Farrar-Hockley decided to make a direct descent from the heights. Reconnoitring, he found a route which led down a 30ft rock face, along a boulder-strewn stream bed, and ended up directly in the rear of the village of Bayn Al Gidr. On the night of 25 May, while C Company picqueted the Jebel Haqla to the right, the main column used ropes to abseil down the rock face and it descended in the darkness, to the village. Sentries posted by the tribesmen around the village rapidly woke the garrison and it promptly fled. By 0600 hours, the upper wadi had been cleared without a shot being fired.

The cliffs on either side were milling with turbanned tribesmen, firing their rifles

X Company of 45 Commando, under Farrar-Hockley's command for this operation, was now advanced down the right side of the wadi, while A Company of 3 Para pushed along the heights to the left. Very quickly, small groups of tribesmen were seen hurrying into positions ahead. They were coming from an ambush position on the better of the two approaches in the upper slopes. Fire opened between the forces, the shots echoing along the sides of the wadi. Meanwhile, Farrar-Hockley, who was talking to Brigadier Blacker, himself just arrived in Bayn Al Gidr, was given map co-ordinates of the marines' position, and he elected to take a Scout to check their progress.

Taking off, Farrar-Hockley's Scout flew towards the map reference given him on the radio. Major Jackson, the pilot, sought the shelter of the cliffs as they skimmed the Wadi Dhubsan, over the battalion headquarters and support elements on the valley floor. They crossed a deserted tract and, suddenly, approaching the map reference point, the ground and cliffs on either side were milling with turbanned tribesmen, shaking their fists and firing their rifles. The noise of the engine obscured the sound of their shots, but then the men in the Scout heard a sound like the opening of beer cans. Fuel began to spray over the forward observation perspex.

'Can you keep flying?' asked Farrar-Hockley. 'This is the last place to put her down.' 'I've got power,' said Major Jackson. Coolly, he turned the Scout towards the head of the wadi, but then the engine or the rotors started making a clattering noise. As they swept forward, the advanced element of battalion headquarters on the valley floor swung into sight. 'Down there,' said Farrar-Hockley. They landed safely and Major Jackson switched off the power. Around them a firefight was in progress; a further 50 tribesmen had moved into position and more waited behind them, no doubt those seen by the Scout earlier on. There were now some casualties to be evacuated, including Lieutenant Ian McLeod who had been shot through the wrist in the Scout. The regimental

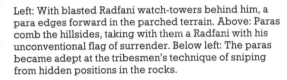

Left: With blasted Radfani watch-towers behind him, a para edges forward in the parched terrain. Above: Paras comb the hillsides, taking with them a Radfani with his unconventional flag of surrender. Below left: The paras became adept at the tribesmen's technique of sniping from hidden positions in the rocks.

sergeant-major led a party from the main element of the headquarters to the damaged helicopter, but was wounded on the way. The Bakri riflemen were shooting with accuracy at 800 yds range. Even as the padre helped carry the wounded back, the heels of his boots were clipped by bullets.

It was a tiresome morning and afternoon. In the end, the difficulty of breaching the tribesmens' well-concealed defences was overcome by C Company. Ordered to outflank them by marching round from the Jebel Haqla, they did so rapidly, surprising the Radfanis' left flank and forcing them to abandon their positions. The battalion then formed a defensive perimeter for the night, within which lay the crippled Scout. By torchlight, two aircraft technicians from the Royal Electrical and Mechanical Engineers worked through the hours of darkness, trying to repair the helicopter before dawn.

Next morning, as the Radfani grain stores were set alight, Major Jackson climbed into the Scout and tried the starter motor. The engine fired, the rotors turned, and when the helicopter lifted, hovered and then rose rapidly into the air, there was a hearty cheer. Major Jackson disappeared through the smoke billowing up from the grain stores and 3 Para, with the marines, began the long climb out of the wadi to the heights. From there, they were airlifted by Wessex helicopters of the Royal Navy to the heart of Aden and the delight of a cold beer.

THE AUTHOR General Sir Anthony Farrar-Hockley was, as a lieutenant-colonel, Commanding Officer of the 3rd Battalion, The Parachute Regiment, during the British operations against guerrilla tribesmen in the Radfan mountains of Aden in 1964. He retired in 1983 and is now a defence consultant.

In the streets of the Lebanese town of Sidon the Israeli paras met fire with fire as they took on the strongholds of the PLO

ON 9 JUNE 1982, a force of Israeli paratroops was faced with the dangerous task of clearing the Lebanese town of Sidon of PLO (Palestine Liberation Organisation) guerrillas entrenched there. Supported by tanks and artillery putting down a barrage 400m ahead of them, the paras advanced along the main road into the town. The tanks fired at PLO positions in small buildings and in the bottom storeys of the high-rise blocks, while artillery fire and air strikes were directed on the buildings where resistance was toughest. In spite of this heavy and well-coordinated support, however, the paras had once more to show their mettle as elite infantry –

Below: On the beaches of Lebanon. An Israeli Defence Forces armoured personnel carrier leaves the hold of its landing ship, ready for the push on the PLO stronghold of Sidon.

fighting at close quarters to mop up the town.

This was strange, dangerous, exhausting work – the paras would often climb up 20 flights of stairs in a tall residential block, expecting to be fired upon at any moment, with death lurking round every corner. Often the sights that greeted them were surreal. As one soldier described it later:

'We burst into one apartment. There was a large living room filled with heavy, antique furniture and glass-doored cupboards. Thick carpets

ASSAULT ON SIDON

PLO IN LEBANON

The Palestinian refugee camps in Lebanon dated back to the earliest exodus of Palestinians from Israel in 1948. It was only after the PLO (Palestine Liberation Organisation) shifted its centre of activities to Lebanon, having been expelled from Jordan in September 1970, that the Palestinian presence in Lebanon became a focus of political attention. Lebanon was now the new PLO base from which to strike at Israel, but their presence also brought problems for their hosts since the actions of the Palestinian guerrillas brought Lebanon into conflict with Israel. This led to clashes between the PLO and the Lebanese Army. The Palestinian involvement in the Lebanese civil war of 1975-76 brought about a distinct worsening of relations with the host population and also led to a clash with Syria whose forces intervened in Lebanon. The potentially dangerous rift with Syria was soon healed, however, when, in 1977, Egyptian President Anwar Sadat launched a Middle East peace initiative that excluded the Palestinians. The PLO united with Syria and other radical Arab states in its rejection of Sadat's policies.

By June 1982, when Israel mounted Operation Peace for Galilee to suppress the threat of Palestinian activity along Israel's northern border, the Palestinians in Lebanon numbered some 400,000 people. The PLO armoury was fairly extensive and was mainly of Soviet design. While the PLO were well equipped with smallarms and support weapons – AK-47s, RPG rocket launchers, machine guns of various types and recoilless rifles – their heavy weaponry was sadly lacking. Their old T-54 tanks, Katyusha rockets and artillery were no match for the modern battlefield weapon systems of the IDF.

were on the floor. In the middle of the room stood a 105mm anti-tank gun.'

This was not the sort of battle for flashy gestures, for vain self-sacrifice. The para commander, Colonel 'Y', preferred a slow, methodical advance, to keep casualties to a minimum. The same tactic was used over and over again: suppress sniper fire with tank

Below: Beside the shattered remains of a blazing armoured personnel carrier, a fully loaded Israeli M113 pulls off the road as the invading forces tighten the ring around the town of Sidon. Bottom: The paras go in. The buildings in Sidon bristled with PLO snipers and the paras were supported by tanks and self-propelled artillery to deal with this threat. As they came under fire, the tanks would swing their main armament into action and blast the snipers' positions at point-blank range.

nd artillery shells and air strikes, enter the building, op up, exit, rest and regroup – then do it all over gain. In this painstaking way, the paras cleared the nain road into Sidon and adjoining streets, but the b was still only half-done. Large numbers of PLO nen remained in the ancient Casbah area of the town nd in the Ein El Hilwe refugee camp – the centre of LO military activity.

Operation Peace for Galilee, the Israeli invasion of outhern Lebanon, had begun on 6 June 1982 with a ombined land and sea assault. The paras were put shore before dawn on the next day, three ilometres to the north of Sidon, in the largest ever mphibious landings undertaken by the IDF (Israeli Defence Forces). The first group to land, paras upported by naval commandos, prepared the landng area for the main force and set up a formal ommand post. They also laid ambushes and mined oads, but the PLO response to the landing was nuted – just a few Katyusha rockets fired out to sea. he main landing force consisted of paratroops in M113 armoured personnel carriers (APCs), suported by naval, tank and artillery fire.

Sidon was an important strategic position, lying on ebanon's main coastal communication route. It was lso an Al Fatah naval base (Fatah was the most imortant group within the PLO) and an arms supply centre from which thousands of weapons were trans-

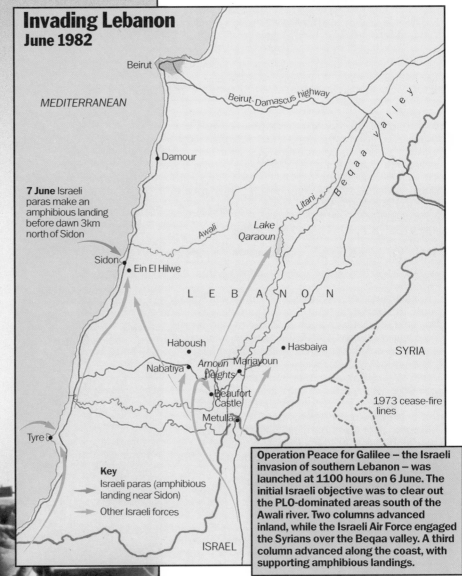

Invading Lebanon
June 1982

7 June Israeli paras make an amphibious landing before dawn 3km north of Sidon

Key
→ Israeli paras (amphibious landing near Sidon)
→ Other Israeli forces

Operation Peace for Galilee – the Israeli invasion of southern Lebanon – was launched at 1100 hours on 6 June. The initial Israeli objective was to clear out the PLO-dominated areas south of the Awali river. Two columns advanced inland, while the Israeli Air Force engaged the Syrians over the Beqaa valley. A third column advanced along the coast, with supporting amphibious landings.

ferred to Arab guerrillas throughout Lebanon. Tanks, missiles, smallarms and ammunition from the Soviet bloc countries, from Syria, Libya, North Korea and even the United States passed through the town. The PLO military infrastructure – military posts, HQs, stores, gun platforms and observation posts – was sited in the midst of the civilian population. Defences were based on a closely built network of high-rise buildings and concealed bunkers, prepared for an Israeli attack from the south. The defenders were some 1500 Al Fatah guerrillas from the El Kastel Brigade, reinforced by units retreating from the IDF invasion of the south that had begun the previous day. The El Kastel Brigade had also built fortifications in the mountains overlooking the coastal strip and was supported by the Palestinians in the nearby Ein El Hilwe camp.

Operation Peace for Galilee was planned as a swift, deep advance, bypassing pockets of resistance, which were to be dealt with later. However, the PLO's secure entrenchment in the heart of Sidon, and the town's strategic position on the coast, made it impossible to bypass. Sidon was duly surrounded on the morning of 7 June and the paras moved in from the north, in a smooth, professional operation.

At noon on the 7th, units of the Golani Brigade with armoured support began an advance on Ein El Hilwe in the southeastern suburbs. Another combined

Right: Covered by a gunner keeping an eye open for snipers in the surrounding apartment blocks, a general-purpose-machine-gun section moves into action. **Far right:** With a rifle grenade to cover the rear, an Israeli officer issues orders to his men before an attack on a gun position. **Below:** A lone para races across the forecourt of a burning petrol station. **Below right:** Paras advance through a deserted building site.

force of Golani infantry and armour moved onto the ridges overlooking the town from the east. The paratroops were now ordered to open the main north–south road, through Sidon, to Israeli traffic on its way north towards Beirut, and then to join up with the southern force for an attack on Ein El Hilwe. This mission was initially to have been given to one of the forces moving north, but because of the fierce resistance that the IDF was encountering in Sidon, it was decided to send in the paras.

The next morning, 8 June, the Voice of Israel radio station broadcast the following message on its Arabic network:

'To the residents of Sidon: Announcement Number 10. IDF forces are about to complete removing the remnants of trapped Palestinian terrorist nests in your city. The IDF is doing its utmost in order to avoid injuring the civilian population in the city, but will uproot anyone holding arms. The fate of the trapped terrorists has already been sealed, after their commanders abandoned them. Residents of Sidon, your brother residents of Tyre harkened to IDF calls and evacuated their town in order to enable the elimination of terrorist nests in that city. Residents of Tyre have been returning to their homes since last night and are better protected and more secure than at any time. Residents of Sidon, the IDF will do its utmost to avoid injuring you – the unarmed citizens of the city. For your own good, quickly distance yourself from the area of danger. The IDF will enable you to return safely to your homes as soon as possible. You have been warned. Remember, your lives are in your own hands.'

This warning followed several others that called on civilians to: 'Deny armed elements the use of your houses and neighbourhoods as combat positions,' 'Stay in your homes and do not go out,' 'Suspend from your windows or balconies a white sheet which is clearly visible from the street,' and 'Constantly listen to announcements that will be broadcast on the Voice of Israel.' At the same time, Israeli Air Force (IAF) aircraft dropped leaflets on the town calling on the civilian population not to be drawn into the fighting, but to leave their homes and gather on the beach within two hours. When this period had passed, the IDF commanders felt that armour, artillery and air strikes could be used against the PLO.

At noon, the paratroopers began their advance, reinforced by more tanks and artillery that had been landed from the sea. In order to save time, it was decided to ignore any building not known as a guerrilla emplacement, or from which there was no firing. The paras, commanded by Colonel 'Y', advanced down the main street in two lines, close to the buildings on both sides. Tanks and more lightly armoured self-propelled 155mm artillery pieces followed. The self-propelled guns, able to lay down high-angle support fire that could hit guerrilla positions on the top floors of the apartment blocks, were a necessity, due to the limited elevation of the tank guns. Resistance was slight at first – just sporadic bursts of sniper fire. This was silenced by point-

ISRAELI TACTICS

Operation Peace for Galilee was planned by Israel as a swift advance in depth, bypassing pockets of PLO resistance; these pockets would be tackled later. At the same time, the advancing columns would aim to cut off PLO bases and forces from the eastern parts of Lebanon and Syria. In the western sector of operations, it was decided that, in order to achieve maximum speed, the narrow mountainous passes of the southwest would be avoided, and a large force of troops would be put ashore three kilometres north of the town of Sidon. This was to be the largest single-force amphibious landing in the history of the IDF and the well-balanced armour and infantry units were provided with considerable firepower and air support.

One of the main problems for the IDF lay in the built-up areas of Lebanon where the civilian population existed side-by-side with some of the main PLO centres of defence. A captured PLO document, dated May 1981, stated: 'The built-up areas in the town of Sidon and the surrounding villages are excellent areas for shelter. The trees enable complete camouflage and concealment for vehicles and personnel.' While some of the smaller pockets and villages could be bypassed and isolated, in the case of major PLO strongholds, such as Tyre and Sidon, the IDF took them on.

First they would outflank and completely encircle the town. This they hoped would have a strong psychological effect on their adversaries and soften resistance. Pressure would then be exerted from the fringes, and increased as the troops came nearer to the main areas of resistance. (The IDF moved into such towns cautiously, having learnt a salutary lesson on the problems of street fighting, and the casualties it causes, in Suez in 1973.) Finally, the troops would engage the enemy positions and gradually winkle them out.

Left: A para looses off an RPG round at an enemy machine-gun nest. Below left: Preparing to go in. A para readies the 40mm grenade launcher mounted beneath his assault rifle. Bottom right: Pinned down. A group of paras, keeping well away from the centre of the street, discuss the location of a PLO position in a high-rise block, before the trooper in the foreground lobs in a grenade from his rifle-mounted launcher.

blank fire from the artillery into the buildings occupied by snipers. But the deeper the paras advanced into the town, the heavier the sniper fire became. Tank and artillery commanders were prime targets for the PLO defenders, and the advance became achingly slow and dangerous. Two Syrian MiGs made a bombing run over the Israeli column, causing no casualties, but adding to the tension. By evening, the para commanders knew that they would not accomplish their mission that day. The southern force attacking Ein El Hilwe reached the same conclusion and both forces withdrew for the night.

The following morning, 9 June, it was decided to give all possible support to the paras. Clearing the main road was now a priority, to maintain a flow of supplies to the armoured units pushing ever northwards. The attack on Ein El Hilwe was delayed and all the artillery in the area was placed at the paras' disposal. This was crucial, for behind a co-ordinated barrage from tanks, artillery and aircraft, the paras, moving steadily from building to building, finally succeeded in winkling out the PLO defenders.

With the main street clear, however, the Casbah remained a problem – the narrow twisting alleyways of this old market providing an ideal site for the remaining PLO men to make a last stand. This was a situation that had been foreseen by the IDF commanders, for at their pre-invasion briefing, the chief of IDF military intelligence, Major-General Yehoshua Sagie, had specifically warned of the folly of streetfighting in the Casbah:

'In 1976, the Syrians attempted to enter Sidon, against the wishes of the PLO. The Syrians were tied down for seven days on the outskirts and could not break a way in. In that battle they lost many tanks, APCs and men.'

This advice was echoed by an anti-PLO Sidon 'Mukhtar' (elder): 'Destroy it,' he said. 'Do not break yourselves and throw away all you have gained so far by trying to enter the place.'

After calling on the PLO guerrillas to surrender, Israeli artillery fired a number of warning rounds into the Casbah. There was no response to the call for a surrender, and so a massive artillery barrage followed, reducing parts of the old market to rubble and forcing the few surviving defenders to capitulate. Thankful that the Casbah no longer posed a threat, the indefatigable paras headed off to join up with the Golani units for the attack on Ein El Hilwe.

The battle for Sidon had been a gruelling test of military skill and courage. The high professional standards of the Israeli paras, combined with armour, artillery and the air force in magnificent inter-arm co-ordination, allowed them to defeat a determined and well-entrenched enemy at a cost of relatively few Israeli casualties.

THE AUTHORS Tony Banks and Ronnie Daniel are military reporters for the Voice of Israel radio station. Ronnie Daniel commands a reserve infantry battalion and Tony Banks serves at the Office of the IDF Spokesman.

LIEUTENANT-COLONEL DAVID CHAUNDLER

David Chaundler joined The Parachute Regiment as a private soldier in 1962; he went to RMA Sandhurst and was commissioned into the 3rd Battalion in 1964 while the unit was serving in Bahrain. He saw service as a platoon commander in Borneo when the Malaysian Federation was being defended against the claims of Indonesia during the 1960s, and in 1970 became adjutant of the 2nd Battalion. During this period 2 Para undertook three tours of duty in Northern Ireland as part of the security forces.

Following a stint at the British Army Staff Training College at Camberley, Chaundler worked at the Ministry of Defence. In 1977 he was posted to Berlin and served until 1979 as a company commander with 2 Para. Then, until 1981, he held a staff position at Army Headquarters at Lisburn in Northern Ireland. It was during this period that a convoy carrying men of 2 Para drove into an IRA bomb ambush at Warrenpoint and 18 soldiers were killed.

In 1982 Chaundler was once again in the Ministry of Defence when the news arrived of the death of 'H' Jones, commanding officer of 2 Para, in the battle at Goose Green. Chaundler flew out to the Falklands and took command of 2 Para for the rest of the war with Argentina; he finally handed over command of 2 Para in August 1984. David Chaundler was awarded the OBE in the 1985 New Year's Honours List.

NIGHT ATTACK

Blooded in the bitter fighting for Goose Green and Darwin, the men of 2 Para tabbed across East Falkland and threw themselves into an assault on the Argentinian forces dug in on the slopes of Wireless Ridge

Far left: On the evening of 3 June the sole surviving Chinook helicopter was used by Brigadier Tony Wilson to fly 2 Para from Goose Green to Fitzroy. Some members of Major-General Moore's staff at San Carlos were angered by the move, believing that it made 2 Para highly vulnerable to Argentinian bombardment and air attack. Above: A Welsh Guard, injured in the attack on the LSL (Landing Ship Logistic) *Sir Galahad*, is helped from a Sea King rescue helicopter by paras. (Padre David Cooper can be seen on the left.) Left: Survivors come ashore from lifeboats at a beach near Fitzroy. *Sir Galahad* blazes fiercely behind them. Right: The sheep-shearing sheds at Fitzroy provided the paras with a chance to sleep and dry out. This para is preparing food with his standard-issue solid-fuel stove.

FOUR DAYS after the death of 'H' Jones, in the battle of Goose Green on 28 May 1982, I joined 2 Para to take over command. Having been flown to Ascension Island, I parachuted from a Hercules into the sea and was picked up by a Sea King helicopter which brought me to HMS *Fearless* in San Carlos Water. Joining the battalion, or rather rejoining it as I had previously been both its adjutant and one of its company commanders, was like coming home. The shock of the battle was still in their eyes, hardly two men were dressed alike, and some were now carrying Argentinian weapons, but there were still many familiar faces. My reception would have been very much the same had it been in Berlin, Aldershot or Northern Ireland. Only the circumstances were different.

My battalion, the 2nd Battalion, The Parachute Regiment, was to become perhaps the most celebrated land force of the Falklands campaign. That we were given such opportunities to confirm our reputation in 1982 was partly a matter of chance. If the Argentinians had invaded a few days later than they

did, the battalion would have been on its way to Belize for a stay of six months. Again, since 2 Para was occupying the southernmost position after landing at San Carlos, it became the obvious choice for the attack on Goose Green. Then, 2 Para, acting as 3 Commando Brigade's reserve battalion in the assault on the mountains around Port Stanley, was to be given the task of capturing Wireless Ridge, thus making it the only battalion to be committed twice against the Argentinians. Chance certainly played a part, but I would like to believe that the battalion's pride, traditions and training all contributed to 2 Para's success in the Falklands.

By the simple expedient of making a call to a Falkland islander's house in Fitzroy via the civilian telephone link with Swan Inlet, it had been established that Bluff Cove and Fitzroy were unoccupied by the Argentinians. Over the evening of 3 June and the next morning the battalion flew forward to occupy the two settlements, using the one available Chinook helicopter. One lift carried 82 fully-armed soldiers – something of a record. There followed nine days of rest to recover from the effects of the battle and cold weather at Goose Green. The sheep-shearing sheds of the two settlements provided shelters through which the soldiers could be rotated to dry out, get a decent night's sleep, and eat a meal.

On 6 June we were relieved by the Scots Guards at Bluff Cove and, with the battalion now concentrated around Fitzroy, we completed our preparations. Rations, radio batteries and medical supplies were issued and ammunition stockpiled. This period, however, was marred by the disastrous attack on the landing ship *Sir Galahad*, which occurred at Fitzroy

and not, as was reported by the press, at Bluff Cove. The Welsh Guards were old friends – we had recently served alongside them in Berlin and then in South Armagh – and the unhappy task now fell to us of pulling many of them out of the sea. It was with some relief that next day I received orders to be prepared to move the battalion to the northern flank. We were ready to go and Fitzroy now held only sad memories.

Two days later the whole battalion flew north by helicopter and once again we came under the command of 3 Commando Brigade (whilst in Bluff Cove and Fitzroy we had been under 5 Infantry Brigade). That night we moved forward. Of necessity we left our packs with their spare food and sleeping-bags behind – we were not to see them again until we were in Port Stanley.

Major Hector Gullan climbed out, and running towards me he shouted, 'Wireless Ridge tonight chaps'

It was a spectacular night. As we moved forward in a single file (known colloquially as the 'airborne snake'), weaving our way around the Argentinian minefields and their periodic artillery bombardments, we could see 3 Para attacking Mount Longdon to our front and No. 45 Commando attacking Two Sisters to our right.

Soon after first light we arrived at our assembly area behind Mount Longdon, which by then had been secured by 3 Para. We dug in and I asked for further orders. Three hours before last light a Scout helicopter arrived, the brigade liaison officer – Major Hector Gullan – climbed out, and running towards me he shouted, 'Wireless Ridge tonight chaps,' surely the shortest set of orders ever given for a battalion attack.

I quickly devised a plan and summoned my officers. Half-way through our conference the boundaries for the attack were changed, and when I got to the point of asking, 'Any questions?' we heard that the assault had been postponed for 24 hours. I was beginning to understand the term 'fog of war'. It was to get worse. Next day, with Major Tony Rice, RA, the BC (Battery Commander) of our artillery support, I flew up to 3 Para's positions on Mount Longdon from where we could see Wireless Ridge. It did not appear as we had supposed from our maps and my plan needed to be altered. Argentinian Skyhawks then came in for the last air attack of the campaign; consequently our helicopters were grounded and the BC and I could not rejoin 2 Para until two hours before last light – the time set for the battalion to move out. The Skyhawks had also delayed the moving forward of our mortars, which only then were beginning to arrive, and the intensive enemy fire onto Mount Longdon had prevented the artillery spotters of 3 Para from registering their targets. There was only one thing for it. I sent the company commanders away for a 'brew' – the army's panacea for all situations – while I replanned the attack.

We were fortunate with Wireless Ridge as the terrain was reasonably flat and open. So far, most of the attacks in the Falklands had been along narrow ridges with little room for manoeuvre; at least on Wireless Ridge we had space. The enemy was the Argentinian 7th Infantry Battalion, with four companies and a platoon on the ridge. My plan called for an attack in four phases, with each axis of attack coming from a different direction. The battalion's experience at Goose Green had taught us the importance of fire support. Up to this point of the

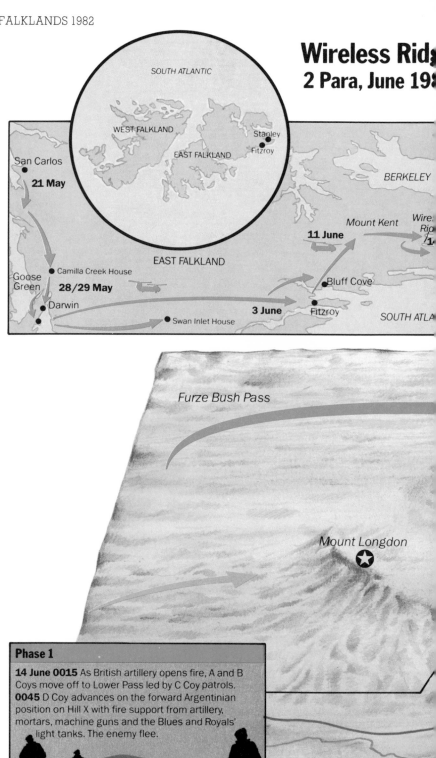

Wireless Ridge
2 Para, June 198

Phase 1

14 June 0015 As British artillery opens fire, A and B Coys move off to Lower Pass led by C Coy patrols.
0045 D Coy advances on the forward Argentinian position on Hill X with fire support from artillery, mortars, machine guns and the Blues and Royals' light tanks. The enemy flee.

Key

→ A Coy	→ 2 Para	★ Argentinia
→ B Coy	→ Blues and Royals light tank troop	→ Argentinia
→ C Coy		
→ D Coy	→ Other British forces	

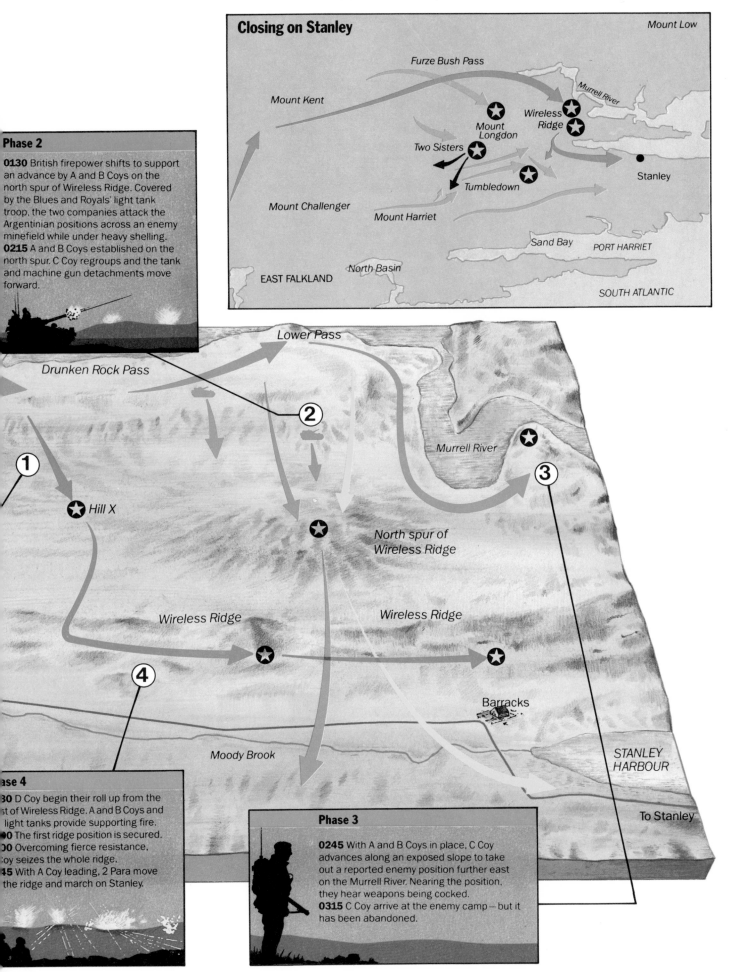

Closing on Stanley

Mount Low

Furze Bush Pass

Mount Kent

Murrell River

Mount Longdon

Wireless Ridge

Two Sisters

Stanley

Tumbledown

Mount Challenger

Mount Harriet

Sand Bay

PORT HARRIET

North Basin

EAST FALKLAND

SOUTH ATLANTIC

Phase 2

0130 British firepower shifts to support an advance by A and B Coys on the north spur of Wireless Ridge. Covered by the Blues and Royals' light tank troop, the two companies attack the Argentinian positions across an enemy minefield while under heavy shelling.
0215 A and B Coys established on the north spur. C Coy regroups and the tank and machine gun detachments move forward.

Lower Pass

Drunken Rock Pass

Murrell River

Hill X

North spur of Wireless Ridge

Wireless Ridge

Wireless Ridge

Barracks

Moody Brook

STANLEY HARBOUR

Phase 4

...30 D Coy begin their roll up from the ...st of Wireless Ridge. A and B Coys and ...light tanks provide supporting fire.
...0 The first ridge position is secured.
...00 Overcoming fierce resistance, ...oy seizes the whole ridge.
...45 With A Coy leading, 2 Para move ...the ridge and march on Stanley.

To Stanley

Phase 3

0245 With A and B Coys in place, C Coy advances along an exposed slope to take out a reported enemy position further east on the Murrell River. Nearing the position, they hear weapons being cocked.
0315 C Coy arrive at the enemy camp — but it has been abandoned.

campaign, all our attacks had been launched in silence in order to achieve surprise. Mortar and artillery fire had been held back until contact was made. I decided upon a noisy attack with an extensive preliminary bombardment, believing that the Argentinians, essentially a conscript army, would crack under a heavy barrage. It was hardly surprising that the impact of fire support was generally underestimated. Before the campaign none of us had either seen or experienced the effects of a bombardment with large quantities of high explosives. On Wireless Ridge we were to do both. We asked for, and got, two batteries of artillery (12 105mm Light Guns), fire support from a frigate (HMS *Ambuscade*) and 3 Para's mortars, in addition to our own mortar and machine-gun platoons. But perhaps the most significant support weapons were Lieutenant Lord Robin Innes-Ker's four Scorpions and Scimitars from the Blues and Royals, which up to this stage of the campaign had not seen action. They made a remarkable journey from Fitzroy over the mountains to join us in our assembly area and, though normally classed as reconnaissance vehicles, were used as light tanks and their fire was to prove devastating.

At last light on 13 June we moved out. It took us four-and-a-quarter hours to reach our FUPs (forming up positions). The night was exceptionally dark with intermittent snow and sleet flurries. Few soldiers had slept for the last two nights (the previous night had been unbelievably cold and sleep was impossible without sleepingbags), we had not seen a ration pack for 24 hours, and, what with the last-minute change of plan, the endurance of the battalion was being tested to the utmost. Also, for most of the soldiers this was their second time into action. At Goose Green they had not really known what to expect. This time there were no illusions.

As we moved forward our Royal Artillery gunners were finding their targets by using illumination shells to spot the fall of shot. This was not an easy task, and we were eternally grateful for their skill in completing it. By this time the Argentinians knew they were going to be attacked and they started to shell our likely approaches and FUPs. As we moved into our FUPs I received the message from Battalion Main Headquarters, about 1km to the rear, that they

Top left: The battalion headquarters at Furze Bush Pass. The force assembled directly south of this point before making the approach to Wireless Ridge. Above left: To the victorious paras on the crest of Wireless Ridge it came almost as a surprise to see the Argentinian base so close over the water of Stanley Harbour. Left: British artillery in the Falklands consisted of 36 105mm Light Guns. With a maximum range of 17000m and a 16.1kg shell, these extremely accurate weapons were formidable in the infantry fire-support role. Above right: The Scorpion (shown opposite) and Scimitar light tanks of the Blues and Royals came into direct combat for the first time at Wireless Ridge.

had something I ought to see. I walked over to the HQ and Major Chris Keeble, the Second-in-Command, handed me a captured Argentinian map which had just been sent up by Brigade Headquarters. It showed a minefield laid right across our main axis of attack. I returned to my Tac HQ (Tactical Headquarters) and met the officer commanding B Company, Major John Crosland. I said, 'John, we've got a minefield out there.' We just looked at each other and shrugged. We knew it was now too late to do anything about it and we had no option but to cross it. Miraculously, although A and B Companies and Tac HQ went through, no-one was blown up.

By now the softening-up bombardment had begun, and Major Phil Neame's D Company, supported by artillery, mortars, light tanks and the machine-gun platoon, with suppressive fire on the other Argentinian positions coming from the second battery and the frigate, attacked their first objective – Phase 1 of my plan. It was quickly overrun, but the Argentinians responded immediately and their 105mm and 155mm guns opened up on the captured positions. D Company rapidly moved off and reorganised, one soldier taking cover in a trench which proved to be an Argentinian latrine!

Mortar illuminating rounds began to burst overhead, casting an eerie flickering light over the battlefield

Our firepower was then switched to support A and B Companies in their attack, which was to be Phase 2 of my plan. Argentinian shells now began to fall to my left. John Crosland came up on the radio – 'It's getting a little hot here, can we move?' I was now satisfied that all was ready. Our two batteries of guns increased their rate of fire to a total of 72rpm and I gave A and B Companies the order to move forward. As they approached their objective, a position held by an Argentinian company and the regimental headquarters, the lines of tracer from our machine guns and tanks were reaching out for the enemy, adding to the already considerable weight of firepower from our guns. An Argentinian artillery salvo homed in on Major Dair Farrar-Hockley's A Company, killing the colour sergeant and wounding several soldiers, but the momentum of the attack did not slow. Our artillery lifted as the companies reached the edge of the Argentinian positions. Mortar illuminating rounds began to burst overhead, casting an eerie, flickering light over the battlefield as soldiers skirmished from rock to rock. The enemy broke and fled, and the machine-gunners in our tanks, aided by their night sights, drove the Argentinians from the ridge.

A and B Companies had captured 37 prisoners and were now quickly digging in. Except for the Argentinian artillery that continued to shell their old positions, there was a pause in the pace of the battle and we prepared for the next two phases of the assault. C Company – who had gained the forward positions in the attack and guided the battalion up to them – regrouped. (C Company was led by Major Roger Jenner, who had been wounded at Goose Green but had refused to be airlifted out). Their next task, Phase 3, was to capture a position held by a platoon. As C Company approached, they heard the sound of weapons being cocked, but the firepower was too much for the Argentinians and they fled. A number of pairs of boots were found, bearing witness to the enemy's hasty departure.

Back at the regimental aid post the medical officer, Captain Steve Hughes, was busy with the first casualties. He had cracked a bone in his foot on the approach to Goose Green but did not admit to it until long after. Though he had only very recently qualified, every wounded soldier treated by Captain Hughes survived, a total of over 50 from both Goose Green and Wireless Ridge. These included Private Gray whose leg he amputated under the most primitive conditions: his was altogether a remarkable achievement.

We now took stock of A and B Companies' position. Many had had lucky escapes. A member of my Tac HQ had been hit in the front of his steel helmet, the bullet passing round the inside and out of the back, without even grazing him; a shell had exploded next to Corporal Curtis of B Company, blowing his clothing to ribbons without him receiving a scratch. Private Philpott had fallen into a freezing pond and a rapid change of clothing was needed to prevent exposure. But the tanks and machine guns, now resupplied with ammunition, had moved up to us, and D Company, having made a wide outflanking movement, was prepared to begin the final phase of the operation.

They had to stand on the baseplates while the mortars fired and four men suffered broken ankles

Once again our firepower swept down upon the Argentinians along the final ridgeline. Back on the mortar line, our mortar crews were making herculean efforts to keep their weapons in action on the soft ground. So as not to let down their comrades in the rifle companies, they had to stand on the baseplates while the mortars fired and four men suffered broken ankles. The artillery was also having problems with the soft ground; one gun had slipped back imperceptibly, and of each salvo fired by the battery one shell was landing on C Company. But we were ready to go again. D Company's movement had gone undetected by the Argentinians who were expecting our next attack to come from the north rather than the west. I gave D Company the order to attack.

FIRE-SUPPORT AT WIRELESS RIDGE

As a consequence of the minimal availability of support firepower, 2 Para had taken Goose Green early in the Falklands campaign without backing from aircraft strikes or concentrated artillery and mortar fire. In contrast, the same unit's assault on Wireless Ridge was a classic British infantry action, one that fully vindicated the tactics of the modern British Army.
According to the textbook, a fully-integrated and well-entrenched enemy should never be attacked by infantry relying on their smallarms and grenades alone. The infantry role is to clear and secure enemy territory only after resistance has been fragmented by heavy, sustained and accurate fire from air strikes, artillery, mortar and machine-gun platoons, and rifle companies. Such a barrage not only weakens and demoralises the enemy, but also forces him to stay under cover as the infantrymen storm forward.
At Wireless Ridge, 2 Para had the benefit of full fire-support. Argentinian positions sustained an intense bombardment from two batteries of 105mm guns, the 4.5in gun on HMS Ambuscade offshore, and 16 mortars. Their Milan Platoon was able to direct precision-guided missiles onto Argentinian emplacements, and six machine guns set up a withering hail of fire. 2 Para also had the invaluable help of two Scorpion and two Scimitar light tanks, armed respectively with 76mm and 30mm cannon and machine guns; they were able to keep pace and supply covering fire over the heads of the advancing paras.
The assault on Wireless Ridge is now regarded as a superb example of the proper deployment of well-supported, trained infantry.

Now began the longest and most difficult part of the operation. D Company was to roll up two Argentinian positions on the final ridgeline from the flank. On the approach they ran into a minefield, and again there was no option but to go through. Once more the firepower had proved too much for the Argentinians and they had abandoned the first position, leaving behind a considerable amount of equipment, including a 106mm recoilless rifle. The company was beginning to advance along the ridge behind our artillery fire when disaster struck. In the confusion of battle, the artillery forward observation officer called for fire on the wrong target number and several salvoes crashed around D Company before the fire could be stopped. Fortunately no-one was killed, but the attack was broken up and it took 45 minutes to reorganise and recheck the tasks of the artillery.

D Company's advance then continued, still undetected by the Argentinians who were directing their fire towards A and B Companies and the tanks; at one stage I had to withdraw the tanks to the reverse slope as they were attracting too much fire. With 90m to go.

Left: One of the four Argentinian 155mm Model 77 howitzers deployed in the defence of Stanley: they were the heaviest ground artillery of the war. Below: On 14 June 2 Para advanced from Moody Brook to become the first British unit to enter Stanley after the documents of surrender had been signed by General Menendez.

surprise was lost when a D Company soldier fired a flare and, instinctively, the whole company went to ground. However, with their commander Phil Neame very much to the fore, the company got up and resumed the advance, charging into the enemy positions.

By now the mortars and artillery had run out of illuminating rounds and so the Royal Navy was asked to provide light for the attack. Soon starshells from the frigate began to light up the night sky as artillery shells crashed in amongst the rocks; lines of tracer crossed the valley, ricocheting off the rocks into the darkness. Above the barrage could be heard the intermittent *whoosh* of a Milan missile and the deeper crack of the tanks' 76mm guns and 30mm Rarden cannon, as the British fire sought out the Argentinian positions.

At first light D Company was well dug in when the Argentinians launched a counter-attack, the only one of the campaign. This was quickly broken up. Just then I heard that Mount Tumbledown had fallen to the Scots Guards after some extremely tough fighting. This was a relief as we were very vulnerable to attack from that quarter.

In a completely impromptu gesture, helmets came off and the paras put on their red berets

It had taken 10 hours to capture Wireless Ridge and, standing on the final objective as dawn rose, we were greeted by the most amazing sight – the complete collapse of the Argentinian Army. Suddenly, several hundred of them, like black ants, were coming off Tumbledown and Sapper Hill across the valley, and out of Moody Brook below us, and walking back to Port Stanley. The break had come and our priority was now to get into Port Stanley before they reorganised. I ordered A and B Companies forward and we began pouring fire down into the valley. The BC asked for, and got, additional fire support. The tanks and machine-gun platoon were now up, and I requested an air strike. This was refused due to the bad weather, but Captain John Greenhalgh, our Scout helicopter pilot, appeared with two more Scouts and engaged an artillery battery across the valley with their SS11 missiles.

The Argentinian defeat was now complete and I ordered a ceasefire. The brigade commander, Brigadier Julian Thompson, arrived behind the ridge in a helicopter and, seeing me in the open, rushed out and pulled me towards cover. I said, 'It's OK, Brigadier, it's all over; we must get into Port Stanley.' He took stock of the situation and immediately gave us the go-ahead.

B Company passed through Moody Brook to the high ground on the other side and then A Company took the Port Stanley road. In a completely impromptu gesture, crumpled berets came out of pockets and pouches, steel helmets came off and the paras put on their red berets. And so, at 1300 hours, 14 June 1982, the exhaustion and tension of battle forgotten, the battalion's leading elements entered Port Stanley – the first British troops to be in the town since the Argentinian invasion 11 weeks before. Our euphoria in victory was tempered only by sadness for the dead we had left behind.

THE AUTHOR Lieutenant-Colonel David Chaundler, was Commanding Officer of the 2nd Battalion, The Parachute Regiment at Wireless Ridge, on East Falkland 13/14 June 1982.

Supporting 5 Infantry Brigade in the Falklands, the combat engineers of 9 Parachute Squadron, RE, were as versatile in battle as they were ingenious in military construction

AMONG THE FIRST professional soldiers of the British Army were the engineers, who gained their familiar name of 'sappers' from the 'saps', or trenches, that they dug to breach the walls of cities under siege. From the beginning, the sappers were tough and idiosyncratic men, combining skill and fortitude with courage and a dour determination, slaving away while the rest of the army waited.

The sapper can be described as a landscaper who alters the terrain to his force's best advantage. As a combat engineer in the attack, he builds bridges and roads, clearing safe routes through the minefields and obstacles of the enemy. In defence, he alters the landscape to make it difficult for the attacker by digging ditches, laying barbed-wire obstacles and sowing minefields. In battle, he is in the thick of the fighting, becoming an infantryman when his sapper tasks are completed.

In the Falklands War of 1982, three squadrons of Royal Engineers carried out hard and dangerous work with the same grim resolution that had characterised their forbears. These were 9 Parachute Squadron, 59 Independent Commando Squadron

Below: Members of 9 Parachute Squadron, RE, are photographed at their barracks at Aldershot during the hectic preparations for the voyage south. In the foreground (left to right) are Sapper 'Jaws' Dunkely, Staff Sergeant Bob Latham, Captain Freddie Kemp and Corporal 'Gaz' Doyle. Bottom: Lieutenant Peter McManners prepares to explode an armed Sidewinder air-to-air missile near Bluff Cove. He is using Cordtex fuze and PE4 plastic explosive for the task.

and 11 Field Squadron and, together with a team from 49 Explosives Ordnance Disposal Squadron, they worked and fought in appalling conditions, clearing safe routes through minefields and completing a wide range of essential construction tasks.

The sappers of 9 Parachute Squadron are volunteers from other units of the Royal Engineers. To qualify, they must first pass the exacting P Company selection tests of The Parachute Regiment, followed by the parachute jumps course. The men remain with the squadron from two to four years at a time. Soldiers first and foremost, many of the para sappers are fierce competitors, and they often win contests of shooting, speed-marching and other basic military disciplines. They have a reputation for being particularly experienced parachutists, and they were selected to test jump the prototype light-scale harness system.

Each man also has a third skill, that of an artisan tradesman. Included among the comprehensive sapper trades are painter and decorator, carpenter and joiner, bricklayer, welder, blacksmith, plant operator, mechanic, fitter, electrician and so on. These artisan skills are maintained at a very high level, and sappers are very much in demand on

FIRST IN
LAST OUT

9 PARACHUTE SQUADRON, RE

The unit that is known today as 9 Parachute Squadron, RE, (see badge above) was raised in Chatham in 1787 as the Chatham Company. Retitled 9 Field Company in 1899, it fought with the 7th Division in the Boer War and with the 4th Division in France in World War I. In June 1942 the unit was redesignated 9 Field Company (Airborne), and on 19 November volunteers from the company took part in Operation Freshman, a glider-borne attack on the Vermork heavy water plant near Rjukan in Norway. Tragically, the two gliders crashed and the survivors were either shot on the landing zone or captured and executed by the Gestapo. No-one survived. As part of the 1st Air-Landing Brigade, 9 Field Company took part in Operation Fustian, an airborne assault designed to capture the Ponte Grande north of Syracuse in Sicily. Going in on 9 July 1943, the 129 gliders were scattered, many landing in the sea, yet 73 members of the company reached the bridge and helped defend it against determined German counter-attacks. Only 19 men survived. At Arnhem, 9 Field Company members were with 2 Para on the bridge and at Oosterbeek. Finally named 9 Parachute Squadron in 1977, the unit is now part of 36 Engineer Regiment. Based at Rhine Barracks, Aldershot, the squadron has a headquarters troop and three field troops, each of about 40 officers and men, plus a support troop. The squadron supports 5 Airborne Brigade in its operations outside Europe. Its field troops are normally divided, one to each of the three battalions of the brigade.

civilian building sites when they leave the army.

Following the outbreak of war in the Falklands, 2 Troop of 9 Squadron sailed south as part of 3 Commando Brigade on 26 April 1982. The rest of the squadron sailed in *Queen Elizabeth 2 (QE2)* on 12 May 1982 as part of the re-organised 5 Infantry Brigade. The war had already started with the recapture of South Georgia on 25 April and 2 Troop's voyage south involved hard physical training and the sharpening of skills. Worryingly, the sappers had minimal data on Argentinian mines, although they did possess an Italian sales leaflet that provided chilling details of special anti-handling fuzes which would make any sort of detection or investigation potentially fatal. Later, Lance-Corporal 'Jonah' Jones went on a patrol to Mount Longdon to collect a couple of mines for examination, killing an Argentinian sentry with a 66mm anti-tank rocket in the process.

As the bulk of the squadron sailed south, it received sobering news from the war zone. A Sea King helicopter had ditched, killing 22 members of the SAS, and an ex-9 Squadron man, 'Lofty' Gallagher, was among those missing. Not long after, they heard that Lance-Corporal Hare of 2 Troop had been seriously wounded while on patrol with 3 Para.

After transferring in bad weather from *QE2* to *Canberra* off South Georgia, the squadron arrived at Port San Carlos and disembarked in LCUs at dawn on 2 June. Ahead of the main body, 2 Troop under Captain Robbie Burns was already ashore and had completed the long walk to Port Stanley with 3 Commando Brigade (2 Troop claims to be the only 3 Commando Brigade unit to walk all the way to Stanley). Following them, 5 Infantry Brigade was to advance eastward to Port Stanley along the southern flank.

'Suddenly the side of the ship opened as an unexploded bomb or rocket crashed through'

The sapper squadron's 3 Troop, commanded by Lieutenant Peter McManners, the author's younger brother, set out with the Scots Guards aboard HMS *Intrepid* on the night of 5/6 June. It was a six-hour trip and, huddling in the bows to escape the worst of the waves, the men were too cramped and cold even to be seasick. Then a British warship, unaware of the operation, illuminated them with starshell. They finally arrived at Lively Island, south of Choiseul Sound, and transferred into LCUs for the long, wet run into Bluff Cove. The sappers landed at the mouth of Bluff Cove and walked the two miles to the settlement in horizontal, wind-driven rain. For the next eight days 3 Troop worked hard to build a water point capable of providing sufficient good water for the sudden huge increase in numbers at Bluff Cove. Water had to be pumped from a stream, purified and installed in a storage tank.

On the night of 6/7 June, Squadron Headquarters and 1 Troop sailed round to Fitzroy on RFA *Sir Tristram*. There, 1 Troop had to repair a bridge blown up by the Argentinians before the advance to Port Stanley. Lieutenant Jon Mullin described the task:

'Captain Richard Willett's Troop completed a

phenomenal job. Thirty metres of bridging with welded joints carried out in the most appalling wet, windy Falklands weather. The welding had to be done underneath a poncho shelter. It showed spectacular ingenuity.'

Mullin very narrowly escaped death in the costly air raids at Bluff Cove:

'I was in the landing craft, alongside the *Galahad*. Suddenly the side of the ship opened as an unexploded bomb or rocket crashed through, 10yds in front of me. There was a roar of jet engines and I hit the deck. I saw the plastic packing from the bombs floating down towards our craft. I assumed they were anti-personnel bombs and that this was it for us. Then there was abject chaos. We started to get the injured out.'

There were two sappers killed and eight wounded.

In spite of the tragedy, operations continued. From 3 Troop, Corporal 'Ginge' Ford with Sappers Mark Sankey and 'Tich' Fortuin accompanied a Scots Guards patrol to Port Harriet House. The house was used as a covert base from which to patrol, and they attempted to locate minefields and suspected Argentinian radar and gun sites. The house was overlooked by enemy positions, but by moving at night they avoided discovery.

After several days, rations – especially hexamine cooking blocks – were running out. Each sapper carried five pounds of plastic explosive, and this they burned, in very small quantities, to make sustaining – and very quick! – brews.

The patrol remained at Port Harriet House until a light helicopter, landing by the house to pick up the patrol commander in order to fly him to a battalion orders group, blew their cover. The Argentinians put down a heavy mortar and artillery barrage and a platoon advanced to attack. The patrol

Below: From a helicopter hovering low over the surface, a para engineer searches for Argentinian minelayers' pegs. Right: Members of 9 Para Squadron at San Carlos, including Lieutenant McManners (left), Staff Sergeant Dave Floyd (fourth from left) and Captain Bill Dick, squadron quartermaster (right). Below right: This FV101 Scorpion of the Blues and Royals was crippled by an Argentinian anti-tank mine. Bottom right: 9 Para Squadron transloads from *QE2* to *Canberra* at South Georgia.

9 Parachute Squadron, RE
Falklands, June-July 1982

Port San Carlos
Douglas
Ajax Bay
Teal Inlet
San Carlos
Big Mt
Mt Simon
Sussex Mts
▲ Mt Estancia   Murrell river
▲ Mt Kent
FALKLAND   EAST FALKLAND
SOUND   Two Sisters ▲   ▲ Mt Longdon
▲
Mt Usborne   Mt Harriet ▲   ▲▲▲ • Stanley
Wickham Heights   Sapper Hill
Bluff Cove
Darwin   Fitzroy •   • Mt Tumbledown
• Goose Green   Mt William

CHOISEUL SOUND

decided to withdraw and, with Corporal Ford in charge, they moved south over high ground to the coast, chased by mortar fire. Sapper Sankey was hit by shrapnel, breaking his ankle, and the Scots Guardsmen suffered casualties as well. The patrol was picked up by a helicopter of No.656 Squadron, Army Air Corps.

On 13 June, 1 Troop finished repairing the Fitzroy Bridge and turned to building an air-portable bridge for the Murrell River. On completion, this was lifted by Chinook from Fitzroy on improvised slings and positioned by 59 Independent Commando Squadron. Such an operation had never been done before and it was very much more complex than can be described here. Suffice it to say that the delivery was rather hairy.

It was the plan of 5 Brigade to attack Port Stanley from the south, in a right hook from Port Harriet to Sapper Hill. However, when Corporal Hick Casswell and his section reconnoitred the route they found mines, their borrowed vehicle losing a front wheel. Sergeant Rob Brewerton confirmed that it was a large minefield that would take 3 Troop at least one night to breach. The operational plan was therefore changed, and it was decided to go across the saddle of Goat Ridge and Mount Tumbledown, along the flank of the ground already taken by 3 Commando Brigade. In order to divert Argentinian attention

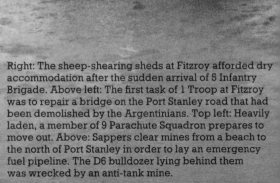

Right: The sheep-shearing sheds at Fitzroy afforded dry accommodation after the sudden arrival of 5 Infantry Brigade. Above left: The first task of 1 Troop at Fitzroy was to repair a bridge on the Port Stanley road that had been demolished by the Argentinians. Top left: Heavily laden, a member of 9 Parachute Squadron prepares to move out. Above: Sappers clear mines from a beach to the north of Port Stanley in order to lay an emergency fuel pipeline. The D6 bulldozer lying behind them was wrecked by an anti-tank mine.

away from their approach route, a diversionary attack from the south was planned, including a troop of Scorpion and Scimitar CVR(T)s (combat vehicle reconnaissance, tracked) from the Blues and Royals, and Headquarters Company of the Scots Guards, accompanied by Corporal Paddy Foran and Lance-Corporal John Pashley.

While the Scots Guards' objective was Tumbledown, the next feature along, Mount William, was to be taken by 1st Battalion, 7th Gurkha Rifles. Meeting the Gurkhas on the afternoon of their attack, Sunday 13 June, Lieutenant Peter McManners, commander of 3 Troop, informed them that their route took them through a minefield. However, a change of plan at this late stage seemed likely to cause as many casualties as the mines, and it was decided to go ahead. Corporal 'Adge' Iles and his section were to lead the Gurkha battalion through, clearing the minefield as they went.

The Officer Commanding, Major Chris Davies, was realistic:

'I thought the battle for Tumbledown would last more than one night and that there would be a lot of casualties. I knew from the bombing of *Galahad* the effect of casualties on the rest of a troop.

'I expected that the 3 Troop commander, Peter McManners, would be killed in the attack. I wanted someone able to grip the troop im-mediately if this happened and keep them going. The Squadron Sergeant-Major came up front with me ready to take over from Peter if necessary.' McManners went forward with the Scots Guards and kept two sections back on the start line in reserve. He now had sappers on either side of the ridge to deal with any mines that might be encountered.

The diversionary attack from the south went in with the two sappers out in front clearing a path through the minefield. The CVR(T)s, following a separate route, struck mines, lost a vehicle and withdrew. Then the main party was hit by machine-gun fire and Lance-Corporal Pashley was killed. This was a nightmare – the men were caught in the middle of a minefield at night and taking casualties. Two Guardsmen, blown up by mines, had lost their legs.

Corporal Foran crawled to the injured men and gave them first aid. Prodding a safe path out of the minefield with his bayonet, he led the patrol, which now had several seriously wounded, to safety. He never talked about this terrifying experience afterwards, but the story emerged from others and he was awarded the Military Medal.

Meanwhile, Corporal Iles and his section, leading the Gurkha battalion, were aware that their para helmets could be mistaken for Argentinian by the men following up. Knowing no Gurkhali, they looped

CLEARING THE MINEFIELDS

According to the Geneva Convention, minefields are supposed to be marked. Often they are not, making mine clearance a very much more dangerous task. First of all, a two-foot wide strip through the minefield is cleared by a sapper officer on his hands and knees, using a wire feeler to detect trip-wires and a metal prodder and bare hands to feel for anti-personnel mines. The strip is carefully marked with white tape.

Anti-tank mines are sown with anti-personnel mines and booby traps to kill or injure foot soldiers. They are also carefully placed to blow up sappers attempting to make a breach. Often a small anti-personnel mine is buried halfway along a trip-wire to catch the sapper as he feels gingerly along the wire for the booby trap at the end. In a silent night attack, the sapper lifts the mines and lays them to one side. Otherwise he attaches a hook and line to each, crawls back 20yds and pulls sharply, blowing any attendant booby traps. Once a two-foot strip has been cleared to the far side of the minefield, the troop, in parties of five, widens the strip using the same laborious and nerve straining techniques. Two men work in front feeling and clearing, one remains in the middle controlling the operation, and two bring up the rear with metal detectors searching for anti-tank mines.

MINES IN THE FALKLAND ISLANDS

While the British forces laid no mines during the Falklands War, over 12,000 mines of various manufacture were laid by the Argentinians.

The majority of these were Spanish non-metallic mines. The round, fat P4B anti-personnel mine is two inches in diameter, and its only metal components are a foil sliver and the percussion cap spring. Impossible to detect with metal-detecting equipment, this type caused most of the casualties and the sappers were extremely wary of them. Troop Commander Lieutenant Jon Mullin gave a terse description of their effects: 'If you stood on one with only your toe you lost your foot and ankle; with your heel, you lost your whole leg – either just above or just below the knee.' The Spanish C3B anti-tank mine, a foot in diameter with its fuze mounted in the top, destroyed several British vehicles, including a Scorpion CVR(T) during the battle for Mount Tumbledown.

The Italian SB33, described by OC 59 Commando Squadron Major Rod MacDondald as 'a high-explosive dog turd' is a sensitive, well camouflaged anti-personnel mine. It can be scattered and operates on both its front and back. The Italian SB81 anti-tank mine can be scattered by helicopter.

The Argentinian FMK1 anti-personnel mine was small, crude and not very effective. It was screwed into the top of the larger FMK3.

Other mines found in the Falklands were the US M1 1944 anti-tank mine of World War II and Israeli No.4 anti-personnel and No.6 anti-tank mines, the latter possibly of Soviet origin.

An Argentinian minefield usually consisted of two to six panels of mines in a straight or dog-legged line. Each panel was 35yds long by 27yds deep and contained about 24 mines.

Above: The FMK1 (with yellow strap) and (bottom left) P4B anti-personnel mines and (centre) the C3B anti-tank mine.

Left: A para engineer undergoes infantry training in Belize. Although the men of 9 Para Squadron are soldiers first and foremost, they are also versed in all the skills of conventional Royal Engineer units. Far left: A cover-from-view screen is constructed from 'wriggly tin' around a security base in Northern Ireland. Below left: A Bedford MK truck lays a 150ft Laird Class 30 Trackway. Bottom: The frame goes up for a 'bund' around a Harrier site at Belize airfield. Eventually the aircraft will be protected from bombs by a 20ft-high concrete wall.

white mine tape over their backs and equipment as a recognition symbol. Peter McManners noted that 'they had yards and yards of the stuff hanging down around their knees'. Tales of sharpened kukris had been taken seriously.

A proper clearing of the minefield through which 'Adge' Iles was to lead the Gurkhas would have taken two days. He had time only to walk steadily through – taking the risk of buried mines – rather than crawling slowly. To detect the tripwires of booby traps he would have to rely on a length of wire similar to a straightened coathanger.

The battle for Mount Tumbledown was cold, hard and brutal. After being shelled several times, Peter McManners and his team crossed the start line immediately behind the leading company, together with Lieutenant-Colonel Mike Scott, the CO of the Scots Guards. It was a dark night and the action was confusing on the steep and uneven slopes of Tumbledown. Progress was hampered, not by mines this time, but by the difficulty of bringing fire to bear on an enemy perched above in rocky outcrops and of clearing out determined Argentinian snipers and machine-gun teams.

From Mount Tumbledown, as the Scots Guards' battle continued, McManners watched the Gurkhas move through, 500 men in single file following Adge Iles and his section. Iles' number two, following immediately behind and ready to take over if he was blown up, was Sapper 'Seth' Roose, aged 17. Iles stuck absolutely to the planned rate of advance and, since the Scots Guards were delayed by fierce enemy resistance, the Gurkhas moved too far ahead up the ridge and had to make a careful withdrawal before the enemy noticed. Once the Gurkhas were through, Corporal Iles reported to Lieutenant McManners on Tumbledown. His section had walked calmly, often under shell-fire, across a medium-density minefield. Iles was Mentioned in Despatches. Sergeant Graham Strettle, Lance-Corporal 'Scouse' Williams and Sapper Mal Mallett, also of 3 Troop, had spent the night carrying wounded under fire off Tumbledown.

In the latter days of the war, mines had been literally thrown about by hand and left unmarked

At dawn on 14 June, Sergeant Ron Wrega led the Gurkhas onto Mount William. As they went, he neutralised anti-personnel mines and booby traps, despite heavy shelling. At the same time, 3 Troop began to prepare for the fight through the town of Stanley, and plastic explosives were unpacked ready to make satchel charges for blowing entries into buildings. But the declaration of a ceasefire that same day made all further preparations superfluous.

Their military duties completed, the sappers immediately switched from combat engineer tasks to civil engineer tasks. That night, 3 Troop returned to Bluff Cove to collect water purification equipment needed at Fitzroy, which was short of water.

The town of Stanley and the surrounding countryside were in a hell of a state. Clearing up was started by 59 Independent Commando Squadron, which then left with 3 Commando Brigade. The airfield and the town buildings had to be cleared of all booby traps and munitions, and the runway repaired for RAF Hercules aircraft to land there. This latter task was completed by Corporal 'Ginge' Ford.

Naval gunfire, brought down on the town late in the war by the author of this article, had destroyed the

roof of the water-pumping station, causing the valves, filters and pipes to freeze up and split. Appallingly bad weather had defeated the civilian engineers, but Corporal Iles and his section took only 24 hours in a blizzard to rebuild the walls and the roof. The pipes were thawed out and kept from freezing up again by heaters from 3 Troop's own accommodation.

Lieutenant Jon Mullin took over the problem of the minefields from the departing 59 Squadron. He aimed, by the time he had left the islands, to have accurately recorded the locations and boundaries of all the minefields and to have fenced off their perimeters. First, the fields had to be accurately mapped. The help of the Argentinian sappers who had laid the minefields was sought, and it was found that documentation was reasonable for some of the fields but non-existent for others – in the latter days of the war, mines had been literally thrown about by hand and left unmarked. Mullin studied an Argentinian minelaying pamphlet found at Bluff Cove and interrogated the prisoners in order to understand the theory behind their placing of mines. He found that they used peg and line, the line marked off at intervals with metal rings to denote where each mine should be placed. Unfortunately, each layer's line seemed to be different. However, once the Argentinian charts had been compared with British maps and the positions of the minefields confirmed by an Argentinian sapper, a reasonably accurate picture of the situation emerged.

On his last afternoon before repatriation, an Argentinian lieutenant pointed out a large culvert mine under the road into Stanley, its command detonation wire leading onto the hillside. On excavation the following day it was discovered that the main charge of two aircraft bombs was covered by two C3B anti-tank mines, with five-kilogram pressure fuzes laying on TNT. The Argentinians, and later the British, had been walking and driving over this lethal bomb, and it had failed to explode only because the ground was frozen hard.

The last few suspected minefields were defined by flying just above the ground very slowly in helicopters, looking for the minelayers' pegs. Snow fell, and on 8 July the Argentinian prisoners of war went home. The minefield markers could not be seen and so the bulk of the work had to stop.

The main body of 9 Parachute Squadron left the Falklands on 17 July and the last man out, Lieutenant Jon Mullin, flew out on the 30th. The homecoming was a huge relief to all.

In the autumn of 1982 the squadron was posted on an emergency tour to Belize, where a huge programme of civil engineering tasks awaited them. Meanwhile, in the Falklands, the sapper work continued. Major Chris Davies sums up modestly:

'I was relieved that all we had to do was fight the war. For the sapper squadrons that followed us, winning the peace was very much harder. The war relied upon some expertise and lots of raw courage. The peace required expertise – and lots of it.'

THE AUTHOR Major Hugh McManners, as a captain, was one of the Naval Gunfire Observers of 148 Commando Forward Observation Battery, Royal Artillery, during the Falklands campaign of 1982. He is author of the book *Falklands Commando*.

The author and editor would like to thank Lieutenant-Colonel Chris Davies and Captain Jon Mullin and Peter McManners for their help in the preparation of this article.

PARAS UNDER FIRE

The Israeli 202nd Parachute Brigade which led the advance into the Gaza Strip during the Six-Day War of 1967, found the defenders ready for a fight

Above: Lieutenant-Colonel Eitan (right), the commander of Israel's 202nd Parachute Brigade during the Six-Day War, in conference with General Tal. Below: Under fire from an Egyptian sniper, paras take cover in a half-track.

MAKING A PARA

The men of Israel's regular paratrooper brigade have always been considered the elite of the Israeli armed forces. To maintain the formation's excellent fighting record, new recruits are put through an exhaustive training programme that pushes them to the limits of their endurance.

After induction, each volunteer is sent on a basic course that is designed to build up his fitness and develop his combat skills. Particular emphasis is placed on both day and nightfighting techniques. Those men who pass this first stage are then sent on a parachuting course.

After this period, the new paratrooper embarks on a course devised to improve his knowledge of combined operations. Joint manoeuvres with tank and artillery units are organised, and each recruit is taught how to work with helicopters, assault craft and armoured personnel carriers.

The next stage of training is the squad commander course, in which the recruit learns the vital skills of a junior NCO. All paratroopers attend this programme and are then assigned to different roles.

Each man is taught a specialised skill including communications, demolition techniques and medical procedures. A percentage of recruits is selected to attend Officer School where they are groomed for higher command.

After serving with the brigade, each paratrooper remains on the reserve list for a number of years. During this time, he undertakes refresher courses at the School of Infantry.

DURING THE Six-Day War of June 1967 I had the honour of commanding the 202nd Parachute Brigade of the Israeli Defence Forces. One of the most outstanding and professional units in Israel's army, it was destined to play an important role in the battles to eject the Egyptians from the Gaza Strip and Sinai.

Tensions in the area had been building for some time before the war began, and both we and the Egyptians had been mobilising our troops. By the beginning of June, the Egyptian commander, General Abdel Mohsen Mortagui, had massed some 100,000 men and 950 tanks in Sinai. As our troops were completing their preparations for our offensive, code-named Red Sheet, I discovered what role we would play in the action. As part of the force led by Major-General Israel Tal, my brigade was ordered to clear the Gaza Strip.

During the previous weeks, Mortagui had fed more troops into the Strip, and our intelligence services had identified Major-General Mohammed Hasni's 20th (Palestinian) Infantry Division and the 7th Infantry Division under Major-General Abdel Aziz Soliman in the area. The enemy had 150 Sherman, T34 and Josef Stalin III tanks to stiffen the defences.

Less than 12 hours before the start of the operation, on the evening of 4 June, I asked Major-General Tal to consider a last-minute change of strategy. I thought that my paratroopers should make a wide, sweeping attack around the southern edge of the enemy's defences at Rafah, and then head northwards to take their positions from the rear. Tal agreed to my suggestions and I was told to attack at the same time as the 7th Armoured Brigade, led by Colonel Shmuel Gonen, made its move from the northeast, near the town of Khan Yunis.

After leaving the meeting I made my final dispositions. I had decided to attack in four groups: the reconnaissance troops in the lead, the paras following, and the 30 AMX13 tanks of Colonel Amnon Reshef protecting the flanks. I placed the brigade HQ in the centre. I knew the fighting would be hard; the Egyptians had thrown two infantry brigades, lavishly backed by artillery, into the defence of Rafah, and had posted a company of Stalin tanks along the road to the south. All was ready.

Shortly before 0800 hours on 5 June, I saw our jets

Above: A combat patrol, foot-slogging through a deserted town, moves out on a mopping-up operation. **Below:** Led by Super Shermans, paras in half-tracks begin the race for the Suez Canal. **Right:** A welcome respite for jeep-borne infantry in Sinai.

streaking towards Sinai and knew that the war had begun. Moments later, the order to start our attack, Red Sheet, was broadcast. The main problem I encountered during the advance was in trying to keep the different formations in order. One of the tank units diverted a little to the west of the planned route and ran into an Egyptian force. A tank was hit, but the black smoke rising from its shattered hull showed where we were to swing north behind the enemy's front line. Our luck held after this first encounter; the young, but highly competent, officer in

charge of our armour spotted the Stalin tanks and destroyed them in only three minutes, and then continued to drive forward.

Striking the first Egyptian brigade side on, my right flank units met with fierce resistance from an enemy holding a series of heavily fortified trenches. The troops on the other flank, however, scythed through the poorly-held rear areas and quickly reached the road between Rafah and El Arish.

Meanwhile, I had taken up position with the brigade HQ in the middle of the battlefield. Suddenly, we found ourselves separated from the other troops and fighting for our lives against the enemy's rear-guard, supported by artillery and mortars.

Holding a radio set in one hand and a sub-machine gun in the other, I informed the divisional commander of our difficulties

I decided to inform the divisional commander of our progress and present situation. Holding a radio set in one hand and a sub-machine gun in the other, I informed him of our difficulties.

After hearing my report, punctuated by bursts of fire, he wanted to despatch an armoured unit to my aid. I told him that the crisis would pass and we would defeat the enemy without any further help. However, it took another two hours of vicious fighting before I was able to reform my force.

Once under control, I ordered the left flank force to join my HQ troops and then push towards the Rafah junction. This point was the northern edge of the enemy's defences, and by taking this objective I hoped to ease the pressure on my right flank force as it pushed up from the south. Between us lay over four kilometres of enemy-held territory.

Once at the junction, I established a communication base and radioed the commander of my southern

Securing the Gaza Strip
Eitan's Parachute Brigade, June 1967

At 0745 local time on 5 June 1967, Israel's devastating airstrike against Egypt was launched. Minutes later, Operation Red Sheet — the invasion of Sinai — began with Israel Tal's attack on the Rafah stronghold at the southern end of the Gaza strip. As the Israeli armour went in, Eitan's para brigade moved on Rafah from the rear.

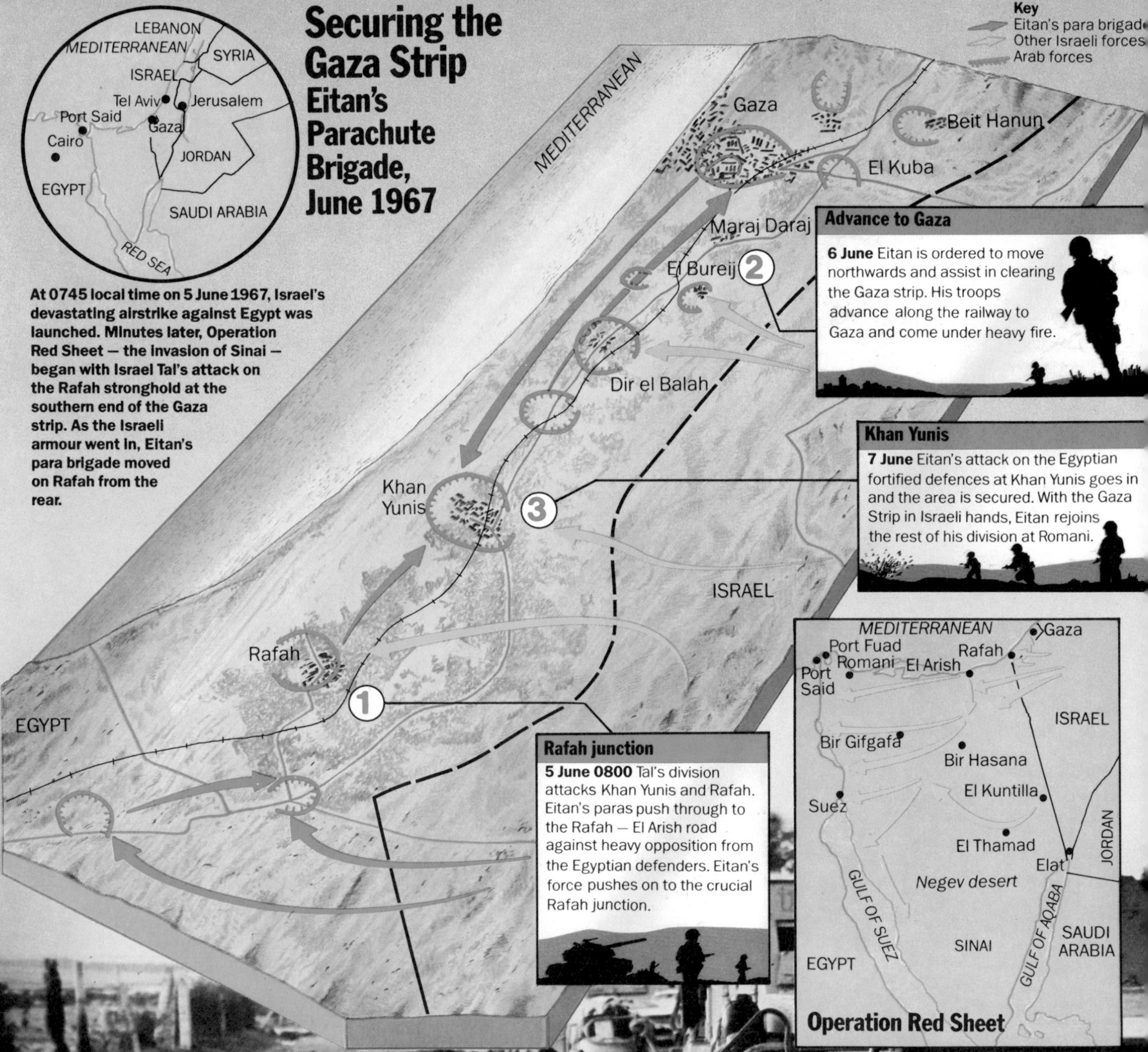

134

Key
Eitan's para brigade
Other Israeli forces
Arab forces

MEDITERRANEAN

Gaza
Beit Hanun
El Kuba
Maraj Daraj
El Bureij
Dir el Balah
Khan Yunis
ISRAEL
Rafah
EGYPT

(inset locator map)
LEBANON
MEDITERRANEAN
SYRIA
ISRAEL
Tel Aviv
Jerusalem
Port Said
Gaza
JORDAN
Cairo
EGYPT
SAUDI ARABIA
RED SEA

Advance to Gaza
6 June Eitan is ordered to move northwards and assist in clearing the Gaza strip. His troops advance along the railway to Gaza and come under heavy fire.

Khan Yunis
7 June Eitan's attack on the Egyptian fortified defences at Khan Yunis goes in and the area is secured. With the Gaza Strip in Israeli hands, Eitan rejoins the rest of his division at Romani.

Rafah junction
5 June 0800 Tal's division attacks Khan Yunis and Rafah. Eitan's paras push through to the Rafah — El Arish road against heavy opposition from the Egyptian defenders. Eitan's force pushes on to the crucial Rafah junction.

Operation Red Sheet
MEDITERRANEAN
Port Fuad
Romani
Gaza
Port Said
El Arish
Rafah
ISRAEL
Bir Gifgafa
Bir Hasana
Suez
El Kuntilla
GULF OF SUEZ
El Thamad
Elat
JORDAN
Negev desert
GULF OF AQABA
EGYPT
SINAI
SAUDI ARABIA

Although the frontline Arab states have voiced their opposition to the continued existence of an independent Israel in their midst almost as an act of faith, the more immediate causes of the Six-Day War of 1967 are to be found in the volatile internal politics of Israel's neighbours and the often fraught international relationships that characterise Middle Eastern affairs.

During the early 1960s, Egypt's president Nasser sought to find a long-term solution to the question in a series of summits. Arab accord, however, proved elusive and several states, most notably Saudi Arabia, were unhappy with Nasser's 'revolutionary' style. At the 1964 Arab Summit, the PLO was created and Yasser Arafat's group, Fatah, dedicated to a military solution to the problem, launched a series of guerrilla raids that prompted the Israelis into retaliatory cross-border actions. The Syrians, who bore the brunt of Israel's response, asked Nasser for tangible military aid, and, against a background of popular support, the president ordered the mobilisation of Egypt's armed forces.

During the latter part of May 1967, the Egyptians deployed in Sinai and requested the removal of the United Nations peace-keeping force which had been manning observation posts along the Egyptian-Israeli border, since 1956. On 22 May, the Straits of Tiran were closed to Israeli shipping and, at the end of the month, the Arab states formalised a mutual defence pact.

The Israelis, faced with hostile forces along their borders, responded by mobilising the Israeli Defence Forces. Unable to maintain such a large force in the field without crippling the economy, the Israelis prepared to launch a pre-emptive strike.

force to get a clearer picture of the situation. He reported heavy casualties, adding that he also was wounded. We tried to evacuate the worst cases by helicopter. I knew that the battle rested on a knife edge and determined to reach the southern force at all costs.

After forming a plan, I called over the senior tank commander, and said: 'We will move with your tanks to the south, straight against the Egyptians and join our southern forces.' He answered: 'We only have enough fuel for one hour, and there are some tanks without ammunition.' I replied: 'We go! Tanks low on fuel will move as far as they can, and those without ammunition will not shoot.'

As if by magic, hundreds of Egyptians left their trenches and fled to the west. We took many of these men prisoner.

I jumped into the leading vehicle and the whole force, consisting of no more than five tanks, roared into action. The move was decisive. Despite heavy opposition, we reached our fellow paratroopers at sunset. As if by magic, hundreds of Egyptians left their trenches and fled to the west. We took many of these men prisoner and those that escaped were later caught by other units of Tal's division in the El Arish area. After clearing the area, we returned to the junction at Rafah to prepare for the next day's fighting. In fact, only one tank made it back, the rest ran out of fuel.

At nightfall, the various units of my command had taken up position at the junction and, though we were all exhausted, we worked until midnight. It was at this point that a young officer came forward to tell me that my nephew had been killed. Although the news was a sad blow, I could not show my true feelings to my men, so I thanked the officer and went back to work.

It was during these hours that I learned the full

Above: Mobility and firepower in action. A pair of AMX13 tanks leading an Israeli column through the Gaza Strip. Below left: Paras snatch some sleep.

story of the right flank force's fight. One of the stories I heard is carved in my memory. As the bitter fighting continued, our wounded were collected by medical personnel and treated in an abandoned trench. Suddenly, an enemy tank appeared from nowhere and bore down on the wounded. Only the medical orderlies were fit enough to fight the tank, and one of them lifted a bazooka, firing at the Stalin III when it was less than 10m away. The shell did not harm the monster, but the noise and impact were enough to force the Egyptians to leave the vehicle.

When I was absolutely sure that all my instructions had been carried out to the letter, I stretched out on the bonnet of a vehicle to get some much-needed rest. My thoughts were filled with memories of our families, our losses and my dead nephew.

On the morning of the 6th, I was ordered to leave Tal's armoured division and move my men north to help in clearing the enemy from the Gaza Strip. I was only given very general instructions and, as I had lost radio contact with headquarters, I decided on my own initiative to head north along a railway towards Khan Yunis. As we approached the town, the lead tank rolled over a mine and was disabled. I then moved out to the east of Khan Yunis to avoid any other unpleasant surprises and pressed on towards Gaza. However, one of my units mistakenly entered the town, and came under very heavy and well-directed fire. It would have been a blunder to leave a strong enemy force in our rear, so I resolved to clear Khan Yunis on the following day (7 June).

That night we parked along the main road to the east of the enemy's positions. We had had nothing to eat over the last two days but a quick search revealed several ducks. I was appointed chef. After the meal, we fell asleep in a convenient ditch. In the morning,

WAR PLANS

Because of the potentially dangerous threat posed by hostile Arab states along its borders, Israel has always held that only pre-emptive action, backed by deep thrusts into the enemy's territory, could save the country from annihilation. The strategy pursued by the Israeli High Command during the 1967 war closely adhered to these strategic doctrines.

Charged with evicting the Egyptians from Sinai and establishing a defensible frontier along the Suez Canal, the commander of Israel's southern forces, Major-General Yeshayahu Gavish, organised his troops into a series of armoured 'fists' backed by infantry and artillery.

Following a massive raid by the Israeli Air Force against the enemy's airfields, armoured units were to race through the enemy's first line of defence, and then head for the canal along the coast and from three points in Sinai.

Although both sides fielded a mixture of old and new equipment, the Israelis were markedly superior in handling tactical formations. Unlike the Egyptians, they eschewed the idea of using armour in small formations. On the eve of the war, the Israelis had 680 tanks in pure armoured brigades, whereas the Egyptians had only 350 out of 950 tanks in similar units. At the local scale, the Israelis were likely to hold the numerical and qualitative edge in the opening encounters.

Despite the Israeli Defence Forces' overall numerical inferiority, the general standard of training and the high degree of initiative displayed by junior officers and NCOs more than offset this weakness.

my force was joined by two tanks that had developed mechanical problems during the earlier stages and had lost contact with their unit.

The attack on Khan Yunis went in as planned, and after a brief skirmish we captured key positions and smashed the enemy's will to resist. As the fighting died down, I received an urgent message warning me to expect an attack by enemy units moving down the coast from the north. I was somewhat taken aback by this information, as our troops were reported to have cleared the Gaza Strip the day before.

However, I decided to investigate the sighting and, after arranging a small force of jeeps and tanks, we headed north along the coast. About 2000m from the village of Dir-el-Balah our column halted and I searched the streets for signs of the enemy. Looking through my binoculars, I saw several tank guns turning, aiming in our direction. At the last moment, I realised that the 'enemy' was a force of Israeli tanks.

Immediately, I ordered our tanks to turn and lower their guns in recognition, and the tanks in the village did the same. After verifying the situation, I moved my men back to Khan Yunis to await instructions.

Later in the morning, I received orders from Tal to move south along the coast and head for the Suez Canal. I was informed that an artillery unit was waiting in Romani to join my force.

I spied several Egyptian tanks massing against the jeeps. I warned the commander and he organised a 'reception committee'

The journey along the coast was in stark contrast to the previous two days. Apart from one attack by Egyptian MiG 21s, we saw no sign of the enemy. By noon, we had linked up with the artillery unit at Romani.

I gathered my officers for a briefing and, as we were finalising our plans, several Israeli Mirage jets flew overhead. I was able to contact the jet formation and discovered that its commanding officer was an old friend. Before the war we had agreed that, if I gave him a certain radio call, he would come to my aid. Using the pre-arranged signal, I asked him to fly towards the Suez Canal and search for signs of the enemy. Coming back after several minutes, he reported that there were Egyptians in the city of El Qantara and that his aircraft had destroyed three tanks with cannon fire. I thanked him for his help, and as a parting gesture I asked him to contact my wife to tell her I was well.

We finished all our preparations and I made my dispositions for the advance on El Qantara. With the command unit leading along the road, the jeeps were spread out along the left flank and the tanks and infantry were massed on the right. The troops would be covered by 105mm artillery.

We soon made contact with the enemy. Looking to my left, I spied several Egyptian tanks massing against the jeeps. I immediately warned the commander and he, noting the location of the advancing tanks, organised a 'reception committee'. Taken unawares, the enemy's tanks were dealt with by 106mm recoilless rifles. The action was so swift that we were soon moving forward on our objective.

Looking to the right, I noticed the tell-tale mushroom of smoke that accompanies the firing of an anti-tank missile, and then saw the small red dot that marked its aiming point. Following it with my binoculars, I told my officers that the missile would pass over our vehicle. It did, but another then shattered a telephone post less than five metres from my position. Scanning the ground for the enemy, I saw several Egyptian soldiers lying in a ditch waiting to ambush my right flank units.

Below left: A grim testimony to the ferocity of the Gaza Strip battles. A severely wounded para, the victim of an Egyptian mine, is helped to safety by a comrade. The Israeli armed forces have always tried to ensure the survival of battlefield casualties by providing first-rate medical facilities. Speedy evacuation by helicopter (above) is a vital part of the life-saving process. Above left: Scenes of jubilation outside the town of El Arish at the end of the campaign. Israel's victory was absolute; up to 80 per cent of the enemy's forces in Sinai were destroyed as fighting units.

As I radioed a hurried warning, I was hit by enemy fire and sank to the floor of my armoured vehicle, trying to keep a firm grip on a metal bar. I knew that I was seriously wounded and remember hearing other officers calling for medics. I was laid on the ground and received expert attention while my men silenced the enemy.

The Egyptian forces at El Qantara were smashed and on the fourth day of the war the paras reached the banks of the Suez Canal

I was unable to talk easily, but I signalled for some shade and whispered the name of the officer to take over the command. A little later, I was evacuated by helicopter. After reaching El Arish, I was transferred to a larger aircraft and flown to the hospital at Beer-Sheva. My part in the Six-Day War was over.

Despite losing their commanding officer, my paratroopers stuck to the task. The Egyptian forces at El Qantara were smashed and on the fourth day of the war (8 June) 202nd Para reached the banks of the Suez Canal. Two days later the war was over, and Sinai was firmly under our control. The paratroopers had played their part in our sweeping victory. The Egyptian armed forces were shattered: over 10,000 men had been killed, 20,000 wounded and 5500 captured; some 500 tanks were destroyed and 300 captured; 450 artillery pieces and 10,000 other vehicles were also taken. Our losses were remarkably light: 275 killed and 800 wounded.

THE AUTHOR Rafael Eitan has had a long and distinguished career with the Israeli Defence Forces, taking part in the 1956 War, the Six-Day War of 1967 and the Yom Kippur War of 1973. He is now a member of his country's parliament, the Knesset.

WITH FIXED BAYONETS

During the night of 11/12 June 1982, the men of 3 Para fought one of the bloodiest land actions of the Falklands War, when they fixed bayonets and cleared the Argentinian forces from Mount Longdon. Here, their commander, Lieutenant-Colonel Hew Pike, tells the story of that heroic engagement

COLONEL H.W.R. PIKE, DSO, MBE

Colonel Hew Pike was born in Hampshire on 24 April 1943. He was educated at Winchester College and attended the Royal Military Academy, Sandhurst before being commissioned into The Parachute Regiment in December 1962. From 1962 to 1966 he was platoon commander and then intelligence officer of the 3rd Battalion. During 1966-67 he was ADC to General Sir Kenneth Darling, the the Colonel Commandant of the Regiment, in Wilton and Norway. He was then posted to the 1st Battalion as a Patrol Company officer, and continued to serve with the battalion as adjutant from 1968 to 1970.

After a spell as an instructor on the Platoon Commanders' Course at the School of Infantry 1970-72, Pike commanded 16th Independent Company, The Parachute Regiment (Volunteers), in Lincoln and Loughborough 1972-74. He became Brigade Major of 16th Parachute Brigade in Aldershot 1976-77 and was awarded the MBE at the end of this tour, when he rejoined the 3rd Battalion as a company commander in Northern Ireland and BAOR. He attended the United States Armed Forces Staff College at Norfolk, Virginia, in 1980 before taking command of the 3rd Battalion, in Tidworth, and taking his unit to the Falklands as part of 3 Commando Brigade in April 1982. Colonel Pike was mentioned in despatches for his command of the battalion in Northern Ireland, and was awarded the DSO after the Falklands operation. After a period on the staff at HQ 1st British Corps in Germany, Colonel Pike was appointed Commandant of the Tactics Wing at the School of Infantry.

Left: A para of C Company on Mount Vernet, just before the main assault on Longdon itself.

MOUNT LONGDON

The men of 3 Para went ashore in the Falklands on 21 May, as part of 3 Commando Brigade's landings at San Carlos. Although they were delayed and were late in getting ashore, they had secured their objectives soon after landing.

On 27 May the battalion moved out of the bridgehead and was ordered to advance to Teal Inlet. The paras marched all night, sheltered in the valley of the Arroy Pedro river during the day of the 28th, and that night pushed into Teal Inlet settlement.

The next step was to flush out the 300 enemy said to be at Estancia House to the east. Fortunately, the Argentinian forces had pulled back, and there was no fighting.

So once more the paras advanced, by now desperately tired after the days of marching and the nights without sleep. From Mount Estancia, they took up positions opposite Mount Longdon, and prepared for action.

Mount Longdon was to be attacked as part of the first wave of British assaults on the Argentinian positions covering the Falklands capital, Port Stanley. The other two assaults in this first wave were to take place on Mount Harriet and Two Sisters.

The force holding Mount Longdon was not expected to provide the bitter resistance it did; but British expectations that only one Argentinian company held the position were mistaken. The infantry company from the 7th Infantry Regiment was in fact supported by Special Forces Unit 601 and by Argentinian Marines, while elements of another company of the 7th Infantry arrived during the battle.

The Argentinians were well dug in, and their mutually supporting positions gave the paras a harrowing night of the most intense close-quarters fighting.

FROM OUR new positions, we had a clear view of Stanley and the airport – looking strangely familiar after our careful briefings – though, significantly, the western part of town was hidden behind the fortress-like bulk of a feature we quickly identified as Mount Longdon. Within a day or two we had been joined by a number of Falkland Islanders from Green Patch settlement, with their tractors, trailers and Land Rovers. Terry Peck and Vernon Steen, having taken to the hills from Stanley, had already linked up with us, proving their quality not only as guides, but as men more than willing to die in the cause of their islands' freedom. The new party was led and organised, however, by a most remarkable woman, Trudi Morrison. She did wonders for my morale by addressing me as 'General'!

The weather now turned against us, and it was not until 3 June that an artillery battery could be flown into the area of Mount Estancia, in order to support us forward. From now until the fall of Stanley (14 June 1982), we received regular attention from enemy artillery, and especially from long-range 155mm guns. A high-level night bombing run by Canberra aircraft added to our discomfort, but caused no casualties.

Nothing like this had been undertaken by the battalion for a generation

On 3 June, A and B Companies moved eastwards beneath the shoulder of Mount Kent, in order to establish secure patrolling bases nearer to Mount Longdon which we knew, by now, was to be our next objective. Extensive patrolling, by the patrol company and by fighting patrols from each rifle company, was conducted in the period 3-10 June. A number of clashes with the enemy resulted, and much valuable intelligence was gained, although not in the detail we would have liked. Frequently, D Company's four-man patrols were able to close to within a few metres of Argentinian positions on the mountain. They normally spent two nights out, returning on the second with their information. Our mortars also regularly engaged the enemy in this period, the Mortar Fire Controllers (MFCs) having something of a field day and relishing this unique chance to prove their skills.

Meanwhile, A and B Companies received increasingly accurate fire from enemy artillery, and

one Pucara mission was flown against their positions, all without loss, as the soldiers were becoming well practised in the disciplines of survival. An Argentinian map, later recovered from Government House, showed our positions in red and proved just how accurately the enemy had pinned the locations which now, of course, had been occupied for some days. It was, therefore, with some relief that on the 10th we received the orders to take Mount Longdon on the night of 11/12 June. Nothing like this had been undertaken by the battalion for a generation.

In the darkness and moving by independent routes under patrol company guides, my CO's party and the three rifle companies (A, B, and C), closed in darkness with the objective, after a three-hour approach. The long, narrow and broken summit of the feature dictated that only one company could effectively fight along it at a time. Outflanking was not a sound option because of known enemy positions on Wireless Ridge to the east and a minefield to the south. (As things turned out, however, there were also mines on our chosen attack route.) The summit of the feature also dominated the very open ground around it for several thousand metres, adding to the hazards of a flanking approach – even one made during the pitch-black night.

The plan was for B Company, commanded by Major Mike Argue, to tackle the Longdon summit (composed of the two features codenamed Fly Half and Full Back), while A Company, under Major David Collett, seized the ridge immediately to the northeast (Wing Forward), which was also thought to

Above left: 'H' Jones (on right) and Hew Pike, commanders respectively of 2 and 3 Para, en route for the Falklands. Below: Packing and sorting man-carrying loads on the *Canberra*. Right: Landing craft hit the beach at Sand Bay, near Port San Carlos.

be held by the enemy. C Company, (under Major Martin Osborne) was to hold back, out of contact, as a much-needed reserve, using what cover it could find in the shallow valleys.

Major Peter Dennison led Fire Support Teams – equipped with Milan missile launchers and GPMGs in the sustained fire role – to a position west of the mountain, codenamed Free Kick, for subsequent redeployment as required. The mortars moved independently, whilst Major Roger Patton was in command of the ammunition resupply and casevac teams, which were equipped with tractors and Volvo BV tracked supply vehicles. We had, most regrett-

Sergeant Major, 3 Para, Falklands 1982

RSM of 3 Para, this soldier wears windproof trousers and combat jacket in DPM (Disruptive Pattern Material) with the distinctive beret of The Parachute Regiment. Footgear consists of DMS (Direct Moulded Sole) boots above which are short khaki puttees. Web equipment is of the standard 1958-pattern although this is supplemented by a 1944-pattern water bottle. The windproofs were issued from a British battalion with a NATO role and feature a small Union flag on the right arm. He is armed with a 9mm L2A3 Sterling sub-machine gun, shown here with its metal stock folded away underneath the barrel.

ably, lost our troop of Scorpions and Scimitars to 5 Infantry Brigade, but we had one battery of 105mm Light Guns in direct support, and further batteries could be called up if needed. We also had the support of the firepower of the 4·5in gun of the frigate, HMS *Avenger*. The latter remained with us for most of the night.

Our start line was along the stream running south from Furze Bush pass and we crossed it just as the moon rose to silhouette the dominant, craggy outline of the mountain. The two assaulting companies (A and B) advanced steadily over the open moorland, shaking out from loose file to extended assault formation as they moved forward, in the bitterly cold night. Throughout the advance we endeavoured to avoid long waits in obvious assembly areas and forming up places, for fear of Argentinian artillery, and all remained silent as we closed unhindered with the mountain. B Company, assaulting the summit, moved stealthily into the rocks at the base of Mount Longdon – and there we lost the advantage of surprise. Corporal Milne, a section commander, stood on a mine, and the Argentinian defenders now opened up on both assaulting companies with heavy machine-gun fire

Mortar and artillery fire was soon adding to our

problems, too. And although initially the shells were landing behind us (and much of the automatic fire was too high as well), as battle was joined the enemy quickly assessed how far we had already advanced. Fire became heavier and more accurate as ranges closed and we gained ground. During much of the subsequent battle, it was often hard to tell whether the explosions amongst us were caused by enemy 105mm, 155mm, and 120mm gun and mortar fire, or by our own artillery and naval support. Directed by the Battery Commander (Major John Patrick) and his Forward Observation Officers (FOOs), the Mortar Fire Controllers and the Naval Gunfire Support Officer (Captain Willie McCracken), our supporting fire became more intimate and audacious as the battle wore on.

Holed out as they were in well-prepared bunkers in the rocks, the enemy could only be shifted by combining intensive fire support with an immediate follow up by the rifle sections, using GPMGs, 66mm LAWs, and grenades before closing with rifle and bayonet. The nature of this battle was of a rush forward, a pause, some creeping, a few isolated shots here and there, some artillery and mortar fire, more creeping, another pause, dead silence, quick orders, more firing, great concentrations of fire followed by a concerted rush. Then the whole process would start again. During this long night of freezing rain and sleet, the weather, the darkness, the terrain and the nature of the task placed great

Left: 3 Para's battalion flag is raised at Port San Carlos by local manager Alan Miller. Above right: Lieutenant-Colonel Pike visits his forward Milan detachment near Estancia House, in preparation for the attack on Mount Longdon. Right: Sergeant Watson of 3 Para leads away an Argentinian captive, the first of many more. The Argentinian is wearing a Royal Marine pullover, possibly acquired at Moody Brook. Below: Men of 3 Para at Estancia House. The standard of 9 Para Squadron, RE, has been set up on a nearby telegraph pole.

demands on the leadership and example of young officers, NCOs and many private soldiers.

Five and 6 Platoons were the first to come under effective fire when surprise was lost. Lieutenant Cox, commanding 5 Platoon, ordered a GPMG team to move up the rock face in order to engage a position which was holding up his advance; the enemy was finally silenced by LAW and Carl Gustav fire. But then, more enemy automatic fire was brought to bear from further east. Some of 5 Platoon were now high on the ridge and made contact with 6 Platoon to confirm their positions and avoid overlapping. Under covering fire from Lance-Corporal Carver and Private Juliff, Privates Gough and Gray tried to take out the enemy position using a LAW; but it misfired twice and finally they charged in, using grenades to put paid to the troublesome emplacement. Gray was later to be shot through his helmet, escaping with stitches to his scalp as the bullet diverted through the crown of his protective headgear.

Meanwhile, 6 Platoon had gained a foothold on the southern side of Fly Half, initially without making contact with the enemy, although they grenaded a number of abandoned bunkers, including a 0.5in HMG sangar, on their way up. But they had missed one bunker, concealed by darkness and rocks, in which at least seven Argentinians were hiding. These men engaged the platoon from the rear with great acccuracy, and undoubtedly accounted for a large number of their dead and wounded. Pressing on forward, 6 Platoon then came under accurate sniper and automatic fire from further positions, that caused four casualties in quick succession. Attempts to aid these soldiers and to destroy the sources of enemy fire led only to more casualties. Six Platoon's position was soon critical, because it had advanced into the killing zone of the weapons engaging 5 Platoon. Our casualties lay among rocks covered by enemy fire, but the men of 6 Platoon treated them as best they could. The attack, pressed with such bravery, had created a valuable foothold; now, however, it was stalled.

Snipers with passive night sights soon made things very difficult

Back on the northern side of Fly Half, 4 Platoon was moving up on the left of 5 Platoon, and although its left forward section was in ground sheltered from enemy fire, the right section was pushing up behind 5 Platoon, and also came under heavy fire. Both platoons had arrived at an area forward of the summit of Fly Half, where the rock ridges had started to break up and the ground to slope away to the east. Their immediate problem was to deal with a well-sited enemy platoon position containing 105mm recoilless rifles, two 7.62mm GPMGs and one heavy machine gun that suddenly opened up on them. This position also included a number of snipers with passive nightsights who proved extremely effective, and were soon making things very difficult.

In the initial burst of fire, the commander of 4 Platoon, Lieutenant Andrew Bickerdike, was shot through the thigh and his signaller hit in the mouth; despite their disabilities, both continued to fire their weapons and to man the radio until relieved some time later, while Sergeant Ian McKay took over the platoon. Five Platoon was already under cover

among the rocks and fortunately avoided casualties. McKay quickly gathered a number of the men of 4 Platoon, and led Corporal Bailey's section against the heavy machine gun that formed the core of the enemy position. This HMG was situated in a well-built sangar and protected by several riflemen who covered all approaches. In the attack, McKay and Private Burt were killed and Corporal Bailey seriously wounded. Sergeant McKay's body was found later in an enemy sangar. The men of 4 Platoon had displayed great gallantry under McKay's leadership, and enemy resistance was greatly reduced in this area, although heavy fire continued to make progress difficult.

McLaughlin crawled to within grenade throwing range of one machine gun, but was forced to withdraw

By now Company Headquarters was forward with 5 Platoon on the ridge, and under heavy fire from the east. Several enemy positions could be identified from their tracer bullets, particularly those firing the distinctive Browning machine guns. Having heard that Lieutenant Bickerdike was wounded, and that Sergeant McKay was missing, Sergeant Fuller from Company Headquarters went forward, to take command of 4 Platoon. He gathered 4 Platoon together and, with Corporal McLaughlin's section providing fire support, pressed forward. Although they cleared several enemy sangars, this force was eventually halted by heavy automatic fire which wounded Corporal Kelly and four others.

Left, from top to bottom: Major Peter Dennison, OC of Support Company, briefs his men before the attack on Longdon, using a model to explain the various stages of the plan; Argentinian prisoners are searched in a cleft in the rocks of Mount Longdon; battle-weary paras snatch a moment's rest behind a rocky outcrop; and wounded paras receive treatment before being casevaced away from the battle zone. Below: A para section – including sniper (centre) – moves out from Longdon towards Stanley. Above right: British and Argentinian wounded are treated by medics, under Argentinian artillery fire.

Mount Longdon
3 Para, 11 - 12 June 1982

The battle for Mount Longdon was the climax of 3 Para's three-week-long campaign, a campaign that began with the battalion's landing at Green Beach near Port San Carlos on 21 May. After consolidating its bridgehead 3 Para 'tabbed' across East Falkland, retaking the settlements at Teal Inlet and Estancia House, and pushing the enemy back towards Stanley. By 3 June fighting patrols were being conducted in the area of Mount Longdon and on the night of 11/12 June the battalion moved off from its start line west of the mountain to attack one of the most important Argentinian defensive positions around Stanley.

Key
→ 3 Para
→ Other British forces

Port San Carlos
San Carlos
Teal Inlet
Estancia House
▲ Mount Estancia
Mount Longdon
EAST FALKLAND
Bluff Cove
Stanley
Fitzroy
SOUTH ATLANTIC
Darwin
Goose Green

Key
→ A Coy
→ B Coy and CO's Tac HQ
— 3 Para start line
OOO Minefields

Drunken Rock Pass
Murrell River
Furze Bush Pass
Wing Forward
Fly Half
Full Back
4 Pltn
5 Pltn
Mount Longdon
① A Coy
C Coy (reserve)
B Coy
6 Pltn
②
Free Kick
Moody Brook
Two Sisters

Full Back

A Coy is ordered to move off Wing Forward and join the assault on Full Back.
Despite tough enemy resistance, A Coy pushes across to Full Back, engaging the enemy with rifle and bayonet.
By daybreak the mountain is in British hands.

③

Fly Half

As A Coy moves on Wing Forward, B Coy goes into the attack on the slopes of Mount Longdon itself. Coming under heavy machine-gun fire. 4, 5 and 6 Platoons of B Coy fan out and work their way towards the summit bunker by bunker. After securing Fly Half B Coy comes under attack from the rear before being pinned down by fire from Full Back. B Coy assaults are beaten off.

Wing Forward

11 June A, B and C Coys move on Mount Longdon.
2100 With C Coy held in reserve west of the battalion start line, A and B Coys cross the stream running north to the Murrell River. A Coy launches its assault on Wing Forward, north of the main feature. The company reaches its objective but is pinned down by Argentinian cross-fire.

145

In addition to providing fire support, McLaughlin's section also managed, however, to obtain a commanding position dominating areas to the east. On their way up they had been temporarily halted by the enemy rolling grenades down the rocks towards them. No casualties had resulted, but although McLaughlin crawled to within grenade-throwing distance of one machine gun, and despite several attempts to silence it with both grenades and 66mm LAWs, he was forced to withdraw under heavy smallarms fire.

Attacks were soon also supported by the GPMG and Milan teams that had moved onto the mountain under Major Dennison. The GPMGs hammered it out with enemy heavy machine guns, while the wire-guided Milan missiles were used to devastating effect against bunkers, the operators homing them onto targets at very short ranges. Unfortunately, all three of the crew of one Milan were killed by a single round from an enemy 105mm recoilless rifle during these engagements. Enemy dead lay in the shadow of the rocks where they had fallen, whilst others, who had been cowering in the rocks, were winkled out by follow-up sections.

Right: One of the most deadly weapons in 3 Para's armoury: the Milan rocket launcher, here being tested on Ascension Island. Below: Private Martin of 3 Para organises a POW working party in Stanley.

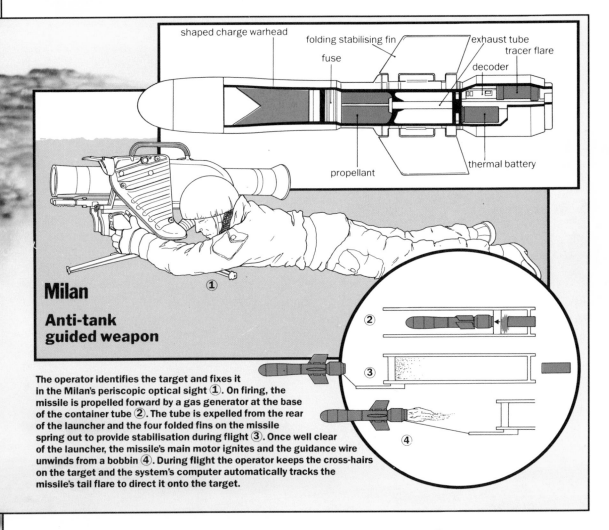

Milan
Anti-tank guided weapon

shaped charge warhead
folding stabilising fin
exhaust tube
tracer flare
fuse
decoder
propellant
thermal battery

The operator identifies the target and fixes it in the Milan's periscopic optical sight ①. On firing, the missile is propelled forward by a gas generator at the base of the container tube ②. The tube is expelled from the rear of the launcher and the four folded fins on the missile spring out to provide stabilisation during flight ③. Once well clear of the launcher, the missile's main motor ignites and the guidance wire unwinds from a bobbin ④. During flight the operator keeps the cross-hairs on the target and the system's computer automatically tracks the missile's tail flare to direct it onto the target.

The fighting had now reached a critical phase, and had developed into a battle of will between attacker and defender. We had established a secure hold on our objective, but were finding the enemy's resistance much tougher than our patrolling had led us to expect. We were also being heavily shelled, and the enemy had no difficulty in adjusting his fire with great accuracy. On the eastern peak, Full Back, the enemy's fire held up both the frontal assault and also B Company's repeated attempts to outflank Argentinian positions. Fire from these positions had also effectively pinned down A Company on their initial objective of Wing Forward.

The grim, dogged courage of small groups of soldiers using rifles, grenades and bayonets at close quarters....

By now I had got forward with my signaller, Lance-Corporal 'Jock' Begg, to the forward groups of B Company and had linked up with Major Argue. The company had been seriously reduced in strength, but was firmly in possession of the western end of the mountain, Fly Half. Every attempt to make further progress by outflanking was now being beaten back, with growing loss. It was at about this time, too, that we got news on the brigade net of enemy Huey helicopters taking off from Stanley and heading our way – perhaps some kind of counter-attack. But this seemed unlikely to make things any more difficult than they already were, and, in the event, the helicopters never arrived!

It was clear to me that I must use A Company, now closer than C, to take the fight through to Full Back and to maintain the pressure of the attack. I reported all this to the brigadier, as I crouched next to three bayonetted enemy corpses, telling him of our situation, but leaving him in no doubt that we would succeed in the end. There were, however, moments when I wondered, almost desperately, what more we had to do to force the Argentinians to give up the fight: positions thought to have been suppressed burst into life again with fire as heavy as ever. There was only one thing to do, of course – to battle on until the will of the enemy was totally broken.

While A Company's attack got under way, the stretcher-bearer platoon was moving in the darkness and over the ice-covered rocks, to locate and evacuate the wounded – a most trying and exhausting task, made a hundred times more so by the constant artillery and mortar fire to which they were exposed. Lance-Corporal Bassey was wounded on a mine as he tried to reach Corporal Milne (the first man to have been wounded that night), while others were hit by shellfire as they struggled down the rocky slopes with their wounded comrades. These stretcher parties, under Major Roger Patton, Battalion Second in Command, also humped forward ammunition for our various weapons, assisted as far as the Murrel Bridge by wheeled and tracked transport. On this lifeline, the battalion's ultimate success in battle was wholly dependent.

A Company now fought a slow, systematic battle forward, well supported by our GPMGs and artillery, in the face of very heavy and accurate enemy

SERGEANT McKAY

Sergeant Ian John McKay won a Victoria Cross (below) for his courage when his platoon commander was wounded and 3 Para was stalled on Mount Longdon. His citation reads:

'It was clear that instant action was needed if the advance was not to falter and increasing casualties to ensue. Sergeant McKay decided to convert this reconnaissance into an attack in order to eliminate the enemy positions... He issued orders, and taking three men with him, broke cover and charged the enemy position.

The assault was met by a hail of fire. The corporal was seriously wounded, a

private killed and another wounded. Despite these losses, Sergeant McKay continued to charge the enemy position alone. On reaching it he despatched the enemy with grenades, thereby relieving the position of beleaguered 4 and 5 Platoons... Sergeant McKay, however, was killed at the moment of victory, his body falling on the bunker.

Without doubt, Sergeant McKay's action retrieved a most dangerous situation and was instrumental in ensuring the success of the attack. His was a coolly calculated act, the dangers of which must have been too apparent to him beforehand. With a complete disregard for his own safety, he displayed courage and leadership of the highest order, and was an inspiration to all those around him.'

machine-gun fire from the rocks above the grassy saddle between Fly Half and Full Back. The impact of artillery, mortar and machine-gun fire, and the stunning effect of Milans, Carl Gustavs and 66mm LAWs at short range, exploited with grim, dogged, courage by small groups of soldiers using rifles, grenades and bayonets at close quarters, provided the best means of overcoming resistance. Nevertheless, it was daylight before Full Back was fully secure. Most of the enemy who had not withdrawn, were strewn dead along the tracks and amongst the rocks – some dismembered by artillery and mortar fire, others shot and bayonetted.

The scene as dawn broke will be perhaps the most haunting memory of this long, cold fight. Groups of young soldiers, grim-faced, shocked but determined, moved through the mist with their bayonets fixed to check the enemy dead. The debris of battle was scattered along the length of the mountain.

Left: Sergeant Ian McKay, VC. Below: The survivors – men of C Company in Port Stanley with their standard, 14 June 1982.

encountered round every turn in the rocks, in every gully. Weapons, clothing, rations, blankets, boots, tents, ammunition, sleeping bags, blood-soaked medical dressings, web equipment and packs had all been abandoned, along with the 105mm recoilless rifles, 120mm mortars, Browning heavy machine guns, and the sophisticated night vision binoculars and sights with which Argentinian snipers had given us so much trouble during the long night. The sour and distinctive odour of death lingered in the nostrils, as we began to dig temporary graves for some of the enemy dead. But it was a slow job, and eventually the task was abandoned when enemy artillery and mortars started again.

Argentinian bunkers yielded not only the particular 'smell' of the enemy, but also Camel cigarettes, bottles of brandy, rounds of cheese, bully beef, and mail from Argentina – a poignant reminder that those we had fought against were also men with families at home awaiting news of them. The flock of prisoners we now had to move to safety from their own artillery

fire were mostly bewildered peasants in uniform, some hardly more than boys, but with professional soldiers made of sterner stuff, to organise them and provide backbone and discipline.

From my position on the forward slopes of Longdon, Wireless Ridge looked to be ours for the taking, and I was anxious to continue our advance if at all possible. But Wireless Ridge was beyond the range of our guns until they moved forward, and was dominated by enemy-held Tumbledown. Further exploitation was not now a feasible operation of war. We held our ground, protecting ourselves as best we could on our hard-won mountain, for the enemy's artillery and mortar fire was to continue to plague us until their collapse three days later, and a number of men who had fought so well and survived through a night of battle were to be killed by sudden barrages of shell fire as they moved of necessity over the mountain, often to help the wounded. It was a grim business, and the battalion continued to lose some of its best soldiers – men like Corporal Stewart McLaughlin, who had been in the thick of the fighting during the night and had received a nasty shrapnel wound in the back just after first light; together with his two escorts, he was hit by heavy mortar fire as he was being evacuated. Or again, Private Richard Absolon, a Patrol Company sniper, had come through numerous recce patrols and a night of battle only to be mortally wounded in the head by shellfire as he helped a comrade to reach safety.

'...certainly, nothing can be more painful than to gain a battle, with the loss of so many of one's friends.'

In the bitter night-fighting and the subsequent shelling among the rocks of this mountain so far from home we lost 23 men killed and 47 wounded. Many of the latter, six of whom had lost limbs, had reason to be grateful to the professional skill and dedication of Major Charles Batty and the members of his Field Surgical Team who had worked tirelessly in the bunkhouse at Teal Inlet during our long battle to take and hold Mount Longdon.

The headlong gallop into Stanley on 14 June, down slopes upon which a few hours before such movement would have drawn a massive weight of artillery fire, seemed scarcely believable. We had been screwing up our courage for another night battle through Moody Brook; and suddenly here we were, requisitioning bungalows and outhouses along the Stanley waterfront. The sense of relief, and of achievement, was profound.

Self-confidence and the will to win – developed through tough selection and demanding training – had seen us through to victory in a remarkable passage of arms. But the overwhelming emotion was not one of elation in victory but of shock and sadness that so many had been killed or wounded, and deep exhaustion. 'Well, thank God I don't know what it is to lose a battle,' the Duke of Wellington is said to have remarked to Dr Hume when he was shown the casualty list on the morning after Waterloo, 'but certainly, nothing can be more painful than to gain one, with the loss of so many of one's friends.'

THE AUTHOR Colonel Hew Pike, DSO, commanded the 3rd Battalion, The Parachute Regiment, during the Falklands conflict in 1982 and was awarded the DSO for his part in the campaign. He was mentioned in dispatches for his command of the battalion in Northern Ireland.

In 1956 the 2nd Colonial Parachute Regiment's jump over Suez gave the world a superb demonstration of state-of-the-art airborne warfare

AT 2300 HOURS on Sunday, 4 November 1956, an officer moved swiftly through the tent, rousing the dozing men into wakefulness. Now alert, the paras immediately dressed and collected their weapons. The camp lay in complete darkness – not even a candle was allowed for fear of Egyptian spies lurking beyond the perimeter fence. Paraded in the darkness, the paras were handed a leaflet: later they would read, 'France and the world have their eyes on you.' The information would do little to calm their nerves, for these men were about to embark upon one of the most hazardous types of military operation, a combat parachute jump into enemy territory.

The paras' destination was Port Said, lying at the northern end of the Suez Canal. On 26 July 1956, President Gamal Abdel Nasser had nationalised the

Anglo-French Suez Canal Company in order to take over the revenue from the canal to finance the building of the Aswan High Dam. There had been serious political repercussions, for not only was he denying the canal owners their very considerable income from the canal, he had also closed the waterway to Israeli shipping, a contravention of an international treaty of 1888 guaranteeing free passage to all nations. In the months following Nasser's move, the British, French and Israelis had initiated a number of diplomatic attempts to redress the situation, but without success. Finally, they took the controversial decision, to use force to seize back the Canal.

During the three-hour flight from their base in Cyprus, the men of the 2e Régiment de Parachutistes Coloniaux (2nd Colonial Parachute Regiment), or 2 RPC, had plenty of time to prepare for the fight to come. Despite having seen much action in the counter-insurgency (COIN) role in Algeria, few of the paras had previously made a combat drop. The handful of veterans of World War II who were among them, and the greater number who had fought in the

FORTUNE
FAVOURS THE BRAVE

Indochina War, summed up the hazards of the jump as a gamble. 'If we achieve surprise, we'll be alright. If we don't, well, remember the regimental motto, "Fortune favours the brave!"'

Suddenly, the time for contemplation was over. A red warning light came on in each plane, accompanied by a klaxon. Five minutes to go before the drop. At the command of a senior NCO, the 34 paras in each transport stood up and completed the routine check of the equipment and harness of the man directly in front. Then, attaching their static lines to the overhead hook-up line, they formed two lines in the centre of the fuselage, each of 17 men, ready to jump out of the doors on either side of the plane. The lead man of each stick crouched in the doorway, bracing himself for the command to jump.

'GO!' At 0530 on the 5th, the green light came on and the leading paras hurled themselves out into the bright sky. Rapidly, the rest of the stick followed, each man jumping close on the heels of the para in front. In 10 seconds the fuselages were empty. Squinting downwards, the parachutists could see French and British warships cruising on the glittering Mediterranean, and in the distance the sun would occasionally catch the wings of Anglo-French strike aircraft as they hurtled onto targets around the paras' drop zones (DZs). To the west, flames were rising from the DZ of their British allies, the 3rd Battalion of The Parachute Regiment (3 Para), who had jumped 15 minutes earlier. Then, with a bone-jarring jerk, the brown and white parachutes opened and the paras were swaying down to earth.

It seemed as though the veterans' hopes for surprise were not to be realised, for the air seemed

Top: Well-equipped French paras file in through the rear door of their Nord Noratlas transport in Cyprus. Above: A paratrooper armed with a 9mm MAT 49 sub-machine gun hugs the ground on the exposed drop zone south of Port Fuad.

Port Said
2e Régiment de Parachutistes Coloniaux
5-6 Nov 1956

After the Egyptians took over the Anglo-French Suez Canal Company in July 1956, France and Britain began preparations for an operation to seize the Canal. The ground forces deployed were approximately the size of a World War II army corps and they were lavishly provided with aerial and naval support — 500 aircraft and 130 ships. The first stage would be a landing by airborne troops to the west and the south of Port Said. The men of the French 2e Régiment de Parachutistes Coloniaux (2 RPC) were assigned to the southern drop zone. Their mission was to seize the Raswa bridges.

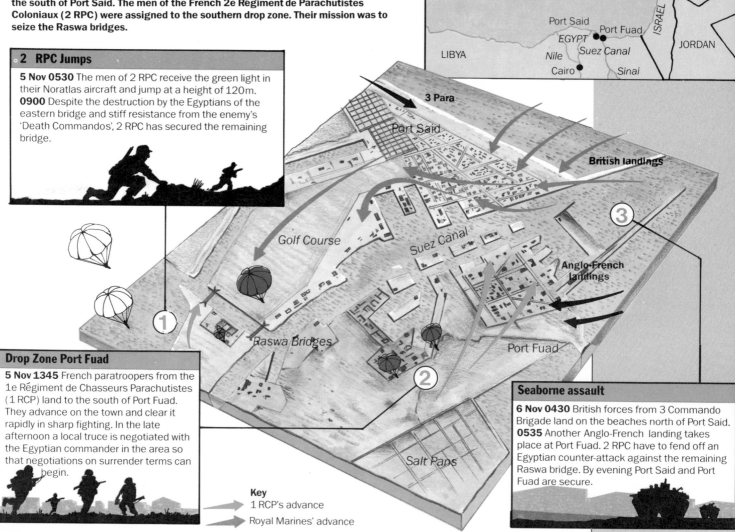

2 RPC Jumps

5 Nov 0530 The men of 2 RPC receive the green light in their Noratlas aircraft and jump at a height of 120m.
0900 Despite the destruction by the Egyptians of the eastern bridge and stiff resistance from the enemy's 'Death Commandos', 2 RPC has secured the remaining bridge.

Drop Zone Port Fuad

5 Nov 1345 French paratroopers from the 1e Régiment de Chasseurs Parachutistes (1 RCP) land to the south of Port Fuad. They advance on the town and clear it rapidly in sharp fighting. In the late afternoon a local truce is negotiated with the Egyptian commander in the area so that negotiations on surrender terms can begin.

Seaborne assault

6 Nov 0430 British forces from 3 Commando Brigade land on the beaches north of Port Said.
0535 Another Anglo-French landing takes place at Port Fuad. 2 RPC have to fend off an Egyptian counter-attack against the remaining Raswa bridge. By evening Port Said and Port Fuad are secure.

Key
→ 1 RCP's advance
→ Royal Marines' advance

---

filled with smallarms fire. Anti-aircraft shells were exploding above them, forcing the Noratlas aircraft to take desperate evasive action. The men struggled to bring their paratroopers' rifles and sub-machine guns to bear, each weapon fitted with a folding stock to enable it to be carried during the descent. At three metres from the ground they bent their legs to absorb the shock of impact – and landed in the centre of an Egyptian defensive position.

The task facing 2 RPC was formidable. The regiment had been ordered to drop at Raswa, lying on the west bank of the Suez Canal, in order to capture the twin bridges which connected Port Said with the road south, and thus isolate the town. This mission, part of the Anglo-French bid to capture the Suez Canal from the Egyptians which had been code-named Operation Musketeer, had been envisaged originally as a British heliborne attack, but that approach had been thought too dangerous and the task had been allocated to 2 RPC instead. Code-named Operation Omelette, their effort was to be supported by 3 Para's drop at Gamil airfield to the west of Port Said, and a drop by annother French airborne regiment to the south of Port Fuad later in the day. Finally, 24 hours later, the main seaborne force would arrive, but until then the paras were on their own.

The principal concern of 2 RPC's commander, Colonel Pierre Château-Jobert, was not so much that of holding out for 24 hours on the ground, but the difficulty of establishing an initial foothold. The DZ was a narrow strip of land, some 800m long by 140m wide, and, bordered by the Mediterranean, the canal itself, roads and trees, it allowed little room for error. The force had been limited by logistical considerations to about 500 men, but to drop even this number into such a restricted area necessitated a jump from 120m, 60m lower than the altitude of the British transports dropping 3 Para at Gamil. The hazards of the drop were increased by the decision to deploy the aircraft in a tight formation of pairs flying only 55m apart, with only 110m separating

each pair from the one following. Château-Jobert was also worried about the degree of Egyptian opposition at the DZ, where dug-in infantry, machine guns and 40mm Bofors anti-aircraft guns were known to be located.

Landing the men took only four minutes. Touching down, the paras hugged every scrap of cover they could find as they received fire from Egyptians well protected in slit trenches. Rapidly extricating themselves from their parachute harness, the French paratroopers prepared to advance. Captain de Klee, the commander of a small British party which had jumped with 2 RPC, one which included sappers and members of the Guards Independent Parachute Company, took in the scene of horror as he raced towards the rallying point. Dead and wounded Egyptian and French troops lay around him, and bullets were raising lines of little spurts of sand, as he later mused, 'just like in a Hollywood movie'. Pierre Leulliette, an NCO of 2 RPC, saw the body of a fellow NCO caught in a palm tree by his parachute, the corpse swaying from side to side as it dripped blood on the sand.

Notwithstanding their initial losses, the paras began to move towards the bridges, but they encountered stiff resistance. The Egyptians in their slit trenches were being given fire support from machine guns and 40mm Bofors guns positioned near the bridges. Occasionally, a para would topple forward as he was struck by a bullet, but the men were under strict instructions not to stop to aid wounded men: that was the job of orderlies following in the rear. Nothing was to stand in the way of the 'maintenance of the objective', the seizure of the bridges.

The advanced machine-gun posts were soon taken out by the French force, together with a Bofors in the centre of the DZ, but the volume of fire from the bridges was causing the attack to falter. The crisis of the battle had arrived. Fortunately, the command

structure of the attack was equal to the problem: circling some 300m above the ground in a converted Noratlas, General Jean Gilles was commanding the action. The aircraft was equipped with a map room and communications centre, and Gilles was able to keep in contact with both the ground forces and his commanding officer, General André Beaufre, who was out to sea aboard the cruiser *Gustave-Zédé*. From this excellent, if risky, vantage point, Gilles was able to call in an air strike.

The air support quickly arrived in the form of French Air Force F-48 Thunderstreaks from Cyprus, and French Navy Corsairs operating from the carrier *Lafayette*. Screaming low over the DZ, little more

Below: Members of the 2nd Colonial Parachute Regiment advance towards Port Faud. The smoke on the horizon was caused by air bombardment. Above right: The para force recieves supplies by parachute. Above: French commandos are taken in by Alligator amphibious tanks to reinforce the paras.

2e REGIMENT DE PARACHUTISTES COLONIAUX

The 2nd Colonial Parachute Regiment was formed around the 2nd Colonial Parachute Battalion (2 BPC), which fought in the First Indochina War. One of the unit's fiercest battles in that war occurred on 14 November 1951, when 2 BPC dropped with parachute battalions of the French Foreign Legion on the town of Hoa Binh and wrested it from the Viet Minh.

After the Suez campaign in 1956, 2 RPC was plunged into one of the toughest actions of the Algerian War of Independence – the Battle of Algiers. In January 1957 the regiment moved into Algiers, as part of the 10th Parachute Division under General Jacques Massu, to crush the nationalist revolt in the city. Following a policy of aggressive 'cordon and search' tactics, raids on houses, and brutal interrogation methods, they destroyed the National Liberation Front (FLN) in Algiers, but French moderate opinion was alienated by their brutal efficiency and Algeria finally achieved independence. The battle-hardened paras of 2 RPC were very resentful of the political settlement of the Algerian conflict but, unlike their comrades in the 1st Foreign Legion Parachute Regiment, they stayed loyal to General de Gaulles's Fifth Republic.

After the Algerian War, the colonial paras were under something of a political cloud, but on 1 January 1968 the old colonial regiments became part of the Infanterie de Marine (marine infantry, not to be confused with the marines of the French Navy). Under the title of 2e Régiment de Parachutistes d'Infanterie de Marine (2 RPIMa), 2 RPC now forms part of the elite 11th Parachute Division, part of the French tactical reserve.

than nine metres above the ground, they poured 20mm shells into Egyptian positions less than 200m ahead of the advancing paras. For the rest of the day, a 'cab rank' of Anglo-French fighter-bombers patrolled above the DZ, homing in on targets indicated by the paratroopers. They could do this because the Egyptian Air Force had been virtually eliminated in pre-emptive strikes by Anglo-French bombers, 72 hours before the paras went in. Encouraged by this massive increase in the firepower at their command, the paras swept forward once again to tackle the defences at the bridges.

Under cover of mortar fire, the paras worked their way in among the trenches and pillboxes

Then, at 0830 hours, the Egyptians cheated the paras of one of their prizes by blowing up the bridge on the eastern side. As the smoke cleared to reveal a broken mass of steel, the assaulting troops headed for the western bridge, praying that their enemy would stay to fight, for it would have been a major blow if the remaining bridge, which carried the main road and the railway, had also been destroyed. They need not have worried – the defenders were Nasser's renowned 'Death Commandos' who, wearing red berets similar to those of their French assailants, proved worthy opponents. Under cover of mortar fire, the paras worked their way in among the trenches and pillboxes commanding the approaches to the bridge, and the area became the scene of intense fighting. Then, overwhelmed by the firepower and ferocity of the paras' attack, the Egyptian commandos began to surrender, one by one. Helped in no small measure by the fighter-bombers prowling overhead, the paras cleared the forward defences, until only the bridge itself remained to be taken. This had to be done by the paras alone, for the steel girders of the bridge afforded excellent overhead cover for the defenders, and a full air strike had to be ruled out in order to capture the bridge intact.

The Frenchmen had no choice but to slog their way forward in a frontal assault. The commandos who remained at the foot of the bridge now effected a withdrawal onto the bridge itself, skilfully covering each other's moves with their sub-machine guns,

until only one Egyptian remained as a rearguard. Single-handedly, he held off the paras for 15 minutes. This stand could have been of the greatest importance, for Egyptian tanks had begun to open fire from the golf course on the far side of the bridge, and the paras feared an armoured counter-attack. Then, inevitably, the lone hero was hit and the paras surged past him onto the bridge. By 0900 their objective had been cleared. The French had sustained 10 fatalities, while 60 Egyptians lay dead.

Once across the bridge, the paras dug in and prepared to clear the area to the north of pockets of resistance. Enemy mortars and guns were keeping up a sporadic bombardment of the bridge, and the paras guided the Corsairs down onto their positions. By 1130 the hinterland was largely secure and the British sappers (from the 9th Independent Squadron, Royal Engineers) and members of the Guards Company set out in two jeeps to push south down the Suez road. They discovered that Egyptian resistance had now become virtually non-existent.

There were still Egyptians in force to the northeast in Port Fuad, however, but their fate was soon to be sealed. At 1345 hours a second French airborne unit, the 1e Régiment de Chasseurs Parachutistes (1st Light Infantry Parachute Regiment), or 1 RCP, landed in the port and routed them. Any men who stood their ground were dealt with ruthlessly by the French. By late afternoon, Château-Jobert had negotiated a local truce with the Egyptian commander, Brigadier El Moguy, and the paras paused to draw breath.

Supported by tanks and self-propelled artillery, these assaults gave the paras a few nasty moments

The following day saw a renewal of the fighting. At 0430 hours the British commenced their seaborne assault on Port Said, and 65 minutes later French reinforcements stormed ashore, in the shape of the 1e Régiment Etranger de Parachutistes (1st Foreign Legion Parachute Regiment), or 1 REP, plus commandos and AMX tanks. Coming ashore to the east of Port Fuad, these units met little resistance, although 72 Egyptian troops were killed when 1 REP stormed a police post lying two kilometres from the town. During the morning, 2 RPC also saw more action as the Egyptians mounted a series of uncoordinated counter-attacks against the bridge. Supported by

Below left: A group of Egyptian prisoners is escorted away from the battle zone by a para. Above: A British general congratulates French paratroopers on their completion of a difficult task. On the right is General Jacques Massu, commander of the 10th Colonial Parachute Division. Below: French airborne troops prepare to depart from Suez. Only hours after their feat of arms, the order of a ceasefire ended the military confrontation and prevented them from exploiting the victory.

The political outcome of Operation Musketeer, in which both France and Britain lost much international prestige, was to have a salutary effect on the subsequent history of the French airborne forces. At Suez they had won a brilliant tactical victory, only to be 'sold out', in their eyes, by the politicians, just as they thought had happened in the First Indochina War. It is not surprising, therefore, that the paratroopers were in the forefront of the military unrest of 1958 and 1961 that resulted from a similar political 'betrayal' over Algeria, leading to the disbandment of 1 REP for mutiny. At Suez, 2 RPC had demonstrated their skill and courage, but the operation proved only that France was no longer a power capable of carrying out military operations against the will of the new global policeman – the United States.

THE AUTHOR W.B. Brabiner is a freelance writer who specialises in 20th century warfare. His numerous articles have described many aspects of military affairs from World War I to the present day.

anks and self-propelled artillery, these assaults gave the paras a few nasty moments, but they were all beaten off with the aid of air strikes. By noon the Centurion tanks of A Squadron, 6th Royal Tank Regiment, had linked up with the paratroopers on the bridge. The Egyptian positions in Port Said were no longer tenable.

The Anglo-French forces had achieved a considerable military victory at Suez: the jump by 2 RPC, in particular, had been a model operation. But the cup of victory was to be dashed away at the very moment of triumph. International pressure, especially that exerted by the United States, forced a ceasefire which began on 6 November. After that, 2 RPC acted as an army of occupation, an unwelcome role which it enacted with ruthless efficiency.

Paratrooper, Suez 1956

All of this para's equipment is manufactured in France, including his M51 camouflaged para uniform, para boots and web equipment. Carried on the belt are rifle grenades and a water bottle. His rifle is a French 7.5mm MAS 1936.

A CONTRAST IN STYLE

Of the two parachute forces that dropped on Suez, the French were far better prepared for airborne operations.
Since World War II, the French had made much greater use of paratroopers in their airborne role. Even when fully engaged in ground actions, they made at least one practice jump per month. In contrast, the last British combat jump had been as far back as the Rhine Crossings in 1945, and The Parachute Regiment had served since the war as elite conventional infantry. Perhaps as a consequence of this different emphasis, the French paras were better equipped. Their Nord Noratlas N2501, a twin-engined, twin-boom, tail-loading transport aircraft, was vastly superior to the aged Valettas and Hastings used by the RAF. It could carry more heavy equipment and disgorge 17 men in 10 seconds, while the Hastings took 20 seconds to drop 15 men. The only piece of heavy kit the RAF planes could carry was the old World War II jeep, and jeeps had to be brought out of mothballs for the occasion. The paras were also armed with the World War II Sten sub-machine gun, which proved alarmingly unreliable. Even worse, the British para was defenceless until he touched the ground and could open the weapon container strapped to his leg, while the French were issued with special para weapons with folding stocks for use on the descent.
In the plane, the French did not waste valuable time by holding a formal inspection immediately prior to the jump. They also recovered their parachutes from the drop zone, unlike the British who regarded them as expendable.
An indication of the differing attitudes of the British and French airborne forces was seen at a party held in Cyprus at the time. The British officers arrived wearing white dinner jackets: the French were in battledress.

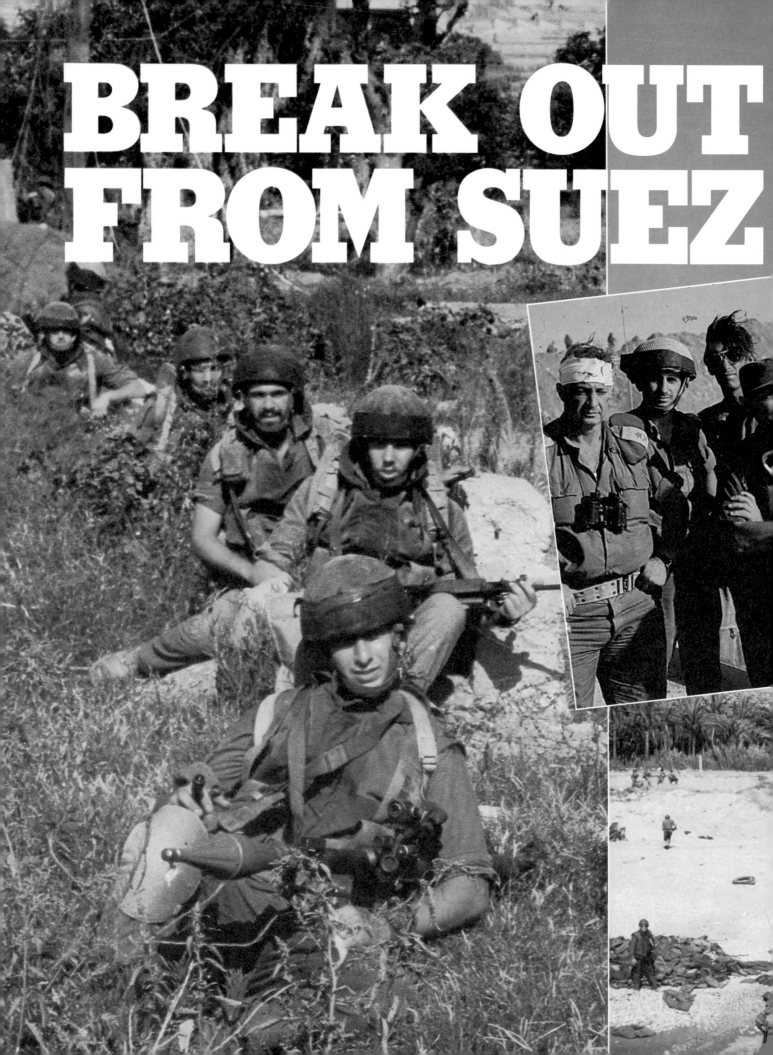

BREAK OUT FROM SUEZ

Pinned down and surrounded by Egyptian troops, the Israeli paras fought a grim battle for survival in the streets of Suez

ON 22 OCTOBER 1973, 16 days after the opening of the Yom Kippur War, the Israeli Defence Forces (IDF) were striking back at the Egyptians, who had so brilliantly crossed the Suez Canal into Sinai on the 6th. After savage attritional battles in the Sinai desert, the Israelis launched Operation Gazelle, their

Left: With an RPG up front, a group of Israeli paras inches forward across waste ground on the outskirts of Suez. Below: On the banks of the Canal. Israeli officers, including Major-General Ariel Sharon (extreme left), discuss Operation Gazelle with Minister of Defence, Moshe Dayan (centre). Bottom: Israeli APCs push forward from the Canal.

own plan to cross the Canal into Egypt. Begun at last light on 15 October, Gazelle, although resisted with great ferocity by the enemy, was ultimately successful and, once across, Israeli columns pushed north and south. The latter thrust was given greater priority with two divisions, under Major-General Avraham Adan and Brigadier-General Kalman Magen, ordered to encircle the Egyptian Third Army from the west. The main axis of advance was along the shore of the Great Bitter Lake towards the town of Suez. By the beginning of the fourth week in October, the Third Army was trapped and on the point of collapse.

During the evening of 24 October, the Egyptians tried again and again to punch a path through the cordon, but the IDF was now strong enough to contain the Third Army and repel any counter-attack by other Egyptian forces. The Israelis then moved to crush the enemy troops in Suez. Adan asked his senior officer, Major-General Shmuel Gonen, for permission to attack, enter and seize the town. Unsure of the precise situation in Suez, Gonen answered, 'If the town is empty, go ahead, but if it is fortified and defended, leave it alone.' There was a lack of basic intelligence as to the situation in the town and the troops did not expect any heavy fighting. It was a misreading of the situation that would lead to enormous casualties almost from the word go.

The attack on the town was to be carried out by two armoured brigades and a battalion of paratroopers – some of Israel's finest fighting men, who had earlier helped force the crossing of the Suez Canal from Sinai into Egypt proper. Initially, all went well. One armoured brigade, commanded by 'Gabi', succeeded in capturing the Suez oil refineries, meeting little resistance. The second brigade, commanded by 'Arieh', advanced along the Cairo-Suez road, running north to south along the Canal, and took a number of buildings at the western approaches to the town. Behind them were two companies of paratroopers, about 100 men, commanded by Lieutenant-Colonel 'Yossi'.

The troops jumped off the half-tracks and began to clear out the nearest buildings

The force moved on the town expecting an easy mopping-up operation, but as the tanks entered Suez, heavy fire rained down on the Israelis from all sides. Within minutes, 20 of the force's 24 tank commanders had been wounded. (Tank commanders were in the habit of riding standing up in their turrets to get a better view of the battlefield). A full scale battle had begun. What happened in Suez during the next two days of fighting was confused. After the war, each soldier was asked to record his impressions to clarify the situation. The following version of the battle is compiled from those reports.

After the tanks had been rebuffed, the paratroopers began to move into the town. In the lead were eight captured Egyptian half-tracks, a jeep and a bus. As the paras entered the built-up area of Suez and moved along the main street, the Egyptians opened fire from all directions. The troops jumped off the half-tracks and began to clear out the nearest buildings. The company commander, 'Buki', who was leading a platoon, made a dash for one of the buildings, he and his men trying to avoid the enemy's bullets. A second platoon of 18 men was following; most of them were either killed or wounded.

CROSSING THE CANAL

Operation Gazelle, the Israeli plan to cross the Suez Canal during the Yom Kippur War in 1973, began at last light on 15 October. The onslaught opened with an armoured push to the east shore of the Great Bitter Lake, followed by a thrust against the open southern flank of the Egyptian Second Army.

Furious fighting broke out around a group of buildings known as the Chinese Farm. Although the battle was to last for three days and cost the Israelis many casualties, the initial advance opened the way to the Canal.

The second phase of Gazelle, the creation of a bridgehead on the west bank, was given to a reserve para brigade under the command of Colonel Danny Matt. The first wave of troops had crossed the Canal by 0135 hours on the 16th and then established a small defensive perimeter. The stage was set for the Israelis to bring up their bridging equipment from a protected concentration area known as 'The Yard', but Egyptian counter-attacks and transport difficulties delayed the crossing.

Surprisingly, the Egyptians did little to threaten Matt's men on the 17th, being content to launch a disastrous armoured attack against the corridor. The Israeli victory eased the pressure east of the Canal and the bridging process began.

The first unit reached the paras during the evening and two further brigades followed on the 18th and 19th. The Israelis broke out of their bridgehead on the morning of the 18th, driving south through the rear echelons of the Egyptian Third Army. The Egyptians, their attacks blunted and their troops all but shattered, were forced to accept the inevitability of defeat.

Right: Israeli self-propelled artillery is ferried across the Suez Canal in preparation for the final thrust against the Egyptian armies.

The rest of the paratroopers had no alternative but to abandon their half-tracks. With them they carried the wounded, but left their dead, ammunition and supplies behind. In the house, the platoon sergeant redistributed the remaining ammunition and ordered the paras to conserve their bullets and prepare the building for a prolonged siege. The Egyptians realised that they had the Israelis trapped. They surrounded the building and placed mines in the road to prevent any break-out attempts or reinforcements reaching the paratroopers.

Buki's radio operator reported that his CO had been killed crossing a road junction, while attempting to make the safety of a house. Two soldiers tried to get out to recover Buki's body, but were forced to retreat under a hail of fire. Within this house were now 18 paras, three of them wounded. They were unaware that the rest of the company had reached the comparative safety of the Egyptian police station, some 30m away. These 18 prepared their defences and repulsed a number of Egyptian attempts to storm the building. All of them were hoping to escape under cover of darkness, reach the half-track that was outside with its engine still running, and make their getaway. Later in the afternoon, the fuel in the half-track ran out, dashing their hopes. They prepared for a night attack by the hundreds of Egyptian troops surrounding the building.

Back at the headquarters, the commanders realised the enormity of the mistake. The paratroopers were cut off and separated into several small groups, with each group having to fend for itself against superior Egyptian forces. There was no possibility of artillery or air support as no-one knew exactly where the different groups were holed up.

During the evening, a relief force made an attempt to extricate the trapped men. The 18 soldiers saw the reinforcements pass not far from their house. They shouted and fired flares, but were not noticed. After a while, the reinforcements withdrew; it had become clear that there was no hope of finding the men in the darkness. Another group of paratroopers had also found shelter in the same building, but in a different apartment. These four soldiers were from Buki's half-track. Surprisingly, neither group was aware of the other, or that the majority of the company was

across the street in the police building.

At first light, a number of aircraft flew a photo-reconnaissance mission over Suez in an attempt to identify the houses where the paratroopers were defending themselves. Towards evening, photography experts had established that four paratroopers were hiding out in the apartment block, but the fate of the 18 and those men in the police station remained a mystery.

To discover what had happened to the main force, we must return to the previous day. As Buki was trying to make the safety of a building, Yossi's half-track was hit by an anti-tank shell that killed the communications officer, the operations sergeant, the battalion medical orderly and the radio operator. Yossi, his operations officer and two other soldiers, who were on the same half-track, were wounded. The only uninjured men were 'Tzachi', an intelligence officer, and the driver, who sped off to the shelter of the nearby police building. The rest of the force followed. One half-track driver, Michael Shor, was shot in the head, but he continued driving until a second bullet killed him. However, he had succeeded in getting close to the police station, where the crew disembarked and found safety.

Outside, Tzachi organised a defence against the vastly superior Egyptian force

The battalion's second-in-command, who was bringing up the rear, got caught up in a fierce firefight with dozens of Egyptians. He and the five soldiers with him fought off the Arabs, turned their half-track around, and sped out of Suez. The wounded Yossi was carried into the police station. In the building itself, a number of Egyptian policemen tried to resist their unwelcome visitors and the platoon commander, First Lieutenant David Amit, led his men to clean out and secure the building. Outside, Tzachi organised a defence against the vastly superior Egyptian force that was trying to retake the station, and provided covering fire for the stray Israelis who were still arriving. Later, a number of Egyptian policemen were captured and thrown out of the building into the street, where they were shot by

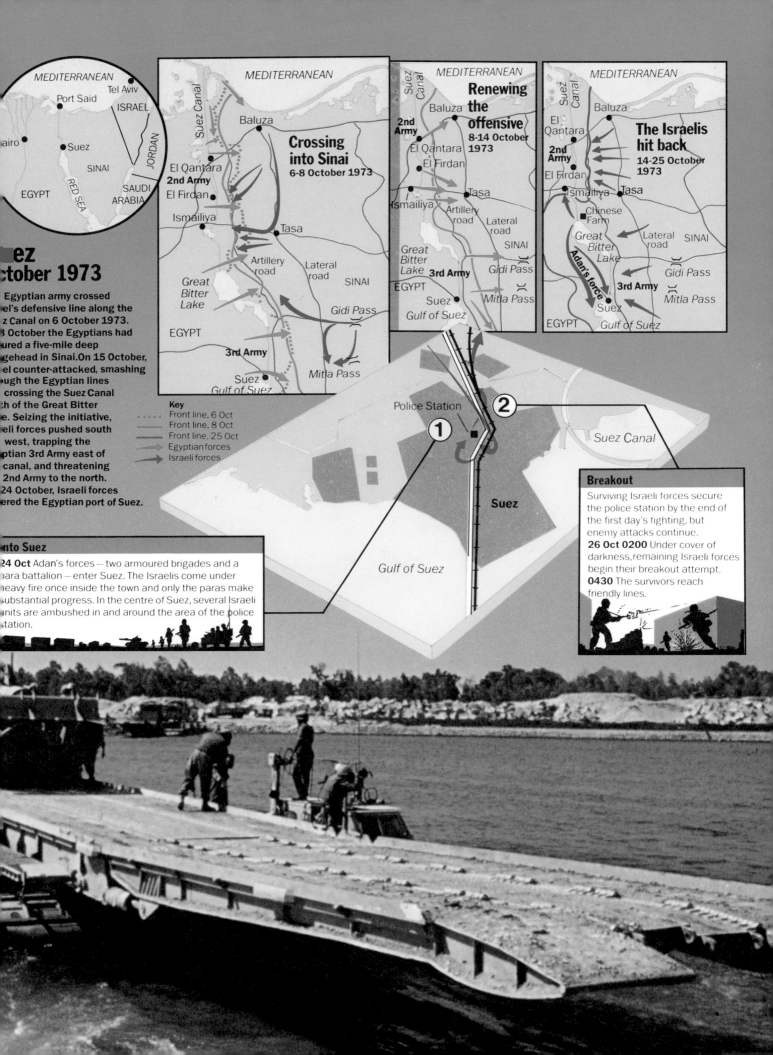

MEDITERRANEAN (inset map)

Port Said, Tel Aviv, ISRAEL, Cairo, Suez, SINAI, JORDAN, EGYPT, RED SEA, SAUDI ARABIA

[Su]ez
[O]ctober 1973

[The] Egyptian army crossed
[Isra]el's defensive line along the
[Sue]z Canal on 6 October 1973.
[By 8] October the Egyptians had
[secu]red a five-mile deep
[brid]gehead in Sinai. On 15 October,
[Isra]el counter-attacked, smashing
[thro]ugh the Egyptian lines
[and] crossing the Suez Canal
[nor]th of the Great Bitter
[Lak]e. Seizing the initiative,
[Isra]eli forces pushed south
[and] west, trapping the
[Egy]ptian 3rd Army east of
[the] canal, and threatening
[the] 2nd Army to the north.
[By] 24 October, Israeli forces
[ent]ered the Egyptian port of Suez.

[I]nto Suez

[24 Oct] Adan's forces — two armoured brigades and a
[p]ara battalion — enter Suez. The Israelis come under
[h]eavy fire once inside the town and only the paras make
[s]ubstantial progress. In the centre of Suez, several Israeli
[u]nits are ambushed in and around the area of the police
[s]tation.

Crossing into Sinai
6-8 October 1973

MEDITERRANEAN, Suez Canal, Baluza, El Qantara, 2nd Army, El Firdan, Ismailiya, Tasa, Artillery road, Lateral road, Great Bitter Lake, SINAI, Gidi Pass, EGYPT, 3rd Army, Mitla Pass, Suez, Gulf of Suez

Renewing the offensive
8-14 October 1973

MEDITERRANEAN, Suez Canal, Baluza, 2nd Army, El Qantara, El Firdan, Tasa, Ismailiya, Artillery road, Lateral road, Great Bitter Lake, SINAI, 3rd Army, Gidi Pass, EGYPT, Suez, Mitla Pass, Gulf of Suez

The Israelis hit back
14-25 October 1973

MEDITERRANEAN, Suez Canal, Baluza, El Qantara, 2nd Army, El Firdan, Tasa, Ismailiya, Chinese Farm, Great Bitter Lake, Lateral road, SINAI, Adan's force, Gidi Pass, 3rd Army, Mitla Pass, Suez, EGYPT, Gulf of Suez

Key
- ········· Front line, 6 Oct
- ――― Front line, 8 Oct
- ――― Front line, 25 Oct
- → Egyptian forces
- → Israeli forces

Police Station, ①, ②, Suez Canal, Suez, Gulf of Suez

Breakout

Surviving Israeli forces secure
the police station by the end of
the first day's fighting, but
enemy attacks continue.
26 Oct 0200 Under cover of
darkness, remaining Israeli forces
begin their breakout attempt.
0430 The survivors reach
friendly lines.

OPPOSING FORCES

In the period between the end of the Six-Day War in 1967 and the outbreak of hostilities in 1973, both Egypt and Israel took the opportunity to expand and modernise their armed forces.

On the eve of Yom Kippur, the Egyptian Army comprised some 285,000 men, backed by 2000 tanks and 600 aircraft. For the crossing of the Suez Canal, the High Command deployed five divsions, divided between the Second and Third Armies, along the waterway, facing the defences of Israel's Bar-Lev Line.

Since 1967, when they lost large numbers of tanks and aircraft, the Egyptians had built up their supplies of missiles, provided by Russia. With a plentiful stock of portable anti-tank missiles, the Egyptians believed that their infantry could hold a Sinai bridgehead against Israeli armoured attacks with man-portable anti-tank weapons.

For their part, the Israelis had also been re-equipping, primarily with US-supplied hardware. However, much of the imported equipment was modified to cope with the rigours of desert warfare.

About half of the Israeli armour consisted of Centurions, backed by 600 M48/60s from America and around 250 of the older Super Shermans. Large quantities of Soviet equipment, captured in 1967, were also available. The air force, although outnumbered, was flying some of the finest aircraft available. On mobilisation, the armed forces had a strength of some 350,000 men, split between 30 brigades.

In crude terms, the Israelis had a rough parity with the Egyptians. However, they would also have to face the Syrians in the north. Only their battle skills and superior hardware could make up for this disadvantage.

their own troops.

Back at the entrance to the town, the rear of the column was being brought up by the headquarters platoon commander, Uri Arbel, and a handful of soldiers. As he followed the main force, he saw a number of wounded tank crew at the side of the road. He left his men, loaded the wounded on his own jeep and then took them out of the town to safety. When he returned, there was no sign of his men. After the war, their four bodies were returned to Israel, but how they died remains a mystery.

After the police building had been secured, the battalion doctor arrived with a number of medics, fighting at close quarters with the Egyptians as they came. They were given covering fire from the building and succeeded in getting inside. They had brought medical equipment with them and managed to save the lives of a number of wounded paratroopers, many of whom would have died without supplies of blood, antibiotics and morphine. The wounded were being treated in a corridor of the station, when a number of Egyptian soldiers, who had been hiding in one of the rooms, burst out and opened fire on the group of casualties. The doctor carried on with his work, treating the wounded with one hand and firing back with the other. David Amit, who had begun the battle as a platoon commander, was appointed senior officer. The other officers had been either killed or wounded.

By the end of the first day of fighting, the paras were in a desperate situation: each soldier was down to one ammunition magazine and one grenade; only two full water-bottles remained, and these had to be saved for the wounded. To make matters worse, the Egyptians had taken up position on a nearby five-storey building and were firing on the two-storey police station with great effect, shooting through the

windows at the 50 Israelis trapped inside. At dawn, an attempt was made to reach the half-tracks parked nearby. Despite cutting enemy fire, men reached the vehicles; ammunition and a few jerrycans of water were brought back to the paras holed up in the station.

Any break-out attempt would mean leaving the wounded behind, and this he refused to do

The brigade commander, who was still outside the town, called Amit on the radio, ordering him and his men to break out during the night. Amit refused to obey the order. He told his superior officer that any break-out attempt would mean leaving the wounded behind, and this he refused to do. Several senior officers tried reasoning with Amit over the radio, but he could not be persuaded. 'Either we all come out or none of us come out,' he argued.

The wounded were taken down to the police station's basement, but Yossi refused to be moved. He was slipping in and out of consciousness all the time, but when he was consious, he would crawl amongst his men giving them encouragement.

The second day of fighting found the Israeli paratroopers in very difficult circumstances. Their morale was dropping, as many of the soldiers believed that they would never get out alive. However, their spirits rose when Amit told them that the four missing soldiers from Buki's half-track were holed up in a building a few dozen metres from the police station. He began planning to bring them into the comparative safety of the police station under cover of darkness. Using their radios, Amit and the commander of the trapped paras, First Lieutenant 'Gil', agreed that the incoming troops would give a series of short flashes with their torches, to let the men in the police station know that they were on their way and to identify their position. Amit was to signal back, giving Gil the direction of the entrance to the police building, and his men were also to give covering fire if the movement was discovered by the Egyptians.

Gil and his men began a slow, wary movement out of the apartment. Suddenly, they heard the sound of men in an adjoining flat. Inexplicably, perhaps miraculously, no-one fired. In fact, the noise came from the 18 paratroopers who, unknown to Gil, had been 'living' almost next door. Their mutual surprise and joy at meeting each other received an added boost when, attracted by the sound of Hebrew being spoken, another eight officers came out of hiding.

This combined force, now 30 strong and buoyed with elation, made for Amit's flashlight and reached the safety of the police building. In the station, the atmosphere was almost festive. It soon became apparent that the soldiers in the apartment block had had no way of knowing that the major part of the force was only a few metres away, despite the noise of the shooting, as there were no windows in the block that faced the police station.

With the arrival of the men from the apartment block, the force in the station numbered 80 men and their situation had been altered sufficiently for them to try a break-out. Amit reported to headquarters that they would make the attempt that night. The plan was to leave the building and then regroup in the courtyard outside. However, Amit's look-outs reported a large Egyptian force on the roof of the buildings overlooking the station. The paratroopers, who had neither eaten nor slept for two days, were loathe to give up the 'safety' of the station. Morale was again so low that Amit decided to postpone the attempt.

Only at 0200 hours did Amit decide that the time was right to move. He radioed brigade command to tell them that they were on their way. This was the message that Gonen, who had been at the brigade's headquarters throughout the battle, was waiting for: all the paratroopers were together in one place and ready to move. Artillery units had been given the exact co-ordinates of the police station and the route out of Suez. The guns were to provide covering fire for the retreat by putting down an accurate barrage of shells around Amit's men, leaving them an 'empty box' to move in.

The wounded refused to be moved on stretchers in order not to slow the force down. Yossi walked all the way, moaning with agony with every step that he took. As they retreated, the paras could hear the Egyptian soldiers calling to each other from the houses where they were entrenched. The paratroopers had been ordered not to open fire unless fired upon, so as not to give themselves away. Surprisingly, the 80 men withdrew without having a shot fired at them. Either the Egyptians were too concerned with the nearby shelling, or they mistook the large force for a friendly unit. Perhaps, they simply did not notice.

Two hours passed before the Israelis reached the water channel on the outskirts of the town. The paratroopers were aware that if they could make the crossing, they would be out of the area controlled by the Egyptians and back into friendly territory. They turned west along the channel, heading for a distant bridge. To their surprise, they almost immediately came upon a bridge that was not marked on their maps. After checking the bridge for mines and booby-traps, 80 tired, hungry and wounded paras crossed to safety. In fact, Egyptian troops in the area had spotted the Israelis, but decided not to engage such a large force. An IDF armoured unit was waiting. The tank crews turned on their searchlights to direct the paratroopers home. The paratroopers, who had gone into Suez for what was to have been a simple mopping-up operation, walked out of the town at 0430 hours, two days after riding in on their half-tracks. Eighty Israeli soldiers died in the fighting.

The paras' heroic defence of the police station in Suez was the last major action of the Yom Kippur War. Both sides had fought close to the point of exhaustion and were eager for some form of political settlement. Prompted by the two superpowers, a UN-sponsored ceasefire had already come into effect on 22 October but the fighting in the south did not end until the 25th.

THE AUTHORS Tony Banks and Ronnie Daniel are military reporters for the Voice of Israel radio station. Ronnie Daniel commands a reserve infantry battalion and Tony Banks serves at the Office of the IDF Spokesman.

Far left, inset: Egyptian soldiers, ensconced in a battered and bullet-scarred building in central Suez, relax during a lull in the fighting. The Israelis grossly underestimated the situation in Suez and what was intended to be a routine mopping-up operation turned into a bitter struggle for survival for the paras sent in to secure the town. Below left: With a dense pall of smoke hanging over Suez, an Israeli tank moves in. Major-General Avraham Adan deployed two armoured brigades and a battalion of paras against the Egyptian town. Below: Ceasefire in Suez. Israeli soldiers maintain a careful watch as UN troops (in blue helmets) police the dividing line.

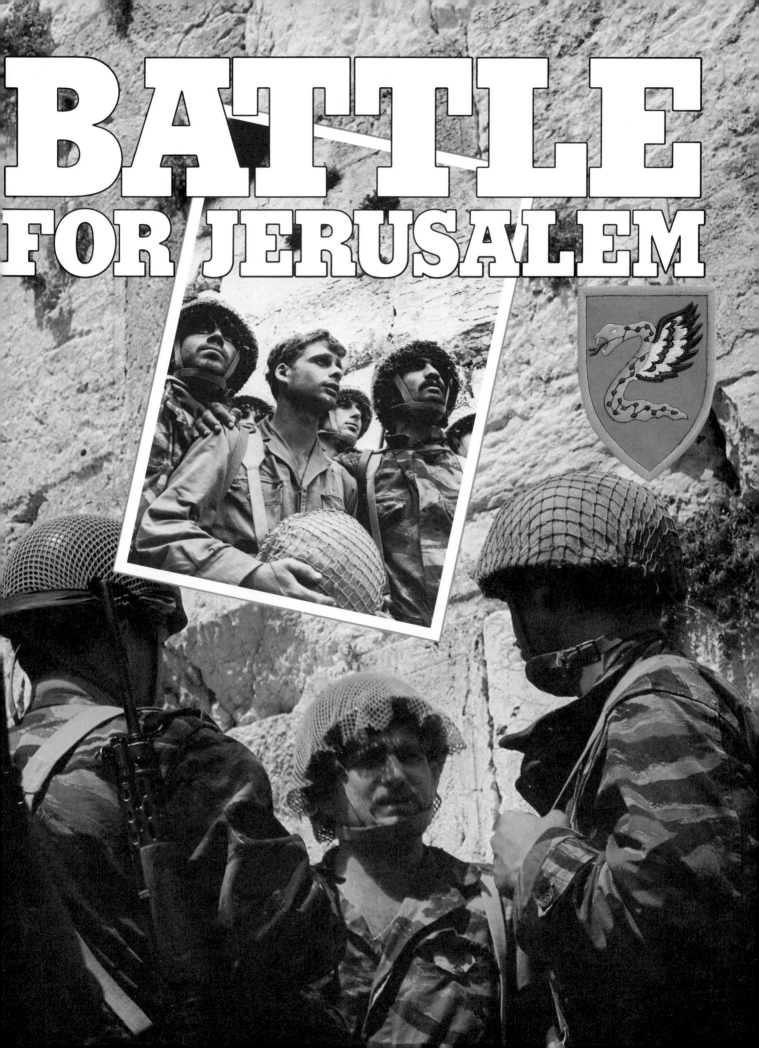

BATTLE
FOR JERUSALEM

The Israeli 55th Parachute
Brigade took on a new assignment
in 1967 – house-to-house fighting in
the streets of the Holy City

Previous page: Men of the 55th Parachute Brigade stand by the hallowed Western Wall of the Old City of Jerusalem after the battle. Inset: The badge worn by Israel's paratroop brigades. Far left: On the point of flying south for action against the Egyptians the 55th is rerouted to Jerusalem. Left: Mordechai 'Motta' Gur (using radio) with paratroopers on the Mount of Olives prior to entering the Old City. Below left: A paratrooper helps a wounded comrade in the narrow streets of Jerusalem.

SHORTLY AFTER 0930 hours on the morning of Tuesday, 6 June 1967, Colonel Mordechai Gur, commander of the 55th Parachute Brigade, spoke on the radio net to his waiting paratroopers.

'We stand on a ridge overlooking the Holy City. Soon we will enter the city, the Old City of Jerusalem about which countless generations of Jews have dreamed, to which all living Jews aspire. To our brigade has been granted the privilege of being the first to enter it.'

The capture of Jerusalem was the most potent symbol of Jewish victory in the Six-Day War of 1967, for the control of the Holy Places, such as the Temple Mount and the Wailing Wall, was enormously important to the young state of Israel. The honour of being the troops who would physically take possession of this great prize had been earned by Gur's men, who had shown great courage and skill over the past two days. In particular, they had wrested control of northern Jerusalem from the experienced and well dug-in forces of the Jordanian Army in the early morning of 6 June.

Tension had been building between Israel and her Arab neighbours for some time when, on the morning of 5 June, the Israeli Air Force launched a sudden strike against the Egyptians. This was totally successful, but in the confusion of that morning's events, King Hussein of Jordan was led to believe that the Israelis had themselves been hard hit, and agreed to send his forces in to attack Israel. At 1100 hours a bombardment began from the Jordanian side of the heavily fortified border, and the Jordanian Air Force flew sorties into Israeli air space. This was a foolhardy move that Hussein was to regret bitterly. Within hours, the rampant Israelis had put his entire air force out of action, and Major-General Uzi Narkiss, in charge of Central Command, was putting into operation his contingency plans for an offensive against Jordanian territory.

The Israelis had to cope with an unpromising strategic situation. Their main problem was that a long, narrow finger of land, inviting attack or artillery barrage from the Jordanian territory on either side, was the only link with the Israeli-held areas of Jerusalem. This corridor had to be made secure, and so Narkiss used the tanks of Colonel Ben Ari's 10th Mechanised Brigade to push north of the corridor and seize the ridge linking Jerusalem with the impor-

tant centre of Ramallah; at the same time, Latrun was attacked and overrun. Meanwhile, to the south of the corridor, the 16th Jerusalem Brigade launched a series of attacks that cut the main Jordanian communications with their forces in Hebron. The success of these two sets of operations, greatly helped by the command of the air that the Israeli Air Force was now exerting, gave the situation a new complexion. Far from being the side with the strategic initiative, the Jordanians were now vulnerable, and their position in Jerusalem under threat.

Within Jerusalem, the possibilities and prospects for either side were complicated by two factors. First, there was a substantial Israeli enclave within Jordanian territory on Mount Scopus, comprising the Hadassah Hospital and the Hebrew University. A prime Israeli goal was to relieve this enclave (which had been maintained, under United Nations auspices, since 1948) while the Jordanians in turn wished to overrun the position. The second factor affecting operations in the city was that in the two decades since the establishment of the existing frontier, both sides had built up complex sets of fortifications. These networks of deep concrete bunkers, carefully sited linking trenches, mines and barbed wire promised to make a frontal offensive a difficult, if not impossible, task.

The main Jordanian force in the city was the 27th Infantry Brigade, under Brigadier Ata Ali. Further brigades were in support to both north and south, while a tank battalion was stationed behind the main built-up areas in the Kidron valley. The Israeli Air Force made every effort to cut the communication lines of these forces with the Jordanian concentrations further to the north and east, but Ali was a competent officer and he had been reinforced. His men, basically the former Arab Legion under a different name, were well trained and confident of the strength of their defensive positions. Against them, the Israelis decided to throw in one of their crack formations – the 55th Parachute Brigade.

The paras had been raised to a fever pitch by the days of waiting before the outbreak of war

The 55th Parachute Brigade was a body of men trained to expect shock action and to be in the forefront of any Israeli offensive. Under its experienced commander, Colonel Mordechai Gur, were many veterans of raids on Arab territory, although some of the most senior officers had not yet seen action. Raised to a fever pitch by the days of waiting before the air strike that marked the beginning of the Six-Day War, the paras had expected to be used against the Egyptians in the Sinai, and at noon on the 5th were told to prepare for a jump against El Arish, to give impetus to the northern axis of advance. However, such was the pace of the Israeli success that by 1600 hours the decision was taken to use the whole brigade against the Jordanians in Jerusalem.

The basic plan was for the 66th and 71st Battalions of the 55th Brigade to attack along a front running from the Mandelbaum Gate to a point opposite the Jordanian-held Police School building. When a breakthrough had been made, the 28th Battalion would push through to exploit southwards, towards the walls of the Old City. Some support would come from the tanks attached to the Jerusalem Brigade, but the paras would have to fight their way through an awesome set of obstacles with only minimum support before the attack could gather momentum.

Labels on the diagram (clockwise):
fore sight assembly · cocking handle · sling swivel · sear · bolt · extractor · bolt guide · return spring · cover · rear sight asse[mbly] · barrel · barrel retaining nut · barrel guide · transverse selector bar · disconnector · safety bar · trigger · selector lever · safety bar · grip safety · follower spring · magazine catch · magazine

Uzi SMG

Calibre 9mm
Length (stock extended) 64cm
Weight (loaded, 25 rounds) 4.1kg
Magazine 25, 32 or 40-round box
System of operation blowback
Rate of fire (cyclic) 600rpm
Muzzle velocity 400mps

SPEARHEAD OF THE IDF

The armed forces of Israel suffered a sharp decline following the demobilisation of the Army of Independence in 1949. On 7 December 1953, General Moshe Dayan was made Chief of Staff. Dayan believed that an elite combat unit was required to inspire confidence in the regular infantry. Accordingly, he merged a small but highly successful anti-guerrilla force code-named Unit 101 with the army's best standing formation, the parachute battalion.

The combination of Unit 101's aggressive spirit and the paratroopers' rigorous discipline created a fine military machine. Its innovatory commander, Ariel Sharon, used the growing *esprit de corps* of the force to execute bold, high-risk tactics which astutely exploited weaknesses in his Arab adversaries. Night raids became standard in order to avoid the accurate fire of Arab snipers, and to take advantage of the enemy's aversion to close-quarters combat in the dark.

The paratroopers' successes roused the Israeli Defence Forces to emulate them, and Dayan ruled that all officers should undergo parachute training. In 1956 the basic paratroop unit was enlarged to a brigade, and the Six-Day War of 1967 saw at least three brigades of paratroopers in action.

The staff of the 55th Brigade urgently prepared for the assault. It was due to go in as soon as possible, but in the event, the battalions would not be ready before 0215 hours on the 6th. The crews manning the 81mm mortars were especially concerned, because the shells they needed were very slow in arriving. They were anxious to start rangefinding, but could not risk running short of ammunition. Units were getting lost as they struggled to find their place in the line and Jordanian shells, falling at random, were causing casualties. In addition, the deputy commander of B Company, 71st Battalion, had mistakenly attached his men to the convoy of buses carrying mortars forward, and with him was all the communications equipment for the battalion. But eventually all was just about in position and, at 0215 on 6 June, the barrage began.

With buildings on the Jordanian side bursting into flame and lines of tracer flicking through the darkness, the first Israeli platoons approached the Jordanian positions. They thrust bangalore torpedoes below the coils of barbed wire, and then hastily pulled back and hit the deck. The 71st Battalion in particular had trouble in their sector: bangalore torpedoes were not exploding, and then further wire obstacles were looming up after the first breach had been made. The delays meant that men moving forward to exploit the expected breach caused overcrowding, and the milling soldiers could have been very vulnerable to Jordanian shells. Eventually the way through was cleared. Waving green torches (usually the recognition signal for assembly after a night jump) to indicate that the path was open, officers led the platoons through into the next phase of the assault.

Once through the wire, the 66th Battalion was to exploit northwards, through the Police School, taking the important position of Ammunition Hill, while the 71st Battalion was to move through the Sheikh Jarrah area and the American Colony towards the Wadi El-Joz. The men of the 66th knew that they would face enormous difficulties. Ammunition Hill was a vital point, and the Police School itself was well fortified. The paras were heavily laden, carrying extra magazines for their Uzi sub-machine guns and

Paratrooper, 55th Para Brigade, Jerusalem 1967

An olive-green combat jacket is worn over this para's French-pattern camouflage uniform. Other items of foreign origin include a British para helmet and a US entrenching tool in a canvas case. Armament comprises a 7.62mm FN FAL rifle – similar to the British SLR.

metal stock

CONFLICT IN THE HOLY CITY

General Uzi Narkiss was leader of Central Command in the Israeli Army, and commander of the Israeli forces in Jerusalem:
'Two weeks prior to the Six-Day War, Central Command received third priority. First priority was given to Southern Command against Egypt, while second priority went to Northern Command against Syria. Thus, the defence of Jerusalem, for which I was personally responsible, was entrusted to only one brigade, with another held in reserve.

'No one took the Jordanian front seriously, but I was concerned because of our lack of equipment. We had only 20 tanks – mostly US Shermans which had seen their finest hour in Libya and Egypt in World War II! Our artillery was laughable – three 175mm guns, 12 25-pounders, and one company of 125mm mortars for the entire Jerusalem Corridor.

'In my opinion the Jordanian Army was the best, and still is, among the Arab armies. There were three infantry brigades and two armoured brigades in the Jordan valley area. It would take only eight hours to move them to Jerusalem. The Jordanians were well disciplined, knew how to use armour, and didn't run away after a local tactical defeat.

'Anything concerning Jerusalem has hundreds of political aspects. An event will immediately become known and generate reactions throughout the world. The main reason for the intensity of the fighting was, I think, that the goal was Jerusalem for both sides. The Arabs needed to defend Jerusalem; but we were determined to take the city.

Above: The 9mm Uzi sub-machine gun was distributed liberally among the Israelis in Jerusalem. Designed by Uziel Gal and first manufactured in 1951, the Uzi is widely accepted to be the most efficient sub-machine gun in existence. Its convenient folding stock makes it an ideal weapon for airborne personnel.

Right: General Uzi Narkiss, with Moshe Dayan, the Israeli Minister of Defence, on his left, walks through the Old City towards the Western ('Wailing') Wall after the defeat of the Jordanians.
Below: Israeli paratroopers shelter from Jordanian sniper fire as they move into the area of the Old City. Behind them is the historic site of the Garden of Gethsemane.

knapsacks stuffed with grenades. In some cases, men were unable to get up when they fell over, and in one narrow trench Israeli troops got stuck because they were too bulky to pass along.

Giant searchlights illuminated the white walls of the Police School; Jordanian flares suddenly lit up the whole scene. Blazing houses made the darkness around them seem even darker, and the constant explosions of tank, mortar and Jordanian 25-pounder shells provided a deadly backdrop as the paras pushed ahead. It was impossible to see exactly where the enemy smallarms fire was coming from. If a trench or emplacement was seen, then it could be attacked and wiped out, but the main priority was to push on to the important objectives. In spite of their loads, and in spite of the fire, the men of the 66th Battalion kept going.

First into the Police School was A Company, cutting a way through a cattle-fence outside. The long passages inside were completely dark, a darkness rendered even more impenetrable by the sudden shell flashes outside. Groups of four men cleared the rooms, two throwing in a grenade and then spraying a room with fire, while the other two moved on to the room next door. But the paras kept tripping and falling in the pitch blackness; in the end, the officers had no option but the dangerous one of using torches. When they had taken the school, A Company moved on towards the Ambassador Hotel, together with D Company; B and C Companies moved towards Ammunition Hill.

As dawn broke (at about 0340 hours) the paras were engaged in a deadly, exhausting fight for the hill. In the trenches and bunkers it was often very difficult to tell friend from foe, and the fighting was further confused by Jordanian sniping from hills to the north. Tanks came up in support, but close-quarters fighting against prepared positions is a

Taking the West Bank

JORDAN
Jenin
ISRAEL
MEDITERRANEAN
Nablus
Tubas
Tel Aviv
JORDAN
Jordan
Ramallah
Ashdod
Jerusalem
Jericho
Asnkelon
Bethlehem
WEST BANK
DEAD SEA
Gaza
Hebron
ISRAEL

The road to Jerusalem

JORDAN
ISRAEL
Beth Haron Pass
Ramallah
Sha'alvim
Latrun
Radar Hill
Bidu
Atarot
Mount Scopus
Maale Hahamisha
Kastel
Police School
Motza
Sheikh Jarrah
Mount of Olives
Jerusalem
UN HQ

Key
Israeli forces
Arab forces
Israeli enclave
Arab enclave

Battle for Jerusalem
Israeli 55th Parachute Brigade, June 1967

At 1100 hours on 5 June 1967 Jordanian artillery and aircraft began attacking targets in Israel. Faced with the problem of defending the corridor to Jerusalem against a Jordanian advance, the Israelis deployed an armoured brigade to secure the high ground north of the corridor. With the northern flank secure the 55th Parachute Brigade began its attack on Jerusalem, entering the Old City early on 7 June. Meanwhile, Israeli forces were clearing the rest of the West Bank, and that evening hostilities between Israel and Jordan ended.

Ammunition Hill

wire defences
command bunker
trench
To Police School

6 June 0215 66th Btn advances north, capturing the Police School and pushing on to Ammunition Hill.
0515 After fierce fighting Ammunition Hill is cleared.

Key – Ammunition Hill
A Coy, 66th Btn
B Coy, 66th Btn
C Coy, 66th Btn
Tank Platoon
Arab bunkers

Key
28th Btn, 55th Para Bde
66th Btn, 55th Para Bde
71st Btn, 55th Para Bde

Nablus Road and Wadi El-Joz

0215 As 66th Btn attacks to the north, 71st Btn advances against stiff resistance to Nablus Road, exploiting as far as the crossroads at Wadi El Joz. Following through, 28th Btn attacks southwards along Nablus Road.
0500 After a brief halt, 28th Btn fights its way westwards to the Rockefeller Museum.

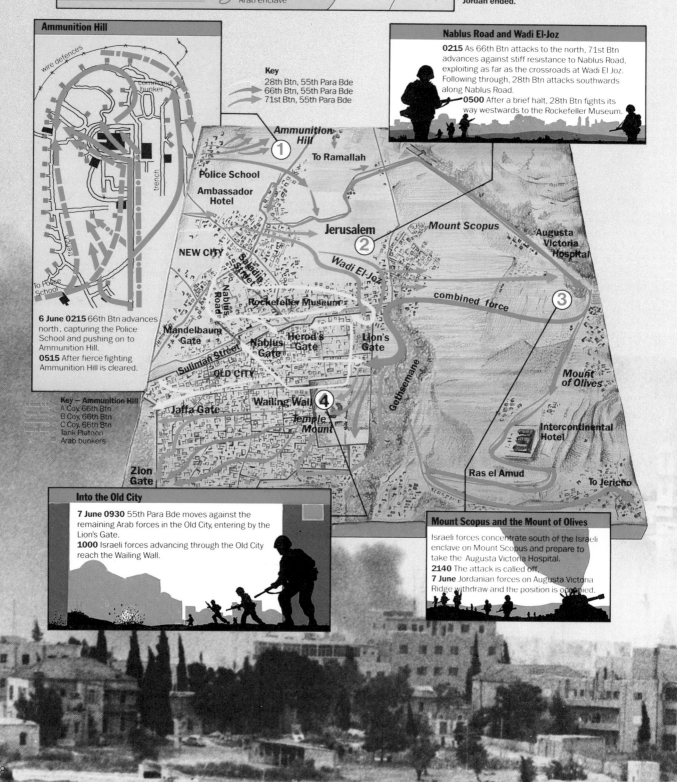

Ammunition Hill
To Ramallah
Police School
Ambassador Hotel
Jerusalem
Mount Scopus
Augusta Victoria Hospital
NEW CITY
Saladin Street
Wadi El-Joz
combined force
Nablus Road
Rockefeller Museum
Mandelbaum Gate
Nablus Gate
Herod's Gate
Lion's Gate
Suliman Street
OLD CITY
Gethsemane
Mount of Olives
Jaffa Gate
Wailing Wall
Temple Mount
Intercontinental Hotel
Zion Gate
Ras el Amud
To Jericho

Into the Old City

7 June 0930 55th Para Bde moves against the remaining Arab forces in the Old City, entering by the Lion's Gate.
1000 Israeli forces advancing through the Old City reach the Wailing Wall.

Mount Scopus and the Mount of Olives

Israeli forces concentrate south of the Israeli enclave on Mount Scopus and prepare to take the Augusta Victoria Hospital.
2140 The attack is called off.
7 June Jordanian forces on Augusta Victoria Ridge withdraw and the position is occupied.

tanker's nightmare, and they needed infantry protection against bazookas and recoilless rifles. Soon, the paras had emptied the spare loaded magazines they had brought with them, and had to refill magazines by hand from ammunition boxes – a tiring, fiddly task when under fire. But gradually, the hill was cleared, and the final, so-called 'great bunker' was taken at 0515.

Meanwhile, the 71st Battalion was also meeting stiff resistance in its attack. Having had the most problems in assembling for the assault, this battalion also had difficulty in finding its way once it was into the Jordanian lines. The difficulty of finding the right road in the darkness with only photographs to guide them was magnified by the need to clear hidden Jordanian positions. Dropping grenades into emplacements, and carefully moving along the sheltered sides of streets, the Israelis began clearing the area between the frontier and the Nablus Road, and had a stroke of luck when the Jordanian defenders of the street leading to Wadi El-Joz were taken by surprise. A company of paras moved rapidly down the street to set up positions at this important intersection.

Although the advance was generally going well, the Jordanian support weapons soon picked out the assembly area of the Israelis, and the brigade's mortar crews and recoilless rifle operators suffered casualties as artillery fire began to zero in on them. The breaches in the front-line defences were soon being crossed by the wounded returning from the fight up ahead, some stoical but others screaming with pain. The medical resources of the brigade were becoming dangerously stretched by the mounting casualties in the attacking battalions and among the support units that were under artillery and machine-gun fire.

One heavy machine gun in particular had caused great concern as it swept the breaches with fire before it was knocked out by a bazooka; and in spite of many efforts, a light machine gun proved endlessly troublesome. It would stop as soon as a shell burst near it, then open up again. A group of staff officers from the 28th Battalion volunteered to finish it off; but when they tried to approach it they were caught in a trap, and the commander of the support company, leading the attempt, was seriously wounded.

With bullets flying and shells bursting around them, the men of the 28th Battalion moved off to begin their part of the assault soon after the 71st Battalion had gone through the breach in the wire. One shell chanced to injure the deputy commander of D Company, while there were serious officer casualties when a Jordanian 25-pounder struck lucky and hit battalion headquarters. After a seemingly interminable wait, it was dawn before the first members of the 28th Battalion had got to the Jordanian side of the wire, and then they had to fight their way south.

Fighting in the daylight proved, in some ways, worse than the night fighting. Now, snipers could fire without the flash of their muzzles giving away their position, and Jordanian artillery observers had a better view of events. Some of the districts through which the men of the 28th were moving were supposed to have been cleared, but the Israelis soon found that enemy troops could easily infiltrate back into good positions. The building of the Moslem Council had to be cleared three times to make certain that a single shot, or a carefully lobbed grenade, would not take its toll of the advancing Israelis.

The task of moving down Saladin Street was given to C Company but, unable to identify the area properly, it went down Nablus Road. Here the paras had to flush out the YMCA building, from which there was considerable fire. Entering it cautiously, they found most of it empty, finding only the base of a machine-gun mounting. Suddenly the squad that was investigating the situation was fired upon, and men went down wounded. Time was too short to waste it on just one obstacle, and a hand-to-hand combat would have resulted in further casualties. The squad pulled out, and a supporting tank put two shells into the upper stories; the advance went on.

About 0500, there was a lull and the men of the 28th Battalion were ordered to halt. This was a nerve-racking moment, because the risk of a sniper's bullet, or of a well-aimed salvo of artillery shells was as great as ever. Then the advance began again with more tank support. The main task now was to get to the Rockefeller Museum, an imposing new building that dominated the approaches to the northeast corner of the Old City. The roar of the tank guns when they fired almost deafened the paratroopers as the sound echoed between the high buildings. The

BANGALORE TORPEDOES

In 1912 trials were held at Bangalore in India to discover effective methods of breaching barbed-wire entanglements. One device was the invention of Captain McClintock of the Indian Sappers and Miners. Consisting of a 5.5m length of water piping stuffed with 27kg of dynamite, his torpedo was so successful that the spectators only narrowly escaped being blown up with the wire. Modified versions of McClintock's weapon were widely used by sappers in the trenches during World War I, but since then its use has declined.

A typical modern Bangalore torpedo consists of a 1.8m light steel tube, 38mm in diameter, packed with 1.8kg of ammonal blasting explosive. Fitted with spring-locking clips at both ends, individual tubes are locked together to form a long charge that penetrates to the far side of the obstacle. The head of the torpedo is streamlined by a smooth, conical nose that helps to prevent the weapon snagging on the wire as it is pushed in. Once slid into position, the connected tubes of the torpedo are fired by an electric detonator fixed to the end of the final section.

The Israeli paratroops in Jerusalem linked up the sections and then carried them forward, one man to a section, to the wire. But there were several problems: if a man stumbled or was hit by shrapnel, for example, sections would come apart and had to be hastily re-assembled. Another difficulty was that torpedoes frequently failed to detonate, or did so just as men were moving forward to replace them.

Below: A pall of smoke hangs over Jordanian positions under attack in Jerusalem.

THE JORDAN ARAB ARMY

When the Jordan Arab Army crossed the Israeli border in 1967, many of the troops will have recalled the attack on Jerusalem made by their predecessors, the Arab Legion of Transjordan, nearly 20 years before. The 1948 Arab-Israeli War had secured considerable tracts of Palestinian land for Jordan, and the nation's population had swelled to three million. Following the war, the Arab Legion had been increased to 10,000 men in anticipation of further war with Israel and to keep order within the expanded state.

Originally a force recruited almost exclusively from bedouin tribes, the Arab Legion received a substantial influx of educated Palestinians after 1948. However, doubts as to their loyalty to King Hussein were confirmed when a newly-formed brigade containing many Palestinians was involved in an attempted coup. Concerned that the army was slipping away from him, Hussein made radical changes in March 1956. He dismissed all his British officers and renamed the force the Jordan Arab Army. Rigorous political screening of recruits was introduced, and bedouins again became predominant in the ranks. Palestinians retained for their skills were closely supervised, with high pay and privileges being relied upon to secure their loyalty. By the time of the Six-Day War of 1967, the army had grown into a highly efficient combat force of 50,000 men.

paras also found it difficult to communicate with the tank crews because the cables for the external telephones had been cut by shrapnel, or were turned off so that the tankers could listen to the stream of orders they were getting on their radio net. But in spite of these problems, the tanks were a real boon, for they drew fire away from the men on foot and they certainly gave the Jordanian defenders second thoughts about opening up at short range.

By 0800, the 55th Brigade had performed brilliantly. All its objectives were secured, and it had set the scene for further advance. From Ammunition Hill in the north through Sheikh Jarrah, the Ambassador Hotel, and down to Wadi El-Joz, a line had been established that gave contact with the slopes of Mount Scopus and promised imminent relief for the besieged garrison; while in the south, the capture of the Rockefeller Museum made an assault against the Old City a practical possibility. Indeed, paras of the 28th Battalion had set themselves up in the Rivoli Hotel opposite Herod's Gate, and when they were not engaging the defenders of the walls of the Old City they were able to sample the delights of the hotel's kitchens, and have a bath.

Left: Troops of the Jordan Arab Army wait impatiently to cross the border into Jerusalem. Below: Israeli paras carrying out a sweep in the Old City climb Temple Mount towards the dome of the Rock.

The casualties sustained by the brigade in reaching these objectives had been horrific – but the achievement had been immense. Gur visited the troops at the Rockefeller Museum. Although many had no previous experience of real action, he noted that already they were comporting themselves like veterans; they knew exactly where enemy fire might come from, and where to find precisely the safest places to sit and relax.

Above: Within the cramped confines of the Old City, shrapnel from Jordanian shellfire and mortar bombs exacted a high toll among the Israeli assault force. Left: Two Israelis, worn out by hours of hard fighting, take an opportunity to eat and think over their experiences.

The ranks of the three battalions were thinned by the pounding they had taken during the assault, but there was no shortage of volunteers to replace the dead and wounded. The mortar crews and anti-tank personnel were now anxious to get into the front line – especially as the Old City was beckoning. Morale was sky-high, and Gur prepared to move the 66th Battalion further south for another day's fighting.

Narkiss, desperate to finish things off and to get into the Holy City, ordered Gur to concentrate on taking the last Jordanian strongpoint in the region, the Augusta Victoria Hospital on a ridge to the south of Mount Scopus, and then to prepare an encirclement of the Old City. The plans for the assault were swiftly drawn up, and it was decided to wait until after 1930 hours, when darkness fell, before attacking.

The assault on Augusta Victoria Hospital got off to a bad start, when some troops strayed too close to the walls of the Old City and were fired on from there; and then, at 2140, Gur was informed that 40 Patton tanks of the Jordanian Army had been seen on the reverse side of the slope his men were to attack. With only four Shermans as support, Gur could not risk the assault. He decided to wait until the next day, when aerial support could be called in. Anti-tank dispositions were made and then the soldiers tried to sleep.

Gur was at last given the order that he was so anxious to receive: he was told to take the old city

Gur's new plan was to attack at about 1130 hours on 7 June, by which time the Israeli Air Force should have dispersed the Pattons. The Israeli high command decided, however, that the attack should go in much earlier in the morning, at 0830. Again, there was frantic haste to reschedule operations, for the new attack was to be mounted from Mount Scopus as well as from across the Kidron valley.

Had the Israelis known it, such frenzied preparations were hardly necessary. Far from being able to bring up substantial armoured reinforcements, Brigadier Ata Ali had been completely cut off by the success of Israeli moves to north and south, and by the Israeli Air Force's devastating attacks on Jordanian road convoys. His troops began a skilful withdrawal in the early hours of 7 June.

At 0804, just before his attacks were to start, Gur was at last given the order that he was so anxious to receive: he was told to take the Old City. Immediately after the air attacks on the Augusta Victoria Ridge, his men stormed over it, and at 0930 he was able to give the historic order to his brigade that the time for waiting was past.

The entry into the Old City was to be via the Lion's Gate, which was the only one able to take tanks, and as the armoured support of the paratroopers approached this point of entry, there was some sporadic defensive fire. Gur himself led the entry into the Old City, and his troops met only light resistance from isolated snipers. At about 1000, he reached the Wailing Wall. The brigade's ordnance officer produced a bottle of whisky, and passed it round. The 55th Brigade had won a victory that no one in Israel would ever forget.

THE AUTHOR Ashley Brown has written various books and articles on military subjects, including *Modern Warfare*. This article has been written using information very kindly provided by Mordechai Gur, the commander of the 55th Parachute Brigade during the battle for Jerusalem.

In 1929 the Soviet Union selected a batch of volunteers to undergo parachute training, and a year later, elements of this battalion-sized force were involved in a large-scale air drop. Another exercise on a similar scale followed in 1931, but it was not until 1933 that a full battalion took part in a training mission.

Soviet paratroopers first saw action in 1940 during an assault on the Bessarabian provinces of northern Romania. Subsequently, little is known of the paras' activities, although it is recorded that a series of brigade-strength operations were carried out between 1943 and 1944.

In general, however, the paras were used as elite shock troops, serving in the Red Army's Guards Divisions, or in conjunction with partisan groups.

In the closing stages of World War II, units were involved in the Far East, fighting with great distinction against the Japanese in present-day North Korea. The crowning achievement occurred on 18 August 1945, when paratroopers captured the headquarters of the Kwantung Army, whose commander then negotiated the surrender of over 600,000 men.

Above: The 1935 version of the Soviet para instructors' badge.

JUMPING UNDER FIRE

Ordered to spearhead the Red Army's offensive against the Dniepr bend, crack Soviet paras waged a spirited fight against Hitler's Wehrmacht

BY SEPTEMBER 1943, the German Army on the Eastern Front, defeated at Kursk, was retreating. Facing an ever-strengthening Soviet adversary, the German forces attempted to take up defensive positions behind natural barriers wherever possible. One of the key lines that the Germans needed to hold was the Dniepr river. To prevent a Soviet breakthrough in this sector, the Fourth Panzer Army was stationed in the north, around Kiev, and the Eighth Army further south, between Kanev and Cherkassy. Between these two armies, however, there remained a lightly defended gap that included the bend in the Dniepr near Pereyaslav.

Operating within this region were a substantial number of Soviet partisans who had been left be-

Below right: Soviet paras, armed with PPSh41 sub-machine guns, emplane on a converted Ant-6 bomber. Their fight for the Dniepr bend in late 1943 was one of the Soviet Union's few conventional airborne operations of the war. Once on the ground, the paras led local partisans in hit-and-run raids. Below: Soviet troops cross the Dniepr.

hind in the wake of Operation Barbarossa in 1941. The closest German formation to the Dniepr bend was the XXIV Panzer Corps. Badly mauled, it was still withdrawing across the river from the east on 22 September when lead troops of the Soviet Third Guards Tank Army began crossing the Dniepr at Zarubentsy and advancing on Grigorovka.

To counter the threat presented by the advancing Russians, the 19th Panzer Division's reconnaissance battalion was sent south from Kiev, where they had recently crossed from the east. Near Grigorovka, elements of the 19th encountered concentrations of Soviet troops, which they attacked. However, despite German resistance, the Soviets continued to cross the river along the Dniepr bend between 22 and 24 September, eventually occupying Zarubentsy.

Meanwhile back at Kanev, by 0600 hours on 24 September, all the men of the XXIV Panzer Corps had crossed the Dniepr, destroying the vital bridge behind them. Realising the increasing danger presented by the Soviet troops on the west side of the Dniepr, the uncommitted portions of the 19th Panzer Division and the 112th Infantry Division were sent into the bend to counter the threat early on 24 September. As the Soviets still continued to cross, portions of the 34th Infantry Division were also sent north from Kanev.

To support their troops crossing the Dniepr, the Soviet High Command decided to commit the 1st, 3rd and 5th Guards Airborne Brigades that had recently been moved from outside Moscow to Lebedin airfield, near Poltava, to reinforce an airhead secured by other brigades. The three airborne brigades had been formed from a cadre of battle-hardened men of the previous Soviet combat

jump at Vyazma in early 1942. Up to 50 per cent of the 1st and 3rd Brigades were, in fact, veterans, but only a few Vyazma veterans were in the 5th Brigade. The airborne brigades at this time each had a strength of about 2500 men, divided into four 500-man battalions, a mortar section, an engineer section, an anti-aircraft section, an anti-tank section, and a medical section. The medical team contained jump-qualified female doctors and nurses.

Had the assault been launched before the XXIV Panzer Corps had completed its river crossing, it would have been most effective; however, lack of transport aircraft, a common problem for the Soviet paratroopers throughout the war, caused the drop to be delayed until 1730 hours on 24 September, when parachutists from the 5th Guards Airborne Brigade jumped near Dudari. Even at take-off time, only 48 of the 65 planes assigned to the 5th Guards had arrived and many of these were the obsolete TB-3 rather than the Li-2s (the Soviet version of the DC-3) expected. As a result, the paratroopers had to be shuttled to the drop zone, thus diluting the effect of their assault. The change in type of plane and general disorganisation also led to equipment being improperly loaded or left behind, and battalions or even companies not being dropped at the same time.

To compound the problems the transports encountered heavy flak over the drop zone and ended up releasing their sticks from 1800ft, a long distance to descend with the hard-to-control Soviet parachutes in the face of heavy enemy fire. The 5th Guards paras, in fact, came under withering fire as columns of the 19th Panzer Division were passing the drop zone and turned their machine guns on the floating targets. Thus, a large number of the men

AIR TRANSPORT

Despite being in the forefront of developments in air assault techniques during the inter-war period, the Soviet Union's para force was poorly supplied with air transporters. Initially, during the 1920s, the airborne forces relied on converted bombers rather than specialist aircraft. Although the air arm put on elaborate, large-scale airdrops in the mid-1930s, using fleets of transporters, Stalin's subsequent purges of senior military men left the paratroopers leaderless and, in consequence, starved of more modern equipment.

In the immediate pre-war period, the main aircraft deployed by paras was the Tupolev Ant-6, a massive four-engined aircraft that had been around since the 1920s. The Ant-6 was capable of carrying up to 10,000lb of either men or equipment to a range of 500 miles; so huge was the aircraft that it was also able to lift a light tank strung between its undercarriage. The Ant-6 saw some service during World War II, but its size and slow speed made it very vulnerable to fighter attack and groundfire; it seems unlikely that many survived the opening months of the conflict.

Desperately short of replacement transports, the Soviet authorities turned to their allies for help. The substitute for the Ant-6 was the DC-3, either supplied direct from the USA or produced under licence in the USSR, where it was known as the Lisunov Li-2. The first Soviet-built aircraft were flying in 1940, and by the end of the conflict over 2000 were in frontline service.

The DC-3 remained the mainstay of the Soviet Union's paradrop force until well after 1945. A replacement aircraft, the larger Ilyushin Il-12, entered service in 1948, but the DC-3 was deployed until well into the 1950s.

were killed before they even hit the ground.

Nevertheless, the drops continued throughout the afternoon and early evening, with 2300 members of the brigade eventually landing in small groups over a 25-square-mile area. As many as 50 per cent of these were killed or captured upon landing; most of the others were so scattered that they could not fight in an organised manner. Still, the Germans reported actions against more than 35 small groups of parachutists during the 24th. Actually, there was one unit of reinforced company strength operating in the forests near Grushevo, where they had withdrawn after landing and been joined by a group of partisans. This unit was commanded by the brigade commander, a lieutenant-colonel, who had rallied as many troops as possible to himself.

The 1st Guards Airborne Brigade dropped west of Pekari and met little German resistance

The combination of bad luck, which had caused them to jump almost on top of a German division, and confusion at the staging area had resulted in a disaster for the 5th Guards. Some pilots had been so confused that they had dropped their loads behind the Soviet lines, which had, at least, saved those men's lives. Another plane-load jumped into the Dniepr and drowned. Poor planning had led to the shuttle system which had cost the lives of many highly trained Guards paratroopers.

Later on 24 September the operation continued as further drops were made to the southwest. About 300 parachutists from the 3rd Brigade were dropped at Shandra and another 400 from the same unit jumped nearby at Beresnyagi. These elements were engaged immediately by members of the German 34th Infantry Division who were in the area. Like the men of the 5th Guards further north, the 700 paratroopers of the 3rd Guards were split into small groups by scattered drops and the immediate German counter-attacks. Rather than cutting off German reinforcements from the Dniepr as had been their mission, those who made it off the drop zone alive were concerned only with survival.

Only the 1st Guards Airborne Brigade managed to land and operate as a relatively cohesive unit. It had dropped west of Pekari and met little German resistance. After assembling, the brigade set up a defensive perimeter and began to clear airstrips for the 2nd and 4th Guards Airlanding Brigades that were to be brought in along with artillery and tanks. Throughout the night of 24/25 September, scattered parachute drops took place in the German rear. Additional Soviet troops also crossed the Dniepr near Zarubentsy and opposite the area held by the 1st Guards Airborne Brigade.

By the morning of the 25th, the Germans were engaged against Soviet units which continued to cross the Dniepr and against pockets of parachutists in their rear. The Luftwaffe had also sent up observers to count the number of parachutes lying around so that a rough estimate of the number of paratroopers who had landed could be reached, and 20mm quad flak guns had also been set up at other likely drop zones in the expectation of more parachutists.

With the drops seemingly over by the 25th, the Germans began systematically to search the countryside for surviving parachutists. The bulk of the German forces, however, were left free to deal with threatened Soviet breakthroughs. Near Pekari,

Below: Paras climb out of the upper hatch of an Ant-6 bomber and clamber onto its wing before making a free-fall jump into action.

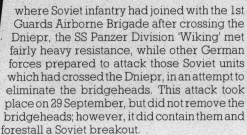

where Soviet infantry had joined with the 1st Guards Airborne Brigade after crossing the Dniepr, the SS Panzer Division 'Wiking' met fairly heavy resistance, while other German forces prepared to attack those Soviet units which had crossed the Dniepr, in an attempt to eliminate the bridgeheads. This attack took place on 29 September, but did not remove the bridgeheads; however, it did contain them and forestall a Soviet breakout.

Despite the failure of the airborne assault to crack the German defences, and despite the heavy losses, the Soviet paratroopers did manage to contribute in a manner which was unique to the Soviet airborne forces. Whereas in the west, the SAS or other such units might be specifically parachuted in to organise or act as partisans, Soviet paratroopers jumped on a mission and then, if necessary, became partisans until Soviet forces had liberated the area and they could rejoin their unit. This system had the advantage of reinforcing the partisans with crack troops and also of salvaging something from difficult airborne operations.

This reversion to partisan warfare was what happened after the Dniepr drops, and during the next 10 days, 43 separate groups of Soviet paratroopers, totalling some 2300 men, began operations in the area between Rzhishchev and Cherkassy. Other individual paratroopers merged with local partisan units and fought with them. The largest groups consisted of 600 men in the Kanev and Cherkassy forests, 200 men around Chernyshi, and 300 men near Yablonovo. Although they suffered ammunition shortages because they had not recovered most of their equipment containers, these groups still struck at the Germans when they got the chance. On the night of 29/30 September, for example, 150 paratroopers hit a German police headquarters in the village of Potok and then ambushed an artillery column south of the village. This group later made its way south, and on 5 October joined the larger group of paratroopers acting as partisans under the command of Lieutenant-Colonel Sidorchuk, the commanding officer of the 5th Guards

Top: Soviet para-nurses line up for an equipment check before going on a mission. Above: Encumbered by his harness, a recruit struggles to control his unusual square parachute.

The Soviet Offensive
Aug–Dec 1943

Key
→ Soviet forces
⋯⋯ Front line, 18 Aug
- - - Front line, 24 Aug
-·-·- Front line, 30 Sept
——— Front line, 23 Dec

POLAND
• Lvov
Zhitomir •
Grigorovka
Kiev •
Pereyaslav
Pzhishev
Dniepr bend
• Vinnitsa
Kanev •
Cherkassy
• Poltava
• Kharkov
Chernovtsy •
HUNGARY
Jassy •
MOLDAVIA
Kotovsk •
Pervomaysk •
Nikolayev •
• Odessa
• Donetsk
Dniepr
CRIMEA
KUBAN
Sevastopol •
BLACK SEA
S O V I E T   U N I O N

In late August 1943 the Red Army launched its autumn offensive in the eastern Ukraine aimed at pushing the Germans back across the Dniepr. By the end of September the German army was in retreat and the Soviets had established bridgeheads west of the Dniepr. Despite stubborn defensive actions by the Germans, the Red Army was able to concentrate its strength at key points and maintain the momentum of the advance. By December, Germany's Eastern rampart was in Soviet hands.

Airborne Brigade.

Sidorchuk's 600 men were by far the best orga-nised of the ad hoc units. Fortunately, they also had quite a bit of their equipment, and on 6 October they established radio contact with Fortieth Army HQ and were able to request resupply. The Germans tried repeatedly to mop up Sidorchuk's group but were unsuccessful. On 19 October, however, Sidorchuk and his men moved south to the Tagancha forest, where they joined with other parachutists and local partisans. With over 1000 men now under his com-mand, Sidorchuk launched raids against German installations around the forest. On 22 October a railway line was blown up, derailing a train. As a result of German attempts to dislodge him, Sidor-chuk had to move again into the Cherkassy forest from where, with a force now numbering about 1200 men, the paratroopers harried German supply routes and gathered intelligence which was radioed to the 2nd Ukrainian Front.

On 11 November, Sidorchuk received orders for his men to participate in the advance of the Soviet Fifty-Second Army across the Dniepr. Sidorchuk's paratroopers were assigned the mission of captur-ing the villages of Lozovok, Sekirna, and Svidovok, from where they could screen the crossing of the main force. The biggest problem faced by the paratroopers was at Svidovok where the Germans had five tanks, for Sidorchuk's men were lightly armed for tank busting. The paratroopers achieved mixed successes in their assaults, taking Svidovok, but the 254th Rifle Division, which had been sche-duled to spearhead the crossing, did not jump off on time and the paratroopers were forced to retreat from their hard-won objectives or be surrounded.

Above: Soviet partisans laying demolition charges along a stretch of railway behind the German front line. Initially poorly led and equipped, the guerrilla groups quickly gained the experience and back-up to carry out devastating attacks against the enemy's vulnerable supply lines. Once the Red Army had gone over to the offensive, partisans were used to prepare the way for more conventional forces. Their activities were often co-ordinated and led by small cadres of paras specially flown in for the job.

The crossing was made the next night, however, and by 15 November the remnants of 5th Guards Airborne Brigade had linked up with the advancing 254th Rifle Division. For his outstanding leadership, Sidorchuk was named a 'Hero of the Soviet Union'. Other small groups of paratroopers throughout the Dniepr bend continued to act as partisans until a chance arose to link up with the advancing Soviet Army, but Sidorchuk's group had been the most successful in battle.

The Dniepr bend operation was illustrative of the best and worst aspects of Soviet airborne operations during World War II. The poor planning and co-ordination of the operation was an invitation to disaster which resulted in the loss of two-thirds of the highly-trained paratroopers. Had the operation been launched just a day or two sooner against the bridge at Kanev, it could have stood a good chance of cutting off large numbers of Germans on the east side of the river. As it was, however, the paratroopers were thrown in piecemeal and wasted.

On the positive side, the Dniepr bend jump illus-trated the strong points of the Soviet paratrooper during World War II. Despite the botched operation, individual paratroopers went on the attack and continued to be a thorn in the enemy's side for many weeks. The paratroopers gave the partisans in this critical area unexpected reinforcements for their operations against the German rear, which played a part in the Soviet advance. Sidorchuk also illustrated those characteristics most desirable in an airborne officer: he took charge and made order out of chaos, turning scattered elements into a cohesive fighting unit which inflicted damage on the enemy and paved the way for a Soviet victory.

THE AUTHOR Leroy Thompson served in Vietnam as a member of the USAF Combat Security Police. He has published several books including *Uniforms of the Elite Forces* and *Uniforms of the Indochina and Vietnam Wars*.